EDUCATION MANAGEMENT SERIES
Series editor: John Sayer

# THE ETHICS OF EDUCATIONAL MANAGEMENT
## Personal, Social and Political Perspectives on School Organization

# THE ETHICS OF EDUCATIONAL MANAGEMENT

## Personal, Social and Political Perspectives on School Organization

Mike Bottery

'They lower their heads to pull the cart
instead of raising their heads to look at the road.'

CASSELL

**Cassell Educational Limited**

Villiers House
41/47 Strand
London WC2N 5JE

387 Park Avenue South
New York
NY 10016-8810

First published 1992
Reprinted 1993

**British Library Cataloguing in Publication Data**
Bottery, Mike
   The ethics of educational management:
   personal, social and political perspectives
   on school organization. — (Education management)
   1. Education. Management
   I. Title   II. Series
   379.15

ISBN 0 304 32409 4 (hardback)
     0 304 32429 9 (paperback)

Typeset by Litho Link Ltd, Welshpool, Powys, Wales
Printed and bound in Great Britain by Dotesios, Trowbridge, Wilts

# Acknowledgements

My thanks to the *Oxford Review of Education*, *Westminster Studies in Education* and
*Curriculum* for permission to make use of material first printed in those journals.

To Christopher and Sarah,
who I hope one day will read it.

# Contents

# Foreword by the series editor

This book opens the Cassell series on educational management, that is to say, ways of managing which will themselves be part of worthwhile educational experience. Some of the books in the series will focus on good practice; but practice has to be informed by values if it is to be described as good. This is not a series about efficiency alone. Currently short-term politically driven priorities will be addressed, but in a context and according to criteria which spring from social values and are informed by a broad and long-term strategic view of development.

Mike Bottery addresses the key issue: what sort of society do we want, and how can the way schools are run be a living experience in active citizenship? This book relates current issues to long-term values in a bold, timely and helpfully clear exposition. It raises the question: what is management practice all for? It broadens the framework in which people can develop their own answers.

There is adequate previous technical literature about skills of pragmatic problem-solving. There is too much about immediate implementation of prescriptive legislation. *The Ethics of School Management* leads us out of those traps, and suggests ways in which school leadership and management may instead offer a foretaste of the open, just society now being sought worldwide.

John Sayer

# Introduction

Imagine an unusual game of soccer. In this game, instead of the pitch being oblong, the pitch is round. Instead of there being just two goals, there are a number of different goals, dotted all round the edge of the pitch. The players do not stay the same throughout the game, but keep changing, sometimes leaving to play on another pitch at a moment's notice. The coaches who train the players also have different tactics and tend to change their mind as to which goal their players should shoot into. Even when the child shoots into the goal and scores a goal, it is not always certain that that goal will count for anything in the overall game. So even the rules governing the game change, and sometimes this information is not very well communicated. To make matters worse, the referees change as well, so you can never be sure that the same rules will be implemented in the same way, assuming that they stay the same long enough for you to get to grips with them. Imagine that you are given the task of organizing and running such a game. How would you go about it?

There must be many in management positions in schools who feel their task is very similar. Not only do the children change, but so do the parents, the teachers, the prevailing educational philosophy, and the economic and social priorities of politicians and society in general. Instead of having one goal to shoot into, those in management positions have several they have to score into at the same time, and quite a number to defend. In most Western societies, the number of goals to be defended and attacked has substantially increased as schools try to cope with a knowledge explosion which increases exponentially, with social problems which show no signs of decreasing, and with economic and political ideologies which demand greater involvement by non-educationalists in the running of the school, and which assert utilitarian priorities which may well run counter to educational philosophies which centre on the value of the individual. As these goals have increased in number, so many of those engaged in school management have found that time for constructive educational planning has diminished, and crisis management has become the norm. The clear danger with this is that, pressed on all sides by increasingly vocal demands, school managers may lose sight of the ultimate purposes of the school, and find themselves driven more and more towards a management of expediency.

Yet it is vital to the management of schools that the practice be based on more than expediency. Good management must stem from an appreciation of the ultimate purposes of that organization, rather than from the exigencies of crisis management. Ultimately, I would suggest, the pursuit of education has to be framed in terms of choices and values, for it is concerned with the thought processes and behaviours of the next generation. If this is the case, then three things immediately follow which must affect the nature of its management.

1

The first is that if education is about choice, then it must necessarily be about selection: one could not, for instance, put everything into the curriculum of a school, even if one wanted to. Biology will probably be placed above bingo, chemistry above checkers. Indeed, not only will some things be placed lower down the list of priorities, others will be positively rejected. Religious education may be chosen: devil worship certainly will not be offered. Choice then implies both a prioritization and a rejection of areas of knowledge, skills, attitudes, values and behaviours.

The second thing which follows is that this selection, because it is made by groups of people or individuals, is *their* selection, rather than everyone's. Even where a national curriculum is adopted, it is still the choice of a particular body of people, informed though they may be in that area. Were another group of informed people to be appointed, it is almost certainly the case that *their* selection would be partly or wholly different. Indeed, twenty years on, the same people may well choose a different list of things.

The point is that choice is inevitably, incurably subjective, for such choice is always limited by viewpoint, and that is determined by such things as age, previous experiences, present inner physiological and psychological states, the cultural or belief system of which one is a member, and historical and geographical location. This does not mean that all choices, in education or in anything else, are all of equal value: there are ways of judging the worth of one viewpoint against another. But one does need to be suitably wary when it is suggested that bodies of knowledge, facts, or values are 'objective', and particularly when a consensus within society suggests that there is no problem. When the management of schools is seen as unproblematical in a value sense, the simple transmission of facts and values from those at the apex of the hierarchy to those at the bottom, then one needs to be doubly cautious.

This leads to the last point, that any selection will be chosen by a particular individual or group, and that this selection will be underpinned by what that individual or group regards as significant and important for the child, the adult, and society. In other words, that selection will be based upon a set of values, which are themselves selective and subjective, for they will stem from that person's or group's beliefs and understandings of the world. And clearly, if these values are selective and subjective, then they need to be scrutinized, and may be contestable.

If, then, education is concerned with values and their subjectivity, it follows that the management of schools cannot avoid these issues, and that it needs to be aware of, and be ready to examine, the values, principles, and attitudes proposed for its practice. Indeed, as Chapter 1 will show, there is a strong interaction between values and management, for the choice of values will have important ramifications for the kinds of management adopted, just as the kind of management chosen will affect the implementation of those values held as most suitable or desirable.

This notion of a dialectic between values and management practice is a point worth emphasizing, simply because this interaction has not always been recognized. Indeed, a fair proportion of the literature treats the management of schools (or of any institution, for that matter) as neutral and unproblematical, as nothing more than the means of implementation for purposes decided elsewhere. Indeed, there has been a spate of books in the last few years dealing with the 'effective' management of schools, as if it were possible to leave the question of the acceptability of such management methods to some other time and body for consideration. But should not ethical questions come before those of effectiveness? Would one want to countenance management methods in education which were effective but ethically unacceptable? Moreover, as all educational decisions are impregnated by judgements of what is or is not to count as valuable or worthwhile, the kind of management adopted will contain within it implicit values about the way in which knowledge and values are viewed, about the status of an individual within the organization, and of the role that individual should play within it. It is simply not possible to consider school management without considering the values underpinning it.

For example, if schools are encouraged to adopt an epistemology which sees knowledge as 'true' and 'objective', or if a set of values is adopted which are seen as 'true' and 'objective' (and the two do tend to go together), there will almost certainly be consequences for the style of management used. As the 'truth' comes from above, education becomes primarily a means of transmission, and it is highly likely that a form of hierarchical, line management will be adopted, where each person is ascribed a certain role and position within the organization. Their behaviours are then defined by that role, and it will constrain the way in which they behave or act. Such a view of management, as will be seen in Chapters 2, 3 and 4, tend to result in hierarchy, alienation, and an inability to voice dissent when it is most needed.

Such a view of values and epistemology also has important consequences for the social and political development of the individual, and ultimately of society as a whole. Where teachers and pupils are defined and treated as low in an objectively defined hierarchy, they are less likely to develop managerial understanding and expertise than those who work in a structure which fosters respect for different opinions and judgements and expertise, regardless of their place in a formal hierarchy. Individuals working within a rigid hierarchical structure are also less likely through this experience to believe that their opinion counts for anything, or their actions can affect anything. This is not fertile soil, then, for the development of a truly democratic form of society, in which citizens genuinely and actively participate.

On the other hand, a managerial approach which appreciates the subjectivity of judgement and the challengeability of approved understandings is much more likely to encourage citizen involvement, both within the school organization, and ultimately within society as a whole. One can anticipate this effect on both teachers and pupils alike, for all working within organizational structures, whether in high position or low, will be affected by the rules and norms of that organization. Indeed, all those involved in a bureaucratic form of organization will be subjected to socializing forces which prevent them from fully developing their potentials, both as individuals and as members of a community. The consequences, then, will be felt not only at a personal level, but at a social and political level as well. Indeed, if morality is defined as

> ... that area concerned with the ways in which people, individually or in groups, conceptualise, treat and affect themselves and other living beings ...
>
> (Bottery, 1990, p. 77)

then ultimately the management of the school is concerned with the *moral* education of those within it. Those who are given little opportunity to experience and exercise involvement and choice within the school are not being given the education which will allow them to exercise these qualities and skills in the wider context of society. The implications for policy-makers are clear: if they genuinely wish to create a really moral and democratic society, in which people feel empowered to play an active, caring, critical and constructive part, then schools need to be developed whose organization gives this experience to people before they enter the larger society. At the present time, it might be argued, this is not high enough on the list of priorities for the purposes of schools.

Indeed, it has been argued that where schools become bureaucratized, they become bound up with the techniques and implementation of the managerial process, and may concentrate on concern with position and self-advancement. In so doing, they may neglect the purpose for which they were set up in the first place. Thus, they do not facilitate the development of those who are part of the school community, and tend to neglect the desires of children, parents and society at large. It is because of such criticisms that there has been an increasing influence in political rhetoric and legislation of free-market theories of organization and society. Such theories suggest that a much more market-oriented, competitive approach is required so that schools reorient themselves towards their 'clients'. By so doing, it is claimed, not only do they once again address the needs of those with whom they should be primarily concerned, but such an approach also unleashes the benefits of individual responsibility, freedom of choice, and reward for personal endeavour.

Though much of this sounds attractive, it has its roots as much in an economic body of thought as in social and political theory, and this must raise the question of whether it can be viably transferred to an educational context. Indeed, if by 'educational' one means the development of *all* within the school community, then free-market theory may miss the mark by concentrating on only one section, 'the consumers'. If teachers are seen as part of this community, then *their* development is just as important. If bureaucracy diverts attention away from the true purposes of schools, it must be asked whether free-market theories succeed in redirecting them back. Further, if one of the problems of bureaucratic forms of management is their adoption of supposedly 'objective' sets of values, free-market theories, based as they are on notions of free choice, face the problems at the opposite end of the value spectrum. If bureaucratic forms of management face the problem of explaining how their values can be objective when they are in fact the product of a particular value orientation, the forms of management derived from free-market theories, suggesting as they do an openness to the adoption of different sets of values, are subject to the charge of relativism. In other words, free-market theories, granted that they are arguing that individuals should be allowed to pursue their own ends, must explain why *any* set of values, including their own, is preferable to another. Chapters 5, 6, and 7 will describe this approach, and assess its difficulties and its possibilities for schools.

The free-market approach, however, is not the only value influence which affects educational management. Indeed, free-market approaches may be seen as but one very powerful subset of *the* major influence upon education on both sides of the Atlantic. This is the business management literature. Its influence upon education has been so strong partly through the need for an educated workforce, but also because of its longer history, and the sometimes fairly unthinking translation into an educational context. Chapter 8 will draw on many of the strands of previous chapters to address directly this question of the transferability of business concepts, aims and purposes to the educational sector, and in particular ask to what extent forms of organization primarily aimed at economic goals are applicable to a form of organization more concerned with the personal and social growth of the individual, and from there to the creation of a 'good' society.

Another very strong influence at the present time, riding on the back of much of the business literature, is that of the example of Japanese management and the Japanese schooling system. The train of argument generally applied is clear: the Japanese economy is booming, whilst ours hovers ever on the brink of recession. Much of the Japanese success, it is claimed, stems from the management techniques they use in business and industry. So should not these techniques – and perhaps those from Japanese schools – be transplanted elsewhere? Chapter 9 will suggest that this is a fascinating but knotty problem, and that glib transferability is neither desirable nor possible. There *are* things for school management to learn, as there are from the other influences examined in this book, but they all need to be examined with the kind of educational scalpel described above.

The last three chapters of the book move directly into the school and confront the question of the form of management for which schools should aim. It will be argued that such a form must be underpinned by prior educational questions concerning the ultimate purposes of school, and that these are of a fundamentally ethical nature. From the place of the pupil in the organization, to that of the teacher, the book moves to examine the form that leadership should take within a school. This question in many ways takes one to the heart of the ethics of school management, for it is from this conceptualization that so much else follows. If, as this book suggests, the management of the school should be a servant to the growth of the person, whether adult or child, then the concept of leadership cannot be tied simply to one person officially designated as being head or principal of that school. Whilst clearly that person *will* have duties of formal management, the role must also encompass a facilitative approach which provides a vehicle for others within the organization to learn to lead. This is not suggesting a flat form of management, nor an abnegation of responsibility by those designated as head or principal. It acknowledges the legal and practical constraints of headship, but also suggests that an acceptance of the personal, social and political aims of management, bounded by an appreciation of the subjectivity of judgement and values, necessarily implies a form of leadership characterized by tolerance, responsiveness, facilitation and progressively greater democracy.

The ethicality of school management must be tested in terms of a number of values. These will be of a personal, social *and* a political nature, for the treatment of the individual and the group within the school must have profound implications for the political processes of the country in which pupils will come to be adult participants, and ultimately for the planet on which they live. The questions which must be asked, then, move along a continuum from issues about individual development at one end to those concerning a world community of citizens at the other. These questions then must include:

- Does the management of the school promote personal growth?

- Does it treat people as ends in themselves or as means to ends?
- Does it foster a rationality which is not only tolerant of criticism, but actually sees it as an essential part of school and society?
- Does it repudiate the view of human beings as resources to be manipulated, and instead see them as resourceful humans?
- Does it create an ethos where measures of democracy can be introduced to be replicated within the society at large?
- Does it foster an appreciation of the place of individuals as citizens within their own communities, states and the world?

The argument of this book is that change must be effected where the structuring of current management practice does not facilitate these functions, or where such management practice actively discourages them. Whilst many writers, administrators and politicians may pay lip-service to such an argument, it is my belief that too often the growth of the person is not at the centre of their vision, and too often people in schools become the victims of organizational structures and practices, rather than these being fitted to their wants and needs. An awareness and acceptance of the ethics of school management could lead to a change in such a perspective.

In the end, whilst being keenly aware of the practical constraints that practitioners are under, this is a book concerning what ought to be done, rather than about what is being done. And if, in the end, people ask why they should read a book which may not immediately help with the design and implementation of the nuts and bolts of management, the answer is that it does. It asks them to reflect, not only on the 'how' of management, but also on the 'why'. The dangers of not doing so are pointed to in the Chinese quotation which forms the epigraph of this book:

> They lower their heads to pull the cart, instead of raising their heads to look at the road.

And if one does not look at the road, who knows where it may lead?

# Chapter 1

# Is value-free management possible?

## INTRODUCTION

It is not so long ago that you would have been hard pressed to find a book in a library on the topic of the management of schools in the UK. Before 1970, you would have found plenty of books on schools, and plenty on management, but very few where the two words were combined. For many years, and for generations of teachers, there existed an ingrained belief that the teacher was an educator, not a manager, and that if you had to be a manager, then the only qualification needed was to be a good teacher. Management as an activity was seen by the vast majority of the teaching profession as dull, boring and uninteresting. The real importance and excitement of the job was in the teaching – that, after all, was why people entered the profession in the first place.

Supporting such assumptions and thus compounding the problem, was the fact that until the mid-1970s schools were very much the preserve of the teacher; what David Eccles, the Minister of Education in 1960, called their 'secret garden' (Lawton, 1980, p. 22). Clearly, when such managers were not very much interested in management theory, and had such control over what went on in schools, there was little that was going to be written on the subject.

Times have changed. Oil crises, balance of payment problems, Black Papers, Ruskin College speeches and monetarist economics later, a new ethos surrounds and infuses education. If the words of the 1960s and early 1970s were progressivism, child-centredness and partnership, the words from the 1970s onwards have been curriculum, testing and accountability. If teachers in the past were seen as individuals in charge of their destinies and those of their pupils, the creators of individual and idiosyncratic curricula and ethos, they are now increasingly seen as members of teams, with specific tasks to perform and to accomplish, which are determined by bodies outside of the school. Increasingly, the determination of ultimate aims has been taken away from teachers, the achievement of short-term objectives now being their sphere of responsibility.

This trend is not peculiar to education. In all areas of life in the Western world where large organizations exist, there has been a continuous move to formalize and systematize, to organize and structure. The reasons for this are many and complex, and one of the purposes of this book will be to show how this movement has come about. Indeed, the tendency has become so ingrained in Western ways of thinking that we find it extraordinarily difficult to think of managing in any other way. For the moment, though, let it just be noted that this is not something peculiar to education. The tendency is widespread, and occurs even in those activities which might appear the exact antithesis of organization and planning, where the creative, the spontaneous and the unpredictable are usually seen as essential for success. Look,

7

for example, at what Dennis Main Wilson said of one area of entertainment. He commented:

> Comedy isn't talent-led anymore. It's management-led. It used to be management's job to support, now they dictate. More and more producers are just given formats to occupy.
>
> (Sedgwick, 1990, p. 5)

This is an immensely insightful remark, revealing the very heart of much management thinking of the present. Activities – even those seemingly dependent upon the unpredictable – are judged to be no longer based upon the decisions of performers. Whereas previously those acknowledged to have the talent were granted the freedom to create, now their job is to perform to scripts dictated by others. Their talent is used to breathe life into something which was essentially stillborn precisely because what was required was the predictable and controllable rather than the creative and the possibly anarchic. And management? Management moves from being the organizer of resources, the provider of facilities, the supporter who makes sure that nothing impedes the creative flow, to being the one who decides what the performer will say or do. The key notions are predictability and control. Now, by 'control' is not necessarily meant some diabolic conspiratorial plot to rule all; rather, what is meant is the need to know where things are, how they are going to work, to be able to predict what will happen next. This has been of the essence of Western thinking for several centuries. It has been the bedrock of scientific thinking, and has been the principal reason for Western economic and military dominance over the globe.

The same process has been increasingly applied to education. Management has moved from an off-stage role to one seen as crucial, central even. Clear signs of the importance being accorded to it are its pre-eminent position in the list of areas of priority designated by the DES, the number of courses being run on it, and the number of books being published in the area. The management of schools is a boom area, and if only for this reason it deserves attention; for what is being suggested within it to the managers of schools will have far-reaching effects upon the job performed by practitioners in the school, and upon the socialization of the next generation. Perhaps the claim that most needs to be made at this stage, then, is that the practice of management is not boring, dull and uninteresting. That might be claimed if the practice was neutral in its effects, but, clearly, both political and ethical issues are raised by the management style and techniques adopted. An examination of the principles underlying the management of schools, therefore, could hardly be more important – or interesting.

## PROBLEMS AND POSSIBILITIES OF TRANSFERENCE

One of the themes which will recur again and again throughout this book is that schools are peculiar organizations, and one must be constantly aware of the danger of transferring concepts from other organizations to schools in an insensitive and undiscriminating manner. Thus, the head and staff of a school might feel their hackles rising when they read Peter Drucker (1968), who suggested (p. 19) that

> Every act, every decision, every deliberation of management has as its
> first dimension an economic dimension . . .

He was, of course, writing for businessmen, and was very quick to follow this remark with the caution:

> . . . the skills, the competence, the experience of management cannot . . .
> be transferred and applied to the organisation and running of other
> institutions . . .

and he lists among those institutions to which one should not transfer and apply such expertise in an unthinking manner that of education. One cannot, therefore, blame *him* for a too eager application of business methods of education.

Nor, indeed, should one be too keen if one is an educationalist to ignore the theories and practices of other organizations. There are real benefits to be gained from taking an overview of organizations in general, and examining their transferability to schools. An example of the kind of thing I am talking about occurs in the work of Charles Handy on different cultures in organizations. This was originally presented in Handy (1985), and subsequently extrapolated to education in his work with Robert Aitken (Handy and Aitken, 1986). Essentially, Handy suggested that there are four major 'cultures' which shape the structure of an organization and relationships within it. These he names after four Greek gods: Zeus, Apollo, Athena and Dionysus. A brief description needs to be given of each.

## (a) The Zeus club culture

Zeus was the king of the Greek gods. He was feared, respected and occasionally loved. He represented the patriarchal tradition of impulsive, sometimes irrational, power which was sometimes benevolent, sometimes malevolent. This god ruled because of and through his charisma and personality. Handy characterizes the organization created by Zeus as one of a 'spider's web', where 'the boss' sits at the centre of the web, is aware of everything going on, and pulls all the strings. Such a culture tends to be an excellent one where speed of decision is needed. Speed, on the other hand, does not guarantee quality, and this of course depends upon the calibre of the Zeus at the helm and his inner circle of trustees. If you belong to this inner circle, this club, it tends to be a very pleasant place to work in, because, within the confines of what Zeus wants, individuals tend to be valued, and their efforts rewarded personally, and there can be real flexibility in the manner in which people do their jobs. It is clear, of course, that the strengths of such a culture are also its weaknesses – those not part of the inner circle are going to have a fairly unpleasant time of it.

## (b) The Apollo role culture

If Zeus is the extreme of personality and unpredictability, Apollo is at the other end of the spectrum. Apollo was the god of order and rules, and thus the Apollonian culture tends to be rather, as Handy says, like a piece of construction engineering, with the parts joined together in a logical, orderly fashion. Roles and duties are similarly rationally divided and fixed, and the individual is slotted into them.

9

Individuality, however, is not a thing to be prized, for the emphasis is upon the performance and completion of clearly defined tasks in carefully prescribed ways. If one person leaves the organization, another can then come in and do the job in precisely the same way. We clearly have here a picture of a bureaucracy. Bureaucracy is fine when predictability can be assumed, but in times of stress, or with activities which depend upon unpredictability, the two may not gel together.

## (c) The Athenian task culture

Athena was the problem-solver *par excellence*, and in this culture management is seen as being basically concerned with the continuous solution of problems. One thus defines the problem, allocates the resources, gives the group or team the go-ahead, and waits for their resolution. Performance can then be judged in terms of ends or results: the means are left to the task group.

Clearly the culture works well for technicians who know their job. Ultimate aims are defined by those outside, and professionalism is therefore restricted to knowing how to get a job done.

## (d) The Dionysian existential culture

In contrast to the Athenian professional, the Dionysian is a self-motivated, self-made individual. Dionysians define and pursue their own ends, seeing themselves as independent, loaning themselves to the organization as experts. Management is tricky, for it is only by the consent of Dionysians that things get done as an organization, and each Dionysian sees him- or herself as beholden to no other. Every individual has the right to veto, and co-ordination is a series of endless negotiations.

Clearly each of these cultures will have marked effects upon how the organization is run and how people within it react to one another. An example of this is given in Figure 1.1, where six dimensions of organizational structure and dynamics are examined.

Perhaps the most important thing which needs to be said about Figure 1.1 is that it, like the sketches of organizations given in the description of the four gods, is sweeping in its scope, but probably limited precisely bcause of its generality. It is certainly true that organizations have many things in common. However, what if organizations fundamentally differ on what they are trying to achieve? Does the fact that a factory tries to make a profit, but a school seeks something very different, make a difference to the way they should be organized?

## THE PROBLEM OF DIFFERING PURPOSES

As an example of these differing philosophies, look at those existing even within one type of organization, that of schools. Schools can be seen as the institutional means of expressing a particular philosophy of education. And it is possible to argue from at least four different philosophical standpoints for the ultimate purposes of education.

The first, the *cultural-transmission code*, values knowledge which is perceived as part of a country's cultural heritage. It sees the child as essentially a passive imbiber, one of many to be graded in their understanding and internalization of such knowledge. Teachers, therefore, are seen as guardians, transmitters of appropriate

| Features / Gods | Who defines the aims? | How is leadership defined? | Is there a hierarchy? How is it arranged? | How is accountability measured? | How is consent reached? | How is individualism seen? |
|---|---|---|---|---|---|---|
| Zeus | The head of the organization | By the personality of the leader | Yes. Head, inner circle, the rest | Head is aware of all strands of the web | By the command of the head | OK as long as Zeus approves of the individual |
| Apollo | Those who draw up the rules and regulations of the organization | By the rules and regulations | Yes. Pyramidal, carefully described in rules and regulations | Clearly laid down in rules and regulations | By the rules and regulations | Irrelevant, possibly impeding the process |
| Athena | Those who set the task | By being an expert | Yes. Hierarchy of expertise | By whether the aims of the task are achieved | By agreement between experts | Part of being an expert, but to be blended with the group |
| Dionysus | Those who do the job | Problematical: everyone and no-one is a leader | Very little. Democratic, moving to anarchic | Problematical: personal assessment by those who do the job | Protracted negotiations | The essence of the job – of existence |

**Figure 1.1** The four gods of management and their organizations.

11

values, and as headteachers will be transmitters, and supervisors of those below them who are also transmitting, the situation will be an essentially hierarchical one.

The second, the *child-centred code*, sees the curriculum as based on each individual child's experiences and interests, each of them being active, involved, unique constructors of their own reality. It sees education as the antithesis of transmission, but as an open-ended activity in which the process of exploration and discovery are seen as being vastly more important than the end-product. The teacher, in this situation, becomes a facilitator, a constructor of beneficial situations for the child, but in no way a transmitter, for he or she must at all times be ready for the movement from one area of interest to another.

The third, the *social-reconstruction code*, sees schools as essentially concerned with pressing social issues which need to be resolved, and therefore the curriculum takes the form of being topic- or problem-based. In this situation, children are active and critical, and gain their educational identity through interaction with others in social groups in which each is seen as a necessary contributor. The teacher in such a situation is a facilitator, a constructor, a selector of relevant problems, issues and materials, but also a guardian of what is to be retained from the past. Here, there is a mixture of democracy and guidance: the pupils have the right and duty to analyse and criticize, the teacher to act as guide and mentor.

The last, the *gross national product (GNP) code*, appears to be the motive force in much educational decision making at the present time, and values knowledge which is conducive to the furtherance of national economic well-being. It sees the child as a being to be trained to fit into this economic machine. Initiative and activity are encouraged only as far as these dovetail with ultimate occupational destinations. The teacher, therefore, is seen as a trainer, constructor and transmitter, a lower-order member of a hierarchy which begins at government levels and proceeds through the headteacher, to the teacher, to the child. It can be seen that the cultural-transmission code and the GNP code are similar in many ways, and yet they differ crucially in what is regarded as valuable, for relevance to the prevailing economic situation is seen as the crucial criterion in one but serves little or no purpose in the other.[1]

One could, therefore, have schools for transmitting the tried and trusted facts and values of the past, schools specifically created for children to explore themselves and their possibilities, schools for fostering a critical approach to changing society, or schools geared to equipping children with the skills and techniques to enable them to get a good job in today's world. Or, of course, one could have a school with a mixture of some or all of these philosophies. It clearly must be the case, then, that 'school' is not a neutral word, but carries a vast array of considerations of value behind it. And if schools transmit particular codes of values, then clearly their management structures and workings should (if the job of transmission is being done at all well) reflect the philosophy or philosophies underpinning the school. We will look at a couple of examples.

If you think that the transmission of tried and trusted facts and values is the proper function of schools, then your aims and objectives will be clear and precise: you know what needs to be transmitted, and you will know when they have been transmitted. The child in such a set-up is an imbiber, a relatively passive recipient of this diet. The teacher is a transmitter and the head a supervisor of this programme.

| Type | Aims and objectives | Role of child | Role of teacher | Role of head | Hierarchical/ democratic | Accountability and evaluation |
|---|---|---|---|---|---|---|
| Cultural transmission | Once selection is defined, clear and precise | Passive imbiber of transmitted knowledge | Transmitter | Transmitter, supervisor in hierarchy | Hierarchical | Clear and precise, probably quantitatively by exams |
| Child-centred | Clear aims, but changeable and impermanent objectives | Active, involved. Creator and constructor | Guide and facilitator | Facilitator, co-ordinator | Democratic | Problematical: subjective and qualitative |
| Social reconstruction | Aims clear, objectives fairly so, but both capable of modification during process | To be informed on issues, hence recipient, but also critic and constructor, hence active | Raiser of issues, guide, facilitator of process | Co-ordinator, raiser of issues, facilitator of process | Mixed: selection and input by teachers suggests hierarchy; criticism and suggestions by children implies democracy | Likely to be problematical and qualitative, multi-dimensional |
| GNP (Economic) | Clear and precise | Generally recipient, though initiative encouraged within overall paradigm | Transmitter of paradigm and facts; facilitator in enterprise initiatives | Transmitter, supervisor in hierarchy, facilitator of economic initiatives | Hierarchical paradigm: possibilities of elements of democracy within it | Usually clear and precise: probably in a quantitative form by exams; some qualitative assessment of initiatives |

**Figure 1.2** Educational philosophies and their management systems.

The system is hierarchical in nature, indeed has to be hierarchical, because of one's view of what a school should be doing.

A very different view of management arises when one considers schools where children are empowered to explore themselves and their capabilities. Here, because children's interests and capabilities are constantly changing, aims and objectives are not so easy to plan; aims may be as strong as in other models, but objectives must remain unclear from one week to the next, for flexibility is the hallmark of this approach. The child here is seen as active and involved, a constructor of his or her reality, whilst the teacher clearly cannot be a transmitter, but must be a guide, a person of infinite flexibility and adaptability, whilst the head becomes a co-ordinator and facilitator. Hierarchy makes little sense, and one moves increasingly towards a model of democracy.

The implementation of management techniques thus differs radically, depending upon which educational philosophy lies behind it. A more complete description of such managerial changes can be seen in Figure 1.2.

One might therefore be inclined to argue that Handy's four gods are really of little value in the school context precisely because of the variations in philosophy even between schools. However, it is still possible to derive benefit from a consideration of them, by applying them *to* the educational philosophies just described. The combination of the two produces some very interesting insights and predictions for the educational process, and management in particular. The application of cultures to philosophies can be seen in Figure 1.3 on p. 18.

## (a) Cultural transmission

The interaction between a philosophy of cultural transmission and the four gods is not as problematical as one might imagine. It will be clear that there is a strong dovetail between this and the Zeus culture. Transmission would be effected through the personality of the head, though clearly the actual selection of what is to be transmitted would be affected by this personality. In many ways, this is the classic 'paternalistic head' for which schools in the UK have been so well known.

Similarly, when one considers the effect of an Apollo culture, there will also be a dovetail here, though now transmission is effected through a less personality-dominated mode, and one might expect something much more systematic and structured, such as through a centrally prescribed curriculum and subject matter, and designated means of transmitting it. Each person in the school would know his or her role in this transmission, and what precisely his or her duties were. There are clear parallels between this model and the kind of very specific legislation on legally prescribed subjects, attainment targets and tasks, and concern for published results characteristic of the 1988 Act in the UK.

Again, with the Athena culture, there would be a good fit between the two. The task for Athena workers, though, is not to work out what should be transmitted, but how to go about the process. The collegial model of school organization, recommended in the 1978 HMI report on primary schools, will be strongly favoured, with each person working as part of a team to accomplish this task. Collegiality, however, will be restricted, and will not be truly professional, for tasks will already be defined by bodies outside the school, generally of a political nature. Again, parallels can clearly be seen between this and recent educational legislation in the UK.

Finally, even Dionysus, the arch individualist, could dovetail with cultural transmission, though a school based on this kind of management would probably be one hovering between democracy and anarchy: each member of the staff would decide what he or she felt it was appropriate to transmit and then continue with it. It could be said, though, that such a school is not an impossibility. Indeed, with no central organization, and a strong belief in some selection of cultural transmission, many UK schools in the past may well have approached this model.

## (b) Child-centredness

The philosophy of child-centredness has real problems with most of the gods, for in a way it is antithetical to any form of organization which tries to structure an environment which moves beyond the single classroom, and this is because each age-group, each child, is different, has different interests and needs, and must be responded to when those needs and interests appear. It clearly demands a very flat form of management, for it is the most democratic form of schooling.

And yet Zeus, by his very nature, is hierarchical. He loves to be in control, to pull the strings. There is clearly a conflict of ideals: a democracy inherent in the philosophy of child-centredness, a hierarchy in the Zeus culture. Forms of accommodation may be found: in primary schools, for example, the paternalist head has in the past overseen the general workings of the school, whilst allowing the class teacher to 'do their own thing'; in secondary schools, with a subject-dominated approach *and* a paternalist head, child-centredness could have little joy.

The relationship with Apollo is probably even more problematical. Child-centredness is founded upon the individuality of children, and teachers' ability to be flexible in their response to them. Yet bureaucracies find individuality an annoyance, a hindrance even, to the pursuance of clearly laid out aims and objectives, rules and procedures; and they dislike flexibility and movement between specified roles – neatness and specification come high on the list of priorities. It might well be argued that the demise of child-centredness in the UK is directly related to the creation of Apollonian educational legislation.

The situation with Athena is slightly more hopeful. There will tend to be a whole-school approach to the child rather than an individualistic approach. In some ways this will benefit the child, for every teacher can bring their own area of expertise to draw out and stimulate the child. The problem with one-teacher/one-child is that any teacher is inevitably limited in his or her pedagogic repertoire, and the child suffers accordingly. Clearly, though, because so many teachers will be involved with so many children, there is the very real danger of the teacher not really knowing the child in the way that is necessary for child-centredness to take place. This is clearly the traditional division between the secondary and primary schools in the UK, and one which has never been satisfactorily resolved. What might well happen with an emphasis on a team-centred approach is a move to an emphasis on curriculum rather than the child, as has happened in the UK for primary schools in the 1980s. The message, however, is clear: whichever course you choose will impose its penalties, and they cannot be entirely avoided.

The picture with Dionysus is a lot simpler. With each individual devising his or her own method, child-centredness could easily be the path chosen. The problem for the Dionysian is the converse of that for the Athenian: if one chooses child-centredness, one loses out on the benefits of the diverse curricular expertise which a team-centred approach could offer. It was the lack of expertise in important areas such as primary science, as well as the lack of continuity between classes, age-groups, and schools, which led to the rejection of a Dionysian approach in UK primary schools. Where each is allowed to do their own thing, the best of practice may result, but so may the worst.

## (c) Social reconstruction

This philosophy has within it strands of both hierarchy and democracy. It has the strand of hierarchy in that there must be teacher guidance in what is to be attended to, and the idea that the teacher might be able to put forward informed points of view to which students should pay due attention is not disregarded. In this sense, then, teachers are seen as guides and helpers, their opinions to be listened to and respected. At the same time, however, there is a freedom of expression, a desire for students to reach their own conclusions on the evidence and opinions put before them. The aim of this kind of philosophy is as much upon the students acquiring the skills of criticism and construction through the dialectical process, as it is with arriving at the 'correct' solution. So parts of this philosophy will appeal to all four gods, and other parts will not.

Zeus, for instance, will be happy to be seen as a guide and mentor. He will be less likely to be happy if children reach conclusions which run counter to his own. Social reconstruction has a deeply democratic strain within it, and the paternalist may find it hard to let go of his fatherly control and allow his charges to reach and act upon decisions with which he does not agree, which he cannot and should not control. The combination of this culture and this philosophy is almost certain to bring conflict.

Apollo will not be much happier. Whilst Apollonian organization is meticulous with regard to stability and predictability, social reconstruction implies change, and demands that it be carried out if the need is felt. Bureaucracies are based on the notion of continuity: a philosophy which is based on change is obviously not going to marry with it. The bureaucratization of education implicit in some of the 1988 Act will very probably have this effect: of preventing quick change and flexibility when needed. It could be argued that in an era of rapid and accelerating change, the very thing one should *not* devise is an education system based around tight rules and regulations, but one based on decentralization and the ability to adapt quickly to changing circumstances.

Athena, on the other hand, will probably work quite well with such a philosophy. Provided that the team of teachers were of like mind on what is to be selected to be discussed, a whole-school approach to the discussion of issues, and ways in which they may be retained, or ways in which they must be changed, would be an extremely powerful way of disseminating this philosophy. Curricula would tend to be holistic in conception, for subject-by-subject teaching would fragment teaching and would inhibit the clear appreciation of the situations out of school which need to be considered and discussed. Clearly, a curriculum which legally demanded that specific subjects were taught, and tested as specific subjects, and a system where ultimate aims were again decided outside the school, would be extremely destructive of such a philosophy. Anyone wanting to prevent schools from being places which facilitated such discussion of social injustice and social change could do little better than to do the things just mentioned.

It should be becoming clear that Dionysians could fit any of the philosophies so far described. As they are individuals who very much design and implement their own programmes, it would be easy for them to adopt such a philosophy and run it. It will, of course, be less effective than an Athenian response, for if a school were filled with Dionysians of different philosophies, the pupil would end up something like the steel ball in a pinball machine: being bumped from one view of education to another, with no explanation, no continuity. For teachers, it might be exhilarating to pursue their own interests and their own designs; for the child it is much more likely to be simply confusing.

## (d) The GNP (economic) philosophy

One might at first assume that there is a simple dovetail between this philosophy and the Zeus culture of management. Are they not, after all, both hierarchical and transmissive? The answer, simply put, is no. Zeus may be in favour of transmission, but it will depend upon his personality as to what is deemed to be suitable of transmission, and there will be many of the Zeus mentality who incline more towards a cultural-transmission philosophy than a GNP one. Similarly, whilst it is clearly the case that Zeus favours hierarchy, the GNP code will applaud a degree of innovativeness and creativity, as long as these are carefully geared to GNP aims – much more than the average Zeus would want to tolerate. Clearly, though, where such a headteacher was in favour of the GNP code, there would be a powerful and effective dovetail. And where a head had grown up within an essentially hierarchical organization which did not necessarily specify any particular philosophy too strongly, it would not be beyond the wit of a government to devise courses, curricula and documentation which led a head down such a path without too much consultation.

In many ways, the Apollo culture would dovetail even more strongly. If the culture is designed around hierarchy and the specification of roles and duties, then discussion of the ultimate purpose of those roles and duties can be taken outside the school, and those within left merely to fulfil their specified tasks. There would then be no friction between the culture and the philosophy. Indeed, this is one of the principal criticisms, as we shall see, of bureaucracy: that whilst claiming to be the most rational form of organization, it is only so in a way which limits that rationality to one of functional and technical rationality – how best to carry out a job. It essentially de-skills the professional, for it takes out of the area of discourse and consideration the examination of those ends for which the bureaucracy's functions and tasks are designed. It dwells, as so many management books of the present time do, upon methods which are 'efficient' and 'effective', without examining whether such methods are acceptable as well.

There is no necessary friction between this philosophy and the Athenian task culture either, for the task would be simply to transmit the philosophy, by means left to a collegial group. It clearly would mean another example of restricted professionality, for again the teachers would not be asked to question what ultimate aims their collegial approach was set to achieve. Their brief would rather be to fulfil a specified set of tasks in the way most suited to their expertise and the children's

| Philosophy / Culture | Cultural transmission | Child-centred | Social reconstruction | GNP (Economic) |
|---|---|---|---|---|
| Zeus | Clear dovetail. Classic paternalism. Personality of head influences cultural selection | Probable conflict: democracy of philosophy, hierarchy of culture | Probable conflict: open criticism by pupils and staff may challenge paternalism | Both essentially hierarchical and transmissive – but Zeus may have different idea of what is to be transmitted. GNP also allows for more creativity |
| Apollo | Dovetail of hierarchy and transmission with designated roles and duties | Conflict – personalities do not fit boxes and roles – flexibility and change does not fit with Apollonian urge for stasis | Conflict – reconstruction implies changes and democracy, bureaucracy likes stability and hierarchy | Dovetail of hierarchy and transmission through designated roles and duties |
| Athena | Good fit, task is to transmit: collegial approach used. Restricted professionality | Possible fit: whole-school approach to each child, tendency towards emphasis on specialism and curriculum rather than child | Powerful dovetail: if aims determined by staff, effect very strong | Good fit: task is to transmit, collegial approach is to be tried. Restricted professionality |
| Dionysus | Dovetail when Dionysian is a cultural-transmission believer. Conflict at most other times | Dovetail when Dionysian is a child-centred believer. Conflict at most other times | Dovetail when Dionysian is a believer in social reconstruction. Conflict at most other times | Dovetail when Dionysian is a believer in GNP codes. Conflict at most other times |

**Figure 1.3** The interaction of organizational cultures and educational philosophies.

talents. But discussion and, crucially, change of such ultimate considerations would not be part of their functioning.

And finally, and as with the other philosophies, Dionysians, provided they subscribed to this philosophy, and precisely because they work alone, could implement a GNP philosophy with little trouble. All of the above comments on the weakness of such an approach – the lack of continuity and specialism, pot luck for the child – apply here as well.

## CONCLUSIONS

A number of things can now be seen.

The first is that general theories of management – usually taken from a business orientation – have some applicability in an educational setting. They provide descriptions of the general kind of running which a school might adopt, or, and probably more importantly, they illustrate the kinds of methods which schools may be compelled to adopt by political forces outside of themselves.

Secondly, it is now clear, however, that there are vast differences between institutions *within the same kind of organization*. The above examination of the effect of differing educational philosophies has shown that schools can be – and are – run in very different ways. And if this is so, how much more so is this likely to be when one considers the values *between* different organizations? This is something that we shall be looking into in detail in the next chapter.

The third point is that there is a clear need to follow through the implications of cultures like that of Zeus, Apollo, Athena and Dionysus for educational philosophies. The consequences are, I have suggested, genuinely predictive. They are in some cases surprising, in other cases cautionary. A close examination of them is essential for those concerned with the consequences of management upon those within the schools – both pupils and teachers.

Finally, neither the culture of a school, nor the educational philosophy it espouses, is value-free. Both culture and philosophy have considerable effects upon the thinking and practices of the inhabitants of such institutions. It is therefore from such a conclusion that a book examining the ethics of school-management practice needs to begin. If the practice of school management cannot be value-free, then it is clear that all managers must be critically aware of the assumptions underlying such practice, for it is only by being aware of and understanding them that one can really understand how schooling will affect the future ethical and political development of the people within the school and of society at large.

## NOTE

[1] A more detailed discussion of the strengths and weaknesses of these different philosophies can be found in Bottery (1990).

# Chapter 2

## The legacy of scientific management

### INTRODUCTION

It should be clear from the first chapter that the managerial practices of a school do not happen in a vacuum. They are undergirded by particular theories, particular conceptions of humankind. Some of these theories and conceptions hardly warrant the name, for they may be little more than the unreflected ideas of one person. Increasingly, though, this is not the case in school. There has been, as noted previously, an explosion in the educational management literature, and it is an unusual individual who gets to a senior position in school without becoming acquainted with some of it. It is essential, therefore, to examine some of the theories proposed for the management of schools. However, these theories have borrowed so widely, and, in some cases, so uncritically, from other fields, that these other fields need to be examined first. It is particularly important to examine the management literature from business and industry. This field is as varied as – perhaps more varied than – that of its younger sibling in education, and an awareness of its key assumptions is necessary because, as Rose (1985, p. 32) pointed out,

> At the core of any theory of industrial behaviour lies an image of the typical worker.

The images and assumptions behind the literature must therefore be closely examined, for they can have profound consequences for the running of the school. Indeed, as it might be argued that there are major differences between business and education, it could well be asked why education has increasingly turned to business for its management theory. There appear to be four major reasons.

Firstly, organizations have many things in common. The very fact that a chocolate factory, a primary school, an architects' partnership and a construction site can all be called 'organizations' suggests that there are some characteristics which they all share. Handy and Aitken (1986, pp. 32–3) suggest that there are seven such commonalities:

- they must decide on their key tasks, and whom they serve;
- they divide up the work to be done;
- they find ways of monitoring what is going on;
- they try to recruit the right people and keep them excited and committed;
- they train and develop them in the competencies required;
- they work out the best way to lead and relate to people;
- they try to create a sense of mission, and a common set of beliefs.

At this level of generality, there is not that much with which to quarrel. There may be different interpretations of these commonalities, but they are stated in such general terms that it is difficult to argue with them as they stand. It is when one moves from generalities to specifics that problems occur. What if an organization has many key tasks rather than just one, and if it serves different, and sometimes opposing, people? What if the nature of the work demands that it be treated in a holistic manner, rather than being divided up in a clean, surgical manner? What if the nature of the work is difficult to monitor because it is as much qualitative as quantitative? Indeed, as seen in the first chapter, Handy describes four very different types of organization, and begins that book with the warning.

> The best way to run an efficient chocolate factory will not be the right way
> to run an architects' partnership, a primary school or a construction site.
> Different cultures, and gods, are needed for different tasks.
>
> (Handy, 1985, p. 11)

The clear implication from this is that if one constructs management strategies for one species of animal, and then applies them to a very different species, the outcomes may be unexpected and unwelcome. One needs to examine the animals in question to understand the problems in transferring from one to another. Those who do not – who know only one beast – will not realize the differences.

The second reason why education has increasingly turned to business for its management theory is that it has had so little of its own. In this country, this is, as argued above, partly due to the ingrained belief of the teacher that he or she is an educator, not an administrator. For many years here it seemed to be an unargued assumption that if you could run a classroom, you could run a school. When school managers are not much interested in management theory, then little will be written on the subject. And when an area is weak in its own theory, it is prey to invasion from the theories of other, more thoroughly worked, areas.

Thirdly, in a socio-political ethos in the UK which gives a major role to free-market economics, there can be little surprise that those in government should attempt to apply their own perspectives to non-business institutions. In the US, the same kind of story has a much stronger pedigree and took place rather earlier. As Callahan (1962) has described, teachers in the US never had the same autonomy, but have been much more at the behest of local politicians and the parental voice. Much of this can be traced back to the early days of this century. In a country that saw itself as the cradle of entrepreneurial capitalism, strengthened by the ability to adopt the latest scientific advances, it is understandable that supposedly 'scientific' theories of management like those of Frederick W. Taylor (1911) would be enthusiastically adopted and applied to education. This mechanistic influence, despite the rise of other movements in organizational theory, has never really been lost. This school of thought, if in modified form, continues to have its adherents, and is so much a part of present-day thinking that its influence may go unnoticed. It is the task of this chapter to trace its influence and to investigate its transferability.

Finally, in an era of financial belt-tightening, there is a generally perceived need for all divisions of the public sector to be more efficient, and efficient in the same manner as businesses have to be, indeed for them to perform as businesses must perform. Those in control of the purse-strings have increasingly applied business analogies to all elements of the state sector, and so have come to feel that the teacher's secret garden should now be opened to the public. The result has been that education has increasingly come to face the kinds of demands met previously only in entrepreneurial concerns.

One further caveat needs to be made. The work in this field derives from the US, and it would be prudent for two reasons to assume that this has some bearing upon its applicability to other countries. The first is, as Campbell *et al.* (1987) point out at some length, that much of the theory is a product of social conditions in the US at the time of writing. If such conditions do not occur in other countries, the theory may well be an incorrect response for a particular time and place. But secondly, the very fact that much of a theory may have been generated by social conditions may lead it to be a prisoner of those times, imbued with their value assumptions. The theory, then, may be as much normative as it is descriptive, and its acceptance may actually *create* the conditions it describes. Such applications will therefore affect social situations and values by instituting regimes for management application, and in so doing transmit a hidden curriculum of values.

This is one very good reason to begin with an examination of the scientific management of F. W. Taylor. Whilst some may be inclined to dismiss it as being rather old hat, having fallen from favour over 50 years ago, there are strong reasons for the educational manager giving it extended consideration. The first is the reason indicated immediately above: that its adoption, or the adoption of neo-scientific approaches, may actually create the kinds of conditions it describes, and the sort of people it suggests. It sees humankind in a very deterministic, machine-like manner, and it is all too easy to create conditions of management which produce such behaviour. Management, as argued above, cannot avoid the issue of values in education. When it does try to ignore them, they continue to have their effects, but in unexpected and possibly undesirable ways. Management, then, must be concerned with the very conception of what we believe humankind to be, indeed ought to be. If this is agreed, it can be argued that it should further be concerned with implementing measures to facilitate the change. The West had been won, and dynamic and aggressive business and industrial empires began to take shape which were a long way from the individualistic, frontiersman attitude that the US had up until then adopted towards life in general. One era was coming to an end, and another and very different one was beginning.

Inevitably there would be two opposing sides in this new period of industrialism. On the one side was the labour of the day, accustomed to a traditional and unsystematic way of life. Not surprisingly, they wished to continue in this style of living. As Montgomery (1976, p. 486) has remarked,

> Working people clung to their traditional, spasmodic, task-oriented styles
> of work and to a social code which was less tightly disciplined . . . and less
> exploitive than that which industralization was forcing upon them.

On the other side, however, were the interests of the management of the new businesses and corporations, seeking to find structures for their organizations which would deliver their demands for efficiency and in so doing replicate the kinds of social relationships to further such calls. What was needed, then, it was believed, was a new means of control over the workforce.

## SCIENTIFIC MANAGEMENT

It was into such a setting that Frederick Taylor stepped. An engineer by profession, Taylor was convinced that there were not one, but two, causes of the inefficiency in the American workplace. The first cause was the workers, primarily because of their habits of 'slacking' and 'soldiering'. The second cause was, perhaps surprisingly, the managers, and this was because of what Taylor perceived as their general incompetence. If one improved the competency of the manager, Taylor believed, one could eliminate the unwanted practices of the workers. How could one do this? Taylor suggested that this was possible by developing effective procedures of supervision and uniform standards of production, and from there integrating the human and the technical sides of the industrial process. This could be accomplished by adopting the following five simple principles:

1. Transfer the responsibility for the organization of work from the worker to the manager. Indeed, it is reported that Taylor told workers that they were not required to think, for other people were paid to do that.
2. Use scientific analysis of the best workmen that you can find on a job to discover the exact series of elementary operations or motions which exactly capture the optimal performance of that task. Eliminate all unnecessary movements, and develop the remaining ones into a perfect sequence.
3. Select the best people to do the job efficiently.
4. Train these people in the optimal manner of performance.
5. Constantly monitor performance to make sure that the optimal manner is followed, and results are achieved.

Much of a critical character has been made of the fact that this procedure was worked out mainly through the study of pig-iron handling and shovelling at the Bethlehem Steel Company. This work was simple, repetitious, demanded little or no brainwork, and, as more than one commentator has pointed out, would probably have been even better suited to a horse or a robot than a human being. Certainly, the man whom Taylor did most of his research on, a Dutchman called Schmidt, seemed to benefit precisely from his limited intellect. Indeed, such was Taylor's mania for the system that he came to believe that those skilled workers who might oppose his system were little more than antediluvian survivors, heretics from a past age to be eliminated from the work process. There was, he believed, no need for them. As they were less efficient than his system, they clearly had no place in a modern workplace. The matter was succinctly put. In the introduction to his most famous work, Taylor wrote

In the past, the man has been first; in the future, the system must be first.

(Taylor, 1911, p. 7)

If Taylor was the ideal theorist for the industrial owners of his time, it was also fortuitous for him and them that he was a passionate believer in the power of science. As noted above, he was an engineer by profession, and this background led him to harbour few doubts about the ability of science to systematize and quantify the world, increasingly to make sense of it. This is clear from the enunciation of his principles of scientific management. What was fortunate as well was the general public's belief in the power of science. Science was in its Victorian inductivist heyday, when practitioners and public alike had a profoundly optimistic belief in the power of science to solve all of society's problems. A post-relativity age, when people would question the scope and power of rationality, and doubt the neutrality of science's findings, was still to come. And because of this, when a professional engineer argued so persuasively for a 'scientific' approach to management, it was hard for a public to argue, and pleasantly acceptable for industrial management not to want to. It is clear, then, that Taylor's system was made all the more powerful and conducive to managers by science providing it with a cloak of impartiality. As Campbell *et al.* (1987, p. 27) put it,

> Such a strategy left the impression that scientific study, and not the desire of managers to reduce costs or meet higher production targets, was chiefly responsible for speedier assembly lines, stricter forms of discipline, and new expectations for extra effort on the part of workers. The inference was simple: it was the stopwatch, not the supervisor who held it, that determined levels of worker performance.

In such a way, Taylor asserted, could the estimation of a 'fair day's pay for a fair day's work' be turned into a purely technical matter. This, however, is clearly fallacious, for by employing the notion of fairness, one moves from simple descriptive statements of work to notions of equity within a society. Mouzelis (1975, p. 87) puts it very neatly when he says that

> ... if it is scientifically possible to determine the length of time in which a certain job could be done, there is no scientific way of determining the time in which a certain job ought to be done.

The most it can say is that within a particular framework of payment, this system is fair. But if the framework is basically unjust, then so must be the payment. What Taylor was doing, whether he meant to or not, was to propose that the wages framework of his time was fair (this being very largely determined by management) and should continue to be so. Those with the whip hand would clearly be delighted with such a convincing argument for their case. There is little wonder then that Rose (1985, p. 54) can assert

> ... Taylor was essentially a man very much of and for his times. No one would have paid him the slightest attention if his message had not seemed a plausible solution to pressing problems confronting economically powerful groups in turn-of-the-century America, and to some extent elsewhere.

Indeed, Rose suggests (1985, p. 31) that many of Taylor's ideas are so silly that there is a great danger that in the present day his work will *not* be studied seriously; and it needs to be, because of the enormous influence it has exerted. It was, however, taken very seriously at the time. For many it was the panacea for virtually all ills. Take, for example, an excerpt from the records of the International Congresses for Scientific Management:

> It [the scientific-management movement] will give people better understanding and cooperation, and realize a new policy, the policy of a human world ... A world organization of scientific management could form a right basis for the foundation of world cooperative production and organized sales, removing the economic causes of war ... the new philosophy of scientific management must help to bring about the Christian philosophy of love and welfare among all nations ... it is absolutely beyond question that a knowledge of the principle of scientific management is fundamental for the success of everybody ...'
>
> (Mouzelis, 1975, p. 84)

## SCIENTIFIC MANAGEMENT AND EDUCATION

Even before scientific management took a stranglehold on the thought of educational administrators in the US, this love affair with the possibilities of science was already taking place in education. The founding father of quantitative psychology, E. L. Thorndike, had already declared in 1903 that

> It was the vice or misfortune of thinkers about education to have chosen the methods of philosophy or of popular thought instead of those of science.
>
> (Curti, 1959, p. 460)

Thorndike was already offering a course in the application of psychological and statistical methods of education at Teachers College, Columbia University, and it was not long after this that intelligence testing became a part of the educational practice of schools in the US, building on work of the French psychologists Binet and Simon, and culminating in the Stanford–Binet test of 1916. Such intelligence tests fitted the times, being acceptable to the growing academic climate, to the public at large, who were clamouring for 'objective' measurements of ability and attainment, and to school administrators who, by such testing, could obtain information which would enable them to sort and compare pupils, and thus more readily place them in suitable educational programmes. Such intelligence tests were increasingly supplemented by similar tests in spelling, arithmetical abilities, English composition and handwriting.

Such testing exactly fitted efforts to match the clarion call from virtually all quarters for the educational service to improve its instructional efficiency. With the dominance of business and industrial thought in American life, and the vulnerability of school administrators to public criticism and pressure, it is not surprising that principles of business efficiency, already a fairly basic assumption of the school, should be even more increasingly adopted.

Perhaps the clearest exponent of the enthusiastic adoption of scientific-management principles is Franklin Bobbitt, whose influence is to be seen down to the present day in the concept of aims and objectives, and the work of people like Ralph Tyler and Benjamin Bloom.

What is perhaps most interesting about Bobbitt's approach, because it has such relevance today, is that he appears to have viewed efficiency in education as a primary rather than a secondary goal. Many people would probably begin with a conception of what 'good education' was, and then move to a view of what problems there are in achieving it, and then to the elimination of these problems. Bobbitt, on the other hand, seems to begin with an acceptance of the notions of efficiency, standards and hierarchy as goods in themselves. This is understandable, given Bobbitt's scientific-management approach. Bobbitt, like Taylor, was fundamentally conservative in his approach to society. Education was to prepare children for their roles in present-day society, not to question or change it. As he explicitly stated,

> The School is not an agency of social reform. It is not directly concerned with improving society. Its responsibility is to help the growing individual continuously and consistently to hold to the type of human living which is the best practical one for him. This should automatically result in an enormous improvement in society in general. But this improvement is not a thing directly aimed at. It is only a by-product.
>
> (Bobbitt, 1926, p. 54)

Bobbitt, like Taylor, failed to see that one cannot derive an 'ought' from an 'is'. Just because lots of people do something, does not make this an acceptable practice. More than empirical evidence is needed to justify it. It requires an ethical argument as well. In Taylor's case, this is encapsulated in his belief that by analysing the most efficient way of doing a job, he could work out what was the fairest way of rewarding it. In Bobbitt's case, it was the belief that an analysis of present-day society could form the foundation of a curriculum:

> The central theory [of curriculum] is simple. Human life, however varied, consists in the performance of specific activities. Education that prepares for life is one that prepares definitely and adequately for these specific activities ... This requires only that one go out into the world of affairs and discover the particulars of which their affairs consist. These will show the abilities, attitudes, habits, appreciation and forms of knowledge that men need. These will be the objectives of the curriculum. They will be numerous, definite and particularized. The curriculum will then be that series of experiences which children and youth must have by way of attaining these objectives.
>
> (Bobbitt, 1918, p. 42)

To Bobbitt's credit, there is a real attempt here to make the planning of the curriculum a rational and meaningful exercise, and to build it from an examination of the practices of existing schools and the society in which they are bedded. But there is no appreciation that this cannot be just a reproductive exercise, but must be a critical and evaluative one as well. The crucial flaw is the flaw of scientific management in general: scientific analysis can tell you what is the case in a very systematic and rational manner, but it cannot tell you what ought to be the case. As one reviewer of Bobbitt's 1924 book *How to Make a Curriculum* said,

> The author seems to be unaware that in the scheme the cart is placed before the horse. How such analyses are to be made unless we know in advance which persons are good citizens, good parents, and true believers is not clear. It is assumed that if we dug up the facts by means of scientific analysis, the appropriate ideals will come to the surface too. . . .
> In other words there is no social vision or program to guide the process of curriculum construction.
>
> (Eisner, 1985, pp. 21–2)

This kind of mistake continued after Bobbitt's day. Tyler, in his curriculum rationale (1950), whilst explicitly asking as a first question 'What educational purposes should the school seek to attain?', devotes only a few sentences to the role of philosophy in curriculum construction, and appears much more interested in the practical questions. And yet it is clear that this must be a task addressed at some length. Any curriculum, national or otherwise, which does not – which fails to engage in debate about its ultimate ends – is making the same mistake.

There is a further flaw in the aims-and-objectives approach in education which again stems from Taylorian days. This is the notion of management as the transmission of such aims and objectives in a strictly hierarchical manner. This, I suggest, is a radical misunderstanding of the true process of education. It simply will not do to be told that the function of a teacher or a manager is to decide upon aims, and the objectives for these aims, and then to pursue them. The result is an individualist, rather than a dualistic, view of relationships. On this view, the individual announces his or her aims, and designs the objectives to achieve them. The criterion for success, then, is the achievement of these objectives, and therefore these aims. The problem for the teacher is that there are other people at the end of these aims and objectives. The teacher may wish to convey certain things: but the person at the other end of this relationship also has his or her aims and objectives for this learning relationship and this learning situation, determined by personal interests, experiences and understanding. What they *need* to get out of the relationship will almost always not be exactly what the teacher thinks they need: it will be a fusion of the two perspectives. Teachers, then, must come with a plan, but a flexible one, where, nimble on their mental feet, they listen to the other and adjust accordingly. A too-rigid version of aims and objectives, where the criterion of success is the success of only one side, defeats the educational purpose.

This, I think, is a major problem. For if aims and objectives are interpreted too rigidly (and there seems precious little qualification of their use in the official literature), then they, of necessity, exclude the interests, experiences and under-standings of those being taught. They prevent the true educational experience from taking place, and ultimately must alienate those taught, for it becomes very clear very quickly that theirs is a voice which will not be heard. There are none so deaf as those who will not hear. A too-rigid adherence to the notion of aims and objectives is only a modern instance of the kind of bad teaching that has been going on in some schools and some classrooms for an awfully long time: only now it seems to be being given official blessing.

It will be clear, then, why Bobbitt placed efficiency, standards and hierarchy as primary goods and demoted other values (which many would see as primary) to a secondary role: it is because Bobbitt began from the adoption of existing values, and assumed other values as problems to be eliminated. Thus, institutional autonomy, instead of being a value to be debated, becomes a problem, a result of the non-adoption of his values of efficiency, standards and hierarchy. As he states,

> It [institutional autonomy] *results* in a constitutional tendency to place the welfare of the worker above the welfare of the organization, and the welfare of both above the welfare of the total society of which school men and school institutions are but the agents.
>
> (Bobbitt, 1913, p. 50)

What happens, then, is that there is no debate about the primacy of the welfare of the system above the welfare of the individual or the individual institution, nor about the fact that this welfare is clearly assumed to be of an economic and profit-making nature. There is no debate about differences between business and education, because

> ... whether the organization be for commerce or for manufacture, philanthropy or education, transportation or government, it is coming to appear that the fundamental tasks of management, direction and supervision are always the same.
>
> (Bobbitt, 1913, p. 8)

There is no debate about hierarchy, because

> The new and revolutionary doctrine of scientific management states in no uncertain terms that the management, the supervisory staff, has the largest share of the work in the determination of the proper methods. The burden of finding the best methods is too large and too complicated to be laid on the shoulders of the teachers.
>
> (Bobbitt, 1913, p. 53)

There is no debate about centralization, because:

> Efficiency implies centralization of authority and definite direction by the supervisors of all processes performed.
>
> (Bobbitt, 1913, p. 89)

If such assumptions about standards, hierarchy and efficiency are made, the solutions to the perceived problem are easily arrived at:

> In any organization, the directive and supervisory members must clearly

define the ends toward which the organization strives ... Directors and supervisors must keep the workers supplied with detailed instructions as to the work to be done, the standards to be reached, the methods to be employed, and the materials and appliances to be used.

(Bobbitt, 1913, pp. 7–8)

The analogy with Taylor's conception of industry is now very clear. There is to be a distinct hierarchy: directors or headteachers are industrial managers, teachers are workers, and pupils are raw materials to be processed. Monitoring this production line is to be performed in terms of educational standards – the testing and assessment procedures mentioned above. And there must also be increasing concentration upon the financial business elements of educational management. This latter aspect was something which scientific management led American school administrators increasingly to emphasize. They began to pay much more attention to accounting procedures, budget preparations, record keeping, annual reports, and all the other aspects of financial management formally associated with the corporate business world. In these ways, it was believed, efficiency, the primary goal, could be achieved.

## EVALUATION

Three issues, perhaps, stand out. The first is the primacy of the goal of efficiency. The second is the model of humanity used in this analysis. The final one concerns the possible problems in transferring business and industrial theory to education. This is such a large issue that it must be left to a further chapter. The first two will be dealt with now.

The belief that there must be an increased efficiency in financing ventures is at the heart of much economic thinking. Lack of efficiency means wasted resources, and wasted resources mean not getting the results you could. So money-saving efficiency is to be recommended. There is a large element of self-evident sense in this proposal, which, it might be argued, only the deliberately obtuse or obstructive would quibble at. It sounds simple, but it has problems at the business level even before one begins an educational translation.

The notion of efficiency tends to be wedded to a simplistic and limited vision of both rationality and science which assumes that one can plan down to the last detail the way in which things will happen. However, it is in the nature of things that there are so many variables to control that the unexpected is just about always more likely to happen than the expected. Building a bridge may make little economic sense at the time of building, but the very act of building it may create demand on opposite sides of the river from industry which will then justify its building. Similarly, in education, one may initially have a choice of running two courses and decide to put on the more costly course, and yet by choosing this course one may provoke such unexpected interest that it becomes the more cost-effective, the more efficient.

Moreover, even if the building of the bridge does not translate economically – fewer vehicles go over the bridge than will pay for its upkeep – this still does not settle the argument. Building the bridge may improve the quality of life of those living around it, so that despite the inefficiency of the bridge in economic terms, it is still deemed worthwhile. We are into value judgements, and we are back to

29

education. A course of study, a particular piece of equipment, may not look cost-effective on paper, but is this the only, or even the major, consideration? Does it not depend on prior (value) assumptions, about what is felt to be worthwhile? Course X may cost less than course Y, but is that adequate justification for putting it on? If education is centrally concerned with values, then efficiency is at best only one of a set of values from which one may choose. Business and industry, primarily concerned with profits, may well play a different tune. And if education is different, then procedures like financial delegation to heads may not be made primarily on grounds of efficiency, but because they are ways of promoting the quality of education provided. It may be that such financial delegation, and an increased quest for efficiency, promote such quality, but it does not necessarily follow.

This demand for efficiency in education also illustrates the preoccupation of scientific management with finding the most rational means of achieving ends. Yet such a preoccupation may do more harm than good, for by concentrating upon the most efficient means for achieving particular ends, the ends themselves may be lost sight of. If the fundamental ends of educational management are not concerned primarily with increasing a society's economic productivity, but rather with the improvement of the quality of relationships within the school, then the irony is that as management strives for increasingly 'rational' means of achieving efficiency, so it may become increasingly irrational in the effects it has on the people affected by it. This is because people do not respond particularly to efficiency as an ideal, but rather to care, trust and responsibility. Efficiency is certainly a value to be accepted, but its place within the overall scheme of things needs to be very carefully evaluated.

The final point – the model of humanity used – is made by the old joke about scientific management that it can organize a job to get the most output for one hour but cannot do this for 500 hours. This is simply because Taylor's work completely ignores the psychology of human beings and their individualities. It has already been pointed out that the major flaw in the theory stems from the assumptions derived from Taylor's engineering background. He unquestioningly believed that he could transfer engineering principles to the human sector, and thus treat humankind like a machine. This, indeed, is the predominant metaphor. However, whilst in engineering one can proceed to work out the simplest co-ordination of optimal operations for one machine, which can then be generalized to all other similar machines, human beings do not work in this way. It is in the end a testament to Taylor's blindness to himself and other human beings that he did not realize this. There are at least two ways in which his blindness manifests itself. Firstly, he completely ignores the feelings, attitudes and private goals of individuals. Partly, this stems from the view of the worker as passive in the process. This is a not uncommon theme in much of the classical management literature: the manager, the entrepreneur, is seen as active, shaping, creative and rational, and the literature may go to great lengths in describing ways of improving this process. And yet workers are depicted as inert and passive, and, as Mouzelis (1975, p. 122) puts it,

> become simply a factor of production that the entrepreneur must rationally combine with other factors in order to maximize his profits.

Further, the notion of 'rationality' is one reserved for the manager, and fails to be applied to the worker. Yet, undoubtedly, what is rational for one is not necessarily rational for the other. The term as used here is one of functionality: something is rational if it contributes towards a given end. And yet, even at the business level, it must be very clear that the aims of management and workers may be very different. Educationally, such a view of rationality is in fact anti-rational, for it fails to deal with the issue of the subjectivity of values and judgements, and so fails to appreciate that a genuine personal, social and political education is centrally concerned with the dialogue, communication and reaching of agreement between different viewpoints. As noted above, this was not just a failure by Taylor, for much of the literature is clearly biased to the managerial perspective, but Taylor was certainly at the beginning of this distortion.

It will be apparent that scientific management has a curiously limited vision of how to cope with the problems of morale and productivity. These problems are seen as solved exclusively by the use of economic reward and punishment. But again, this fails to take into account the psychology of the individual. What may motivate one worker may not motivate another. The simple wage may have been the only necessary motivation for Schmidt, but research and common sense both show that there are other things which are as important to many people. There is a holism to human work and activity, grounded in personality, involvement, self-esteem and previous experience, which cannot be encapsulated in simplistic mechanical analogies, simply because much more than mechanism is involved.

However, to leave a description of human beings here would be to commit the same kind of error as Taylor did. An examination of motivations will show that the meaning and importance that individuals give to situations can be largely determined by the groups with which they affiliate. This was perhaps the most important insight of the human relations theory which followed scientific management. By concentrating upon the individual, Taylor failed to see the importance of the social. Indeed, one can go further than that, and say that even human relations theory did not present the whole picture, for even a portrayal of the individual as influenced by the group in which he or she associates is still deficient. One needs to look beyond the physiological, the psychological and the social to the sociological – to the structuring of the organization and the society in which it works, and to the influence of these upon the individual. Only by focusing on each of these levels does one see the range of influences brought to bear, and is one able to evaluate the total situation.

## CONCLUSIONS

In reflecting upon the impact of scientific management, four issues affecting present-day practice need to be drawn out.

The first concerns the notion of rationality. There are at least two ways of looking at this term in a managerial context. The first form of rationality is the limited kind, where, within a particular (given) problem situation, the individual works out the most appropriate method of achieving a solution. This is clearly how Kuhn (1970) envisaged the work of what he called the 'normal scientist' – one who works away within a particular field or paradigm of science throughout his or her life, without ever questioning the validity of the paradigm itself. Morgan (1985, p. 37), in a managerial context, described this as 'functional' or 'instrumental' rationality, a rationality which is limited to an ability to perceive the application of rules and a consequent ability to apply and obey them. This kind of rationality is very different from the second kind of rationality, that of 'substantial' rationality, where people are encouraged to develop not only a facility for conforming to directives, but also a talent for evaluating the appropriateness of those actions, and acting accordingly. The danger of an adherence to a scientific-management paradigm – where those higher in the hierarchy determine what is to be achieved – is precisely that opportunities to demonstrate substantive rationality are increasingly diminished. This has potent consequences for the people – adults and children – within school, for their development, and for the nurturing and encouragement of their abilities to build a just community within the school as a blueprint for the larger society. It therefore has major implications about their ability to exercise influence outside of the school as well. Again the purely managerial is left behind, and the social and political take on more significance.

The second concern is that of the role of values in curriculum construction and development. The practice of scientific management clearly illustrated the dangers of the adoption of a cloak of scientific respectability for what amounted to desired management practices. The same kind of thing can be said for Bobbitt's approach to the curriculum, which, by assuming that what was the case ought to be the case, took a profoundly conservative and uncritical view of curriculum building. By so doing, it maintained as objectively true one view of the curriculum and of values, which, coming from only one quarter, was necessarily subjective, and therefore contestable. It is the kind of lesson which other constructors need to be aware of, whether local or national. Description of what is the case cannot be translated into what ought to be the case without acceptance of subjectivity, contestation and consensus.

The third concern is the lesson from US educational history, and the preoccupation, in the heyday of scientific management, with financial concerns. Where these concerns are stimulated by the recognition of their place in the development of a better-quality education, then they have a part to play. Where, however, they are stimulated by the ideological assumption that financial efficiency necessarily means better education, then they should be questioned, for an over-concentration upon financial matters may lead to the neglect of other and more important matters within the school. Initiatives in the UK, such as the local management of schools, may be a particular case in point.

The final concern is with theories like scientific management which place their focus of concern on the individual, at the psychological level. This kind of theory undoubtedly has its part to play in a complete understanding of organizational functioning. What it tends to do, however, is to prevent the examination of the context within which the individual acts. It is precisely by taking an organizational and societal perspective on management that one can see that it is in many ways the embodiment of a much broader principle of systems organization. Scientific management is a particular case in point, being an example of a much wider and more pervasive type of organizational influence, that of bureaucratization. The next chapter will attempt to trace the growth of bureaucracy, assess its influence, and ascertain its effects and acceptability.

# Chapter 3

## Bureaucracy and educational values

### INTRODUCTION

Anyone visiting Egypt for the first time will almost certainly want to visit the pyramids at Giza. They will learn, if they did not already know, that the Great Pyramid alone contains some 2,300,000 blocks of stone, each weighing over two-and-a-half tons, all cut some distance from the pyramid, all having to be transported to the eventual site. It is estimated that 10,000 people were engaged in building the pyramid over a period of twenty years. Reactions to this accomplishment are likely to be mixed. One might wonder at the sheer size of the edifice, be astonished at the lengths people will go in order to have themselves buried in a manner appropriate to their standing, amazed at the amount of planning and organization needed to complete such a construction, awed at the amount of sheer back-breaking labour involved in positioning the blocks, and, finally, perhaps disgusted at the way in which people were used to perform this labour, and then discarded when no longer capable of performing.

It is possible to see this wonder of the ancient world, in part at least, as the product of a bureaucracy, for without the careful and detailed planning, and meticulous organization, the assignation of different functions and roles, it is unlikely that the feat could have been accomplished. At the same time, it is likely that the employment of the bureaucratic processes just described was a major factor in the inhuman treatment of those who built the pyramids. Wherever one may find it, it can be argued that bureaucracy has its uses but it also has its abuses. This is as true of education as anything else. As this book argues that education should be fundamentally concerned with personal, social and political growth, its view of bureaucracy can be expected to be fairly critical. Nevertheless, the baby must not be thrown out with the bathwater. Wherever education is provided on more than a one-to-one basis, there will be a need for some form of plans, rules and regulations, and therefore for some measure of bureaucracy. These rules and regulations will reflect the need for:

- a fair provision of teachers, schools and equipment for any child in the administrative area;
- the co-ordination of planning such that similar systems of curriculum, pedagogy and discipline are experienced by the same children in different classes and schools;
- the co-ordination of the purchase of equipment to benefit from economies of scale;
- an effective means of providing specialized teaching activities such that children get the kind of in-depth knowledge of an area needed to fully appreciate its complexities;

- a means of recruiting and training teachers who reach a minimum standard of ability for the job at hand;
- the assessment and grading of pupils such that employers have a fair and unbiased system of choosing between them;
- the fair and impersonal assessment of teachers' abilities with regard to promotion.

There will always be a tension within educational management between the need for such impersonal rules, and the need to adjust these rules to the growth of the person and the group. If there is a paradox in educational systems, then, it is that to be truly effective and meaningful, an educational experience needs to be an individual, unpredictable encounter, whilst to be truly effective and fair, the educational organization needs to be impartial and predictable. A system of education, then, needs both individuation of treatment and a measure of bureaucracy. It is the balance between the two which is the problem.

Of course, the kind of fully fledged bureaucracy one sees today did not happen overnight. It was a gradual process, in which elements of patronage and hereditary title continued to exist for a long time alongside the more 'rational' aspects of organization. A good example of this development was given in 1916 by Tout in describing the evolution of the English Civil Service. He traces the birth of bureaucracy to the earliest days of the English state. Anglo-Saxon monarchy had just about recognized a need; Norman kings with a need for centralized administration, and an ever-increasing desire to know and understand, and hence control, accelerated the process. At first, however, organization was very haphazard: administrators were virtually indistinguishable from the court retinue, following the king round his kingdom, rather than remaining in one place; positions of responsibility and administration were shared between officials rather than specific duties being specialized; and appointment was made on a hereditary or patronage basis rather than through open competition. Only gradually did the civil service separate itself from the king's domestic servants and permanently locate itself in London; only gradually were offices seen as needing an expert to do one particular job; and it was a very long time before such occupations were put out to open competition through public examinations. Bureaucracy, then, has been around for a long time, but its 'purer' form took a considerable time to develop.

These kinds of descriptions of the growth of bureaucracy indicate the need for such a form: there are no pejorative overtones here. Rather, it is increasingly seen as the most sensible, most rational form of organization to deal with such tasks. Reports of abuses appear a little later, though there can be little doubt that they were there from the beginnings, parasitic on the host.

A more recent description of the evolution of bureaucratic structures can be seen in education with Katz's (1977) description of the development of the different forms of organization of nineteenth-century American schools. Moving through what he calls 'paternalistic voluntarism', 'democratic localism', and then on to 'corporate voluntarism', Katz shows how deficiencies in each allowed 'incipient bureaucracy' gradually to gain centre stage. He argues, though, that the need for this bureaucratic form of organization did not stem purely from the need for order, rationalization and efficiency. As he suggests,

It stemmed equally from a gut fear of the cultural divisiveness inherent in the increasing religious and ethnic variety of American life. Cultural homogenization played counterpoint to administrative rationality. Bureaucracy was intended to standardize far more than the conduct of public business.

(Katz, 1977, p. 391)

By arguing that control of a population was a prime mover in the institution of bureaucratic procedures, Katz moves to consider bureaucracy in a wider role within society as a whole. He quotes (Katz, 1977, pp. 393–4) a critic of the Massachusetts Board of Education, who suggested that the board saw education as 'merely a branch of general police', and 'schoolmasters' as only a 'better sort of constables'. The board promoted universal education only 'because they esteem it the most effectual means possible of checking pauperism and crime, and making the rich secure in their possession'. In some respects, then, Katz's thesis is an example from education of a much better-known theory, that of Karl Marx.

## THE CLASSICAL WRITERS

For Marx, bureaucracy was an important, but dependent, institution. It was, and could never be more than, an instrument of the dominant (capitalist) class. Thus, in the *German Ideology* he asserted that the state was

... nothing more than the form of organisation which the bourgeois necessarily adopt ... for the mutual guarantee of their property and interests.

(Marx, 1965, p. 78)

The functions of bureaucracy were seen as two-fold: to impose upon society the kind of order which perpetuates its domination, and to conceal this domination by means of the unending flow of form-filling, task division and constant supervision. With a population unable to see the wood for the trees, the dominant group maintains its grip on the reins of power.

If these are bureaucracy's functions, its effects upon the general population are similarly far-reaching. As in a Kafka novel, its regulatory effects are there for all to see, but precisely who is doing what within this bureaucracy is never clear. This force is omnipresent but mysterious, for none can pinpoint precisely the people or forces involved. The effect is a corrosive alienation of the individual citizen from the process of government, the feeling of helplessness before a force not fully understood and beyond control. This has been well brought out in this century by Mackintosh (1977, p. 116), professor of politics and Member of Parliament, in commenting upon the state of British politics:

When the electorate now pause and survey the government, they see a massive complex of authorities with no clear sign of public control, with no clear channels by which pressure can be exercised and results achieved. To put one party in power and then, four or five years later, to replace with another seems to make little difference. Much that affects the individual can be traced to no specific person or institutions; decisions seem simply to emerge from the machinery and local or individual complaints apparently have little effect.

Perhaps surprisingly, such 'representative' forms of democracy have been championed by a large number of democratic theorists, the most famous being Joseph Schumpeter, who argued (1942) that such alienation and apathy was in fact a necessary part of democratic functioning, for the mass of the population, unskilled and uninterested as they are in the actual running of a country, must be rendered apathetic in order to ensure the stability of the system. Too much involvement would produce friction, disturbance and influence by those least capable of using it sensibly. Democracy, then, for Schumpeter is nothing more than 'that institutional arrangement for arriving at political decisions in which individuals acquire the power to decide by means of a competitive struggle for the people's vote' (Schumpeter, 1942, p. 269). Democracy provides the opportunity to exercise choice in selecting a leader and government, who will then perform the real running of the country. Bureaucracy, according to this description, has effects which may seem negative at first, but have an ultimately beneficial outcome.

Such a conception of democracy, widely accepted in modern times, is based mostly on the findings by political scientists that the general population *is* apathetic and generally politically illiterate. Common sense, then, dictates that a practical, representative form of democracy be adopted, rather than an idealistic and impracticable participative model. The adoption of such a model has had profound repercussions upon the ways in which governments have actually functioned, as well as upon the role of schools and their function within a democratic society. Yet it is important to note here that such a view entirely ignores, or misdescribes, a complete tradition of 'participative democracy', the espousal of which could lead to radically different outcomes for society and school, and which would allow one to continue to accept that the corrosive, alienating and apathy-producing effects of bureaucracy are not ones which need to be accepted. Much more will be said about this later.

Besides alienating people in society at large, Marx also suggests that it alienates individuals working *within* an organization, for they fail to see how their actions relate to the whole. Because the overall purpose cannot be seen, bureaucrats lower their sights, and instead become involved in a manic attention to rule-implementation, or to internal struggles for advancement and prestige. The results for both those inside and outside the bureaucracy are the same: an inability to understand the pattern of their lives, and the consequent alienation.

Modern Marxist writers like Bowles and Gintis (1976), Harris (1979) and Apple (1982) similarly argue that education systems act through their bureaucratic machinery to reflect and reproduce the divisions of society in which the capitalist class is dominant. Schools, they argue, are not built to stimulate widespread class and social mobility, but rather are there for the production of people for different jobs in a technological society, and it is this society which defines what counts as acceptable knowledge and behaviour. Schools, in performing such functions, will have strong alienating effects upon their inhabitants. For teachers it may result in a myopic view of the causation of pupils' behaviour, and a spiritless approach to the job; for pupils it will be the prime reason for indiscipline and deviancy. The conclusion is reached that schools, and more particularly society, are the prime producers of deviancy simply because they define what is acceptable behaviour.

The only way forward, then, for Marx, is through revolution. If bureaucracy is the product of the capitalist class, created as a smokescreen for the maintenance of divisions and differences between classes, then sweeping away such classes must result in the similar destruction of bureaucratic organizations, and the consequent elimination of alienation, and much of the indiscipline and deviancy, in schools.

In his arguments, Marx makes the explicit connection between class-based society and the use of bureaucracy to further its ends. Bureaucracy then takes a secondary and functional role. It is possible, however, to conceive of bureaucracy taking on an autonomous existence, one in which it acquires so many powers that those who initially created it now find themselves in a position where it is dominating them. A different class structure, or a classless structure, would then make very little difference to its power and influence. Clearly, for Marx's theory of the state as a power struggle between economically based classes, governmental organizations such as bureaucracies must remain subordinate to these classes, otherwise the theory becomes seriously imperilled.

A very different tradition of criticism stems from the work of John Stuart Mill (1859), who saw no necessary subordination of bureaucracy to the class in power. Rather he saw an increase in bureaucracy as an unnecessary and dangerous increase in the power of government. He therefore developed a critique of bureaucracy into an argument against governmental interference, the result of which would be that as governmental bureaucracy grew, the more the most talented would see the summit of their ambition as residing within such a structure. This being the case, '. . . not only is the outside public ill-qualified, for want of practical experience, to criticise or check the mode of operation of the bureaucracy, but . . . no reform can be effected which is contrary to the interests of the bureaucracy' (1963, pp. 246–7).

Mill was much concerned specifically with the political expression of bureaucracy, and became convinced that a government, democratic in name but centralist in nature, provides no real political freedom, but in fact 'creates a spirit precisely the reverse' (1963, p. 229). It is only by providing models of participation at the local level that people can come to be educated to become democratic citizens. As he says (p. 186),

> We do not learn to read or write, to ride or swim, by being merely told how
> to do it, but by doing it, so it is only by practising popular government on
> a limited scale, that the people will ever learn how to exercise it on a
> larger.

The parallels for schools and children's gradual participative induction could not be clearer.

Mill's writing has strongly influenced present-day writers like Friedrich Hayek and Milton Friedman, whose writings have had considerable effect upon the running of state bureaucracies, including education, on both sides of the Atlantic. Both Hayek and Friedman argue that bureaucratization is an inevitable consequence of adopting the kinds of political institutions which attempt to structure or engineer the shape of society. As Hayek (1973, p. 2) says,

> ... the predominant model of liberal democratic institutions, in which the same representative body lays down the rules of just conduct and direct government, necessarily leads to a gradual transformation of the spontaneous order of free society into a totalitarian system conducted in the service of some coalition of organised interests.

This malignant growth of bureaucracy is given an air of inevitability in the work of Robert Michels (1949). Bureaucracy is seen as the necessary end-result of any attempt to incorporate democratic measures into the functioning of an organization. Both the complexity of organizational problems and the need for all members to participate prevent genuine democracy from emerging. Moreover, as a party is elected to power, party activists will be placed in full-time employment to carry out the wishes of the electorate. This role-filling, by both civil servant and politician, leads inexorably, says Michels, to the position where both take on attitudes and perform actions which maintain themselves rather than fulfilling the wishes of those they initially represented. As Michels (1949, p. 370) says,

> ... from a means, organization becomes an end. To the institutions and qualities which at the outset were destined simply to ensure the good working of the party machine (subordination, the harmonious cooperation of individual members, hierarchical relationships, discretion, propriety of conduct), a greater importance comes ultimately to be attached than to the productivity of the machine.

The process of institutionalization, then, becomes progressively bogged down, until structures become so detailed, so conservative, so antiquated and so oligarchic that another democratic reform is needed to shake the system up again – and the process begins once more. As Michels says (quoted in Mouzelis (1975), p. 29), democratic movements 'break ever on the same shore' and 'are ever renewed'.

Michels' work has genuine relevance to education in two ways. Firstly, it is usually quoted in connection with literature suggesting that genuine participatory democracy is not possible within society, and that a limited form of representative democracy is all that is desirable or possible. His argument, then, might be taken to mean that genuine participation is also impossible in school. This is an important question which will be dealt with later, when a picture of the desired school is developed. Secondly, though, a description of the usurping of power by bureaucracies highlights the possibility of a concentration upon means rather than ends. Michels' work, then, draws attention to the need to re-focus upon a school's purposes, and, within this re-focusing, to reflect upon the quality of service to the intended beneficiaries – the clients.

Max Weber's thesis of the evolution of bureaucracy is probably *the* classic description upon which most modern writers draw inspiration or begin by criticizing. It suggests that the structure of organizations is increasingly affected by a 'rational' approach to knowledge and society in general. This 'rationality' sees human activity as being based on the clear specification of ends, and the similarly clear analysis and specification of the means to attain these ends. Like Michels, Weber thought bureaucratization inevitable, but for different reasons. It was only inevitable because rationality is the distinctive mode of thought which Western society uses, and hence the institutions it creates will increasingly reflect this dominant mode. Other societies need not necessarily follow such a trend.

Moreover, Weber (1947) argues that as power is a crucial concept in understanding the dynamics of society, so leadership and bureaucracy are intimately bound together, for it is through the evolution of particular forms of leadership that one finds bureaucracy evolving. Weber suggests that there are three different kinds of political authority possible: charismatic, traditional and rational–legal (or bureaucratic). It is important to understand each to appreciate how bureaucracy is seen to evolve. The first kind, as Weber (1947, p. 370) suggests,

> ... is a phenomenon typical of prophetic religious movements or of expansive political movements in their early stages.

Thus one has a Mohammed, a Jesus, a Napoleon, a Martin Luther King, a Piaget or a Montessori, or any charismatic educational thinker: individuals who through sheer force of personal magnetism carry all before them. People follow them, not only because of the ideas they express, but also because of their personal qualities. During his or her career, it is never quite certain whether the ideas are valuable in themselves, or because they are embodied so well in this particular individual. Of course, once this individual dies, such charisma disappears, and one is left with the ideas only. Others may try to live off them, and the second form of leadership, the traditional, develops. All subsequent leaders in the tradition claim an inheritance from the great one which gives them the authority to 'rule'. It is only with the passing of time that people may come to see that such traditional authority lacks appeal and conviction. Then there may be a movement towards a charismatic individual outside the tradition, and the process may begin once more.

At the same time, however, as those following seek to justify their authority once the charismatic leader is gone, so they increasingly routinize the actions and structures of the movement, for they rely upon contributions to keep the organization running and keep themselves in work. In so doing, they may increasingly rationalize its activities, more clearly specify the organization's goals, employ the best qualified to fill positions, generate a clear set of role descriptions so that people know exactly where they are, and implement clearly defined hierarchies of authority so that each person knows what is his or her responsibility and to whom he or she is responsible. This routinization of charisma, then, inevitably involves an increasingly bureaucratic component. One then has the basis for the rational–legal, or bureaucratic, form of leadership.

Weber argues that from an economic point of view, routinization and bureaucratization are ideally suited to a capitalist system of organization, for they have many 'virtues' which this economic system will value. If the ultimate aim is one of profit-making, then the more efficient the structure, the more likely are profits to be increased. And efficiency is greatly aided by the main characteristics of bureaucracy: a high degree of specialization, a hierarchical authority structure with limited areas of command and responsibility, an impersonality of relationships between organizational members, the recruitment of officials on the basis of ability and technical knowledge, and the use of impersonal rules which apply to all equally, so that anyone new to the enterprise can immediately understand such rules and their own position within the organization. A fairly extreme example of this is given in Figure 3.1, where the desired behaviours of counter staff in a fast-food restaurant are broken down into segments which can be checked, changed and improved. If members of staff fail to meet these criteria, they can be fired and the same process can be applied to the next employees.

Whilst Weber is quite explicit in maintaining that his is merely a description, not an evaluation or a recommendation, there are clearly strong elements within it which he sees as immensely appealing to the modern age. This comes from the premise of 'rationality' with which the description begins. If you want this ... then you design a system like this; and who would not wish for organizations to state their purposes clearly so as to hire the best people for the job? Is this not both more efficient, more rational, and more fair? When viewed like this, bureaucracy seems an ideal vehicle for both a more efficient and a more egalitarian society.

There are, indeed, many within educational bureaucracies who would agree with such a positive description. Anderson (1968), in his study of American secondary schools, found that teachers within more bureaucratically organized schools felt more secure than those in less organized schools. This probably is also at the bottom of Nias' (1986) findings for primary teachers in the UK, who preferred the head to run the school in a paternalistic manner if they were left to run their own classrooms, for this meant clear role definitions and hierarchy, little ambiguity, and hence much more security. And in terms of equality, Broadfoot (1979) has pointed out that public examinations, maligned by some nowadays for, among other things, the way in which they seem to (unfairly) favour the middle class, were instituted precisely to provide greater fairness in society – selection on the basis of merit and ability, rather than on background or wealth. Bureaucracy, for many, has a great deal going for it.

One can see where scientific management fitted into this picture: beyond the details of handling pig-iron, this was a system which also stressed detailed job descriptions, clear hierarchy, an absence of ambiguity, and the search for the right person for the right job. If it took its application to extremes and thereby defeated itself, it still had many of the attributes of its parent. Weber appears (1970, p. 261) to share in this celebration:

> With the help of the appropriate methods of measurement, the optimum profitability of the individual worker is calculated like that of any material means of production. On the basis of this calculation, the American system of 'scientific management' enjoys the greatest triumphs in the rational conditioning and training of work performances.

It will be clear, then, that, for Weber, rationality in a bureaucratic system is essentially functional. Being 'completely rational', then, is not a recommendation as such, but a description of what will be created if a particular end is desired. For Weber, rationality in this context suggests the appropriateness of means to ends; and within a bureaucratic organization, this means efficiency. And both rationality and efficiency, it is claimed, are gained by the specification of rules which direct the behaviour of members of the organization, making such behaviour consistent and

| Greeting the customer | Yes | No |
|---|---|---|
| 1  There is a smile. | | |
| 2  It is a sincere greeting. | | |
| 3  There is eye contact. | | |
| Other: | | |
| **Taking the order** | Yes | No |
| 1  The counter person is thoroughly familiar with the menu ticket. (No hunting for items.) | | |
| 2  The customer has to give the order only once. | | |
| 3  Small orders (four items or less) are memorized rather than written down. | | |
| 4  There is suggestive selling. | | |
| Other: | | |
| **Assembling the order** | Yes | No |
| 1  The order is assembled in the proper sequence. | | |
| 2  Grill slips are handed in first. | | |
| 3  Drinks are poured in the proper sequence. | | |
| 4  Proper amount of ice. | | |
| 5  Cups slanted and finger used to activate. | | |
| 6  Drinks are filled to the proper level. | | |
| 7  Drinks are capped. | | |
| 8  Clean cups. | | |
| 9  Holding times are observed on coffee. | | |
| 10  Cups are filled to the proper level on coffee. | | |
| Other: | | |
| **Presenting the order** | Yes | No |
| 1  It is properly packaged. | | |
| 2  The bag is double folded. | | |
| 3  Plastic trays are used if eating inside. | | |
| 4  A tray liner is used. | | |
| 5  The food is handled in a proper manner. | | |
| Other: | | |
| **Asking for and receiving payment** | Yes | No |
| 1  The amount of the order is stated clearly and loud enough to hear. | | |
| 2  The denomination received is clearly stated. | | |
| 3  The change is counted out loud. | | |
| 4  Change is counted efficiently | | |
| 5  Large bills are laid on the till until the change is given. | | |
| Other: | | |
| **Thanking the customer and asking for repeat business** | Yes | No |
| 1  There is always a thank you. | | |
| 2  The thank you is sincere. | | |
| 3  There is eye contact. | | |
| 4  Return business was asked for. | | |
| Other: | | |

**Figure 3.1** A management observation checklist used to evaluate the performance of counter staff in a fast-food restaurant.

predictable, and individuals easily replaceable. Through elaborating this formal structure, the aim is to obviate the effect of unpredictable human beings. The influence of this kind of logic has continued through into the present century. F. W. Taylor was not the only individual wholeheartedly to espouse the position. Alfred Krupp, the German industrialist, said much the same thing:

> What I shall attempt to bring about is that nothing shall be dependent on the life and existence of any particular person; that nothing of importance shall happen or be caused to happen without the foreknowledge and approval of the management; that the past and the determinable future of the establishment can be learned in the files of the management without asking a question of any mortal.
>
> (Anderson, 1968, p. 112)

It should be noted that if bureaucracy is so appealing to a capitalist form of economic organization, and if this form of economic organization affects the forms that other institutions take within society, then bureaucratic forms and procedures might be recommended for institutions which are not ideally suited to it. Education might be a good example. If education is about the dissemination of information, and the training and socialization of individuals for a job market, then such forms will do very well. If, however, education is more concerned with the development of individual creativity, of personal, social and political development, a spirit of seeking for the unpredictable, then bureaucracy would not be so suited. In the real world, there is clearly going to be conflict between these two aims and their forms of organization.

## TWENTIETH-CENTURY PERSPECTIVES

Educationalists should, then, be cautious about the rather optimistic manner in which Weber describes bureaucracy. Is this, one must ask, a desirable end state for education, and if not, why not? If one of the benefits of studying the nineteenth-century writers is that, taking a societal perspective, they enable us to ask these questions, one of the benefits of studying the twentieth-century writers is the way in which they bring these general theories down to particular contexts. For example, the work by people like Merton (1952) and Anderson (1968) has shown that the creation of rules, rather than making organizations more predictable, controllable and efficient, may instead make them dysfunctional through people's blind adherence to these rules. Their research showed that individuals, realizing that their own job security or advancement rested upon the adherence to these rules, followed these rules for their own sake, regardless of whether such conformity was functional or not. A further consequence of such rule-centred behaviour was for the individual to conform to rules, and to avoid doing anything more. In other words, the specification of rules laid down for individuals the minimum standards which were acceptable within the organization, and this then became the standard to which people worked. They ceased, then, to be personally involved with the organization, and attempted only the minimum standard required. Anderson (1968, p. 23) puts the situation nicely when he says

The end result is that bureaucratic controls intensify the problem that they are introduced to mitigate – lack of commitment and motivation. In a very real sense, controls beget additional controls, making it necessary to devise still other means of coping with the original problems. Participants become functionaries, simply exercising the authority vested in them by the rules. The vast reservoir of experience, skills and knowledge, the product of the diverse backgrounds of the members of the organization, is left untapped. The originality, initiative, or the insight that comes with experience is wasted.

Such bureaucratic controls, then, increase the likelihood that teachers will cease to innovate, and instead teach to the letter of the law. This is, of course, the great danger of a national curriculum and national testing, for describing in exhaustive detail which hoops are to be jumped through, and when, may quite possibly cause teachers to see this as their whole job. Whether such dictates correspond to the children's needs, abilities or interests, and whether they become outdated and irrelevant, cease to be central questions. The main aim becomes to teach the legal requirements, and to get the children through the test, regardless of its value.

Moreover, where circumstances change, the individual continues to follow the rules, irrespective of their ultimate effect. The original purpose for the rules is lost, and individuals cease to be creative, to seek for the solution which will fit the individual case. Instead, hiding behind the rules, they develop what Merton (1952, p. 366) called a 'ritualism' towards rules, and from this results a trained incapacity to behave in an intelligent (i.e. adaptive) manner.

Indeed, if one of the virtues of bureaucracy has been seen by some as its predictability, others, like Handy (1985), have argued that predictability is a liability where change is common and an ability to cope with unpredictability is at a premium. Indeed, as a bureaucracy gets bigger, it undermines itself by importing uncertainty, for it becomes involved with more and more outside groups and is thereby exposed to a much wider range of forces. When society is changing so rapidly, and schools are being asked to change at least at the same rate, bureaucratization can become positively dysfunctional.

This increasing dysfunctionality of originally functional procedures is also seen when organizations begin to compartmentalize, to increase their number of subunits, as when schools increase in size from several hundreds to several thousands. As Selznick (1949) has demonstrated, these subunits may then set up their own goals, which conflict with the overall purpose of the organization. The traditional remedy for this has been to set up new departments to counteract this tendency, but this may only result in more of the same kind of empire-building.

This is part of a more general difficulty, that the control of bureaucracies is usually attempted through the creation of more (supervisory) bureaucracy, which only produces more of the same problem. What may well happen is what Gouldner (1954) termed a 'punishment-centred bureaucracy'. In this, those charged with improving production resort to increased supervision and bureaucratization through more detailed rules and regulations. The result, however, is that such rules have an 'apathy-preserving function', and instead of increasing production and controlling behaviour, only make the situation worse. What happens is that such behaviour locks the organization into a vicious circle of repression, subversion and further repression. Nobody wins, for the workers become increasingly dissatisfied and alienated, and the management finds itself having to deal with increasing apathy, disenchantment, disloyalty and absenteeism. It is a point which policy-makers in education would do well to heed.

In the light of the above, some of Anderson's (1968) predictions on control in education look particularly prescient:

- bureaucratic rules will vary inversely with the administrator's perception of their members' competence (which is substantiated by the poor press given to teachers and teaching since the mid-1970s in the UK, resulting in this country in the 1988 Education Act).
- such rules will vary inversely with the degree of the subordinates' perceived commitment (the same as above).
- controls will vary directly with the 'routinizability' of tasks, and there will be a constant attempt to make activities 'routinizable' (through, for instance, national curricular requirements).
- controls will vary inversely with how specific objectives are. Where, as in education, aims can be seen as varied and diverse, constant efforts will be made by administration to prescribe behaviour through rules which direct behaviour towards particular desired ends.

This also points to a central dilemma of all bureaucracies, and particularly public services, such as education, which are peopled by human beings who must deal with other human beings. This treatment ideally should be carried out on an individual caring basis, through the discretion of the practitioner. Yet in reality the service is delivered through a form of organization geared to mass treatment, detachment, equal service and consistency. It is a dilemma and contradiction which all 'street-level bureaucrats', as Michael Lipsky (1980) calls them, have to confront daily. The new teacher, enthused at the prospect of helping the child to reach his or her full potential, finds a reality geared more to controlling and organizing classes of 30-plus children, which actually allows minimum time for the kind of individual attention which inspired them in the first place. Teachers, like street-level bureaucrats from other public services, are faced with work- or case-loads which, on a one-to-one basis, are impossible to fulfil in a satisfactory manner. The bureaucratic organization, by its very design, then, prohibits and contradicts one of the ultimate aims of its practitioners.

Individuals within these organizations may cope with this situation in a variety of ways. They may simply become so distraught with a situation which they cannot ultimately resolve that they leave. They may, on the other hand, continue struggling onwards, fighting to maintain their personal ideals, attempting to resolve the unresolvable. If this becomes impossible, they may come to accept the reality as described by the organization, and lose their ideals. Then they become cynical, and children become merely so many products to be processed. Finally, they may develop coping strategies which allow them to partially fulfil their personal ideal at the expense of the bureaucratic ideal. In teaching, this may occur through tracking, streaming or creaming, or simply through concentrating on some rather than all children in the same class. As Lipsky (1980, p. 107) says,

> . . . they attempt to succeed with some clients when they cannot succeed with all.

This tension between individual and organization is heightened the more that the organization attempts to place accountability controls upon its members, and one may well move into the kind of punishment-centred bureaucracy mentioned above, where alienation leads to apathy, disloyalty and reduced creativity and involvement.

This is not something just related to public-service bureaucracies. Kanter (1983) has shown in great detail that bureaucratic, 'segmentalist' companies can, by their very structure, inhibit the kind of innovative activity which companies depend on to keep them abreast of the latest technological developments and changing consumer tastes. She derives ten rules for stifling initiative from her observations of bureaucratic companies in America, which are sadly amusing, and cautionary for all types of organizations, including schools:

1. Regard any new idea from below with suspicion – because it is new, and because it is from below.
2. Insist that people who need your approval to act first go through several other levels of management to get their signature.
3. Ask departments or individuals to challenge and criticize each other's proposals. (That saves you the job of deciding: you just pick the survivor.)
4. Express your criticisms freely, and withhold your praise. (That keeps people on their toes.) Let them know they can be fired at any time.
5. Treat problems as signs of failure, to discourage people from letting you know when something in their area isn't working.
6. Control everything carefully, make sure people count anything that can be counted, frequently.
7. Make decisions to reorganize or change policies in secret, and spring them on people unexpectedly. (That also keeps people on their toes.)
8. Make sure that any request for information is fully justified and that it isn't distributed too freely. (You don't want data to fall into the wrong hands.)
9. Assign lower-level managers, in the name of delegation and participation, responsibility for figuring out how to cut back, lay off or move people around.
10. Above all, never forget that you, the higher-ups, already know everything important about this business.

Such behaviours benefit neither the client, the organization, nor themselves. The tragedy is that this is not the individual's fault as much as the organization's, for it is the organization which has set up a system of rewards and punishments, and it is only the brave or foolhardy who attempt to change it – unless, that is, they are at the apex of the organization, and therefore have the power to change the rules.

Indeed, one of the key weaknesses of the bureaucratic organization is precisely that of the location of authority at the top of the pyramid, when in fact real expertise may be located further down. Peter Blau (1956) talks of the myth that rationality only comes from the top of an organization. Clearly, we are bound up with a confusion over rationality. Rationality for the scientific manager can come only from the top, as only those at the top can specify what needs to be done; any action which comes from below and which runs counter to these specifications and rules is, by definition, irrational. In any everyday meaning, however, it is totally rational to go counter to orders from above in order to achieve the ultimate aims of the organization and resolve a problem. It runs against common sense to suggest that it is rational to uncouple people's creativity and resourcefulness from the organization's functioning. And yet this is what a bureaucracy tends to do.

It seems inevitable that conflict will arise in any organization where authority and expertise are separated, for members then have to choose between those with the designated right to command and those with the greater expertise. Service bureaucracies such as welfare agencies, the police, medicine and education will all exhibit this tension. It is a point we shall return to in the chapter on leadership.

One further point needs to be made here. This is that whilst change may be directed from the top, it is almost certainly easier to make there, and more likely to be resisted at the bottom. This is because those at the bottom – classroom teachers, for example – develop coping strategies, a *modus vivendi* between the realities of the classroom and the dictates from above. Any changes from above will probably unbalance these survival strategies, and will therefore be strongly resisted. This explains why teacher participation is not, as I will argue later, only a right of teachers, but also a necessity for healthy organizational functioning. For it is only by careful consultation, and teacher participation, that decisions can be made which those at street level will not find threatening to their survival in the classroom. It is all very well to make decisions at the managerial, boardroom or cabinet level – but it is the street-level bureaucrat whose professional life and self-concept is at stake.

For many, then, there is a fundamental contradiction between the ideal of the individual and the ideal of the bureaucracy. A teacher may have to live with the belief that much of teaching is essentially artistic and unpredictable, and yet may have to work within a bureaucracy which constantly tries to mechanize it. As Jackson (1968, p. 167) said, the path of educational progress more closely resembles 'the flight of the butterfly than the flight of the bullet'. Much of education cannot be standardized, and many of the activities of teaching and learning necessarily are ones which are personal to pupil and teacher, and which in many situations will be spontaneous and intuitive. The more that rules dictate such interactions, the more communication becomes impersonal, meaningless and ineffective, and the more both teachers and pupils are demotivated.

This demotivation through bureaucratization can be seen in at least three different ways. Firstly, motivating students requires meaningful and affectionate relationships between teachers and students, and yet the imposition of impersonal disciplinary rules mitigates against such possibilities. Secondly, as Anderson (1968) suggests, if schools are simply allowed to grow, with no attempt being made to break them down into more personal units, the more rules will be introduced, and the less meaningful relationships will be nurtured. Finally, with increased and increasing demands from central government for paperwork and form-filling, such bureaucratic duties eat into the time which could be given to such relationships. When student teachers voice the opinion that their main concern with starting a teaching career is keeping abreast of the paperwork (and this has been voiced to the present writer on a number of occasions) then it must be argued that something has gone seriously wrong.

## STRATEGIES FOR CHANGE

To be effective, strategies for change need to have both practical and philosophical sides. They need to be able to relate to the realities of schools, and they need to be informed by an undergirding philosophy. This philosophy could be drawn from the personal, social and political perspectives being suggested in this book. A start could be made by considering the three areas for improvement of bureaucratic performance suggested by Lipsky (1980). These recommendations, whilst not specifically related to education, are interesting not only because of the broad perspective they provide, but also because of the way they have been increasingly taken up by government since their initial suggestion.

Lipsky's initial recommendations refer to the need to develop client influence over policy. He suggests that essential strategies in this area would include:

- finding out what clients actually want;
- decentralizing bureaucracy so that client input has more effect;
- the education of clients in the ways of bureaucracy;
- the demystification of its jargon.

A final strategy, which has gained increasing popularity, is that of the notion of educational vouchers, so that clients become voluntary buyers rather than involuntary recipients of services. Such a change in role and perception by both themselves and the deliverers might make services much more responsive to client demands.

If these recommendations are made in such a manner as to suggest that the 'client' or 'customer' is both adult and child, then they dovetail quite nicely with the perspective suggested above. They suggest that teachers should be more responsive to the wishes of both parents and pupils, that both parties should be listened to more carefully, and that both should be given increased input into the management of the school. If schools are about partnerships, and education is about personal discovery, then the inclusion and valuing of these points is an essential part of the building of such a community.

Lipsky's second series of recommendations revolve around the improvement of current practice. Such improvement might begin at the training stage, when more emphasis could be placed on dealing with the realities of teaching, which in effect would mean more help and training in the management and organization of large groups. Training for practised teachers would also be more appropriate were it to centre upon the solving of actual job problems, rather than on the dissemination of research information, which practitioners must do their best to apply, but which might simply be inappropriate to their needs. This process might be aided if, as Lipsky suggests, trainers spent part of their time returning to the classroom to reacquaint themselves with classroom realities. It might be a further help if reward and promotion were more related to performance with clients, and less to seniority. This would entail real attempts to find out what clients thought, as well as greater development of peer assessment. All of these suggestions are very practical and down to earth, but need to be undergirded by the perspectives mentioned above. Such training and re-training must be embedded within a philosophy which focuses on the purposes of education and the individuation of treatment, just as reward and promotion need to be assessed in terms of the effectiveness with which these criteria are implemented.

This point can also be made for Lipsky's third set of recommendations, where he suggests that street-level bureaucrats should be helped to become more effective agents of change. This would entail, he suggests, the decentralization of decision-making, so that bureaucratic routines could be developed at lower levels. This would be beneficial, in that they would almost certainly be more responsive to client demands than routines intitiated from on high, as well as being developed by those who have to cope with the street-level situation. By being developed at this level, then, routines would be evolved which would also function as coping strategies, but without the particularity and possible unfairness of coping strategies developed on an individual basis.

It is significant to note that many of Lipsky's recommendations have been implemented in various ways in British education. There is, for example, an increasing recognition of the need to be responsive to clients. There is increased emphasis on training geared to the actual problems of teachers in the classroom. Trainers now have to return to the classroom to upgrade their teaching skills after a specified amount of time. There is increasing talk in the management literature of teacher participation in decision-making. Peer appraisal is gaining increasing acceptance both at teaching and higher education levels. Many of Lipsky's recommendations, therefore, are being seriously attended to.

There are, however, some genuine problems with the implementation of these recommendations, which further chapters will pick up. An initial problem for education, as we have seen, lies in defining who is the client. Parent, child and industrial producer have all at one time or another been put forward as candidates. Clearly, the definition of who is the client has important repercussions for policy and school structuring, and present initiatives do not necessarily see the child in this role. Similarly, the subject of educational vouchers has had intensive examination on both sides of the Atlantic, and the majority of opinion suggests that its implementation is not as simple as some might believe. Teacher training has been asked to increase its concentration on response to problems of classroom management, but there is concern that this may lead to a neglect of questions in training about the purposes of education, which may lead to the deprofessional-ization of practitioners, and to the failure of any attempt to implement an individually liberating form of education. Finally, whilst there is plenty of rhetoric about teacher participation, it is not always carried out in practice, either by senior management, or by those at policy-making level.

What is needed, as much as nuts-and-bolts suggestions, then, is an overview which provides the intellectual resources and movement in thinking necessary for the achievement of the form of schooling argued for in this book. No one aspect of the organization of schools can be singled out as all-important; rather, it is the cumulative effect of a philosophy upon the workings of a school, the way in which schools can be turned to face in one particular direction rather than another, which will make the difference. If bureaucratic forms of organization are necessary parts of systems of schooling, then their dangers, from personal, social and political points of view, need to be recognized, and their applicability to particular contexts challenged. The rule of thumb, I suggest, should be: can we do without bureaucratization? Where aspects of schooling can be achieved without its use, then this should be the aim.

A useful step along this path is provided in an article by Edward Pajak (1991), in which are detailed a number of areas of school organization within which 'bureaucratic' and 'educational' paradigms contest. These areas are presented in modified form in Table 3.1. The delineation of such areas not only sensitizes one as to where in the school's organization such contestation takes place, but it also suggests the form of education which will develop as one particular paradigm takes hold. A conclusion to be swiftly reached is that progress can be achieved gradually, in one area at a time. 'Bureaucracy' need not be some monolith which is impossible to tackle because it is so all-pervading. By distinguishing the areas, forms and influences through which bureaucracy works, it is possible to work within specific situations towards the achievement of a more 'educational' paradigm.

Table 3.1

*'Bureaucratic' and 'educational' approaches to schooling.* Adapted from Pajak (1991).

| Issue | Bureaucratic | Educational |
|---|---|---|
| Communication within the organization | Initiated from top down, usually as written reports | Initiated at any level, going up, down or horizontal |
| Staff development | Driven by needs assessed from above, planned and co-ordinated from above; teachers seen as passive imbibers | Teachers are actively involved in assessment of needs and planning for fulfilment. Help seen as only making sense when applied by teachers to *their* contexts |
| Instructional programmes and materials | Designed and planned by experts, implemented by teachers who act as technicians rather than as professionals. Co-ordination from above | Designed and planned by teachers who act as professionals, in conjunction with others in school community. Co-ordination achieved by establishing networks |

| Planning and change | Changes identified and planned from above, teachers there to adopt and implement. Schools viewed as transmission stations for central commands | Changes identified and planned at school level. Schools viewed as centres of inquiry, of personal, social and political education |
|---|---|---|
| Motivating and organizing | School members notified as to required behaviours, and evaluated according to degree of conformity, with uniform criteria expressed in measurable terms | Participation encouraged in development of shared vision. Leaders seen as facilitators rather than monitors or rule enforcers. Evaluation made using multiple criteria |
| Observing, helping and learning | Observation of practice made by those higher in hierarchy such as heads or inspectors. Seen as inspecting and criticizing rather than advising | Hierarchy not relevant: observations made by any who can help. Pupils, parents, teachers, heads and inspectors all seen as advisers and helpers |
| Curriculum | Written by experts for implementation by teachers, to be imbibed by pupils. Revised at pre-set intervals | School community involved in curriculum construction. Curriculum revised as and when necessary, seen as ongoing, never-ending process |
| Problem-solving, decision-making | Seen as best handled by those at top of hierarchy. Solutions developed and communicated to practitioners as rules, regulations and procedures | Seen as best handled, for pragmatic, ethical and developmental reasons, by those who face them, with solutions designed for particular situations |
| Resources for teachers | Resources identified as necessary by those higher in hierarchy, made available on basis of remedying perceived teacher deficits | Resources identified by teacher groups engaged in process of self- and school development |

| Personal development | A matter for each individual, within a framework of rules, regulations, and policies | Seen as a process of dialectic between the needs, interests, values and practices of the individual and school community |
|---|---|---|
| Community relations | Seen as a matter of public relations, of keeping parents and taxpayers happy. An 'us' and 'them' situation | Seen as the necessary involvement and education of parents and taxpayers, so that they can contribute meaningfully to school policies |

## CONCLUSIONS

In an ideal school community, the ethical ideal would be to treat people as ends in themselves. In such a community, each person would be regarded as unique, and this uniqueness would be celebrated by the fullest use of individualized techniques of teaching and learning. Bureaucracy works precisely counter to these ideals. By its very nature, it seeks to de-individualize learning contexts, and to treat people as means to ends. Rather than creating a community within which individuals come to explore and negotiate their goals with others, it attempts to condition individuals to its own objectives.

In an ethical school environment, members would be aided not only in their personal development, but in their social and political development as well. This would apply not only to pupils, but also to adult members, for not only should the school's benefits be felt by all within it, but also it might be asked how pupils can learn to use these benefits unless they see the older members of the community acting as role models. Ultimately, such developmental enhancement can only be achieved by the shaping of a community which moves beyond what Pateman (1970) calls 'pseudo-participation' (the use of techniques to persuade employees to accept decisions already made by management), through to 'partial participation' (where individuals can genuinely influence decisions, but not decide them) to, in some exceptional cases, 'full participation' (where each member has equal power to determine the outcome of decisions). Bureaucracies, again, are incapable of these ideals, for they attempt to impose hierarchy, and condition individuals to limit their aspirations and abilities.

An ethical form of educational institution necessarily has before it the question of the destination to which each individual is travelling. Ideally, there will not be one vision of where people are going, but as many visions as there are people travelling. This is not, however, to abnegate responsibility to a form of value relativism: schools cannot be supermarkets of values where people pick and choose as they like. An appreciation of the individuality of judgement and the subjectivity of values does not imply relativity: rather it implies a guardedness against strident espousal of ethical positions, a tolerance of others, and an awareness of personal fallibility. It suggests, instead of the cut-and-dried objectivity of bureaucratic values, a sensitive dialogue between all those within the school community (and this includes parents, taxpayers, and other interested bodies) in the progressive definition and redefinition of ultimate purposes and ends.

This also implies more than just individual rights. It implies a recognition by the individual of the overarching values of the school, of each person's place within it, of the duties and responsibilities both to the school and to others within it and to society at large. The need to achieve such a balance between rights and responsibilities, between undergirding values and a tolerance of differing opinions, will unsettle some, for whilst it encourages thoughtfulness, creativity and communication, it does not make for certainty. It is no easy option. But then genuine ethical commitment is more than the adoption of another's values; it is the constant striving to define one's own within the context of the community at large. This is the ultimate educational purpose of the school.

It is clear, then, that teachers must constantly ask themselves the question of why they are doing what they are doing. The consideration of ultimate ends in education comes to be seen as constantly important and relevant, as they continually inform and re-inform a teacher's practice. A teacher's role becomes one of providing a framework for the child, and

> ... whilst they cannot climb the ladder for their children, they can secure it, adjust it, and advise on ways of ascending.
>
> (Webster, 1985, p. 25)

Bureaucracy, in effect, emasculates these functions, for it is of its essence that it predetermines ends, and then allows the practitioners only the freedom of implementing them. Clearly, in a school with ethical guidelines, bureaucratic ends can never be sufficient because they cannot accommodate to the individual case, and they prevent the investigation and interpretation of these guidelines.

What should be clear is that whilst some bureaucratization is an inevitable part of the organization of education systems, it is still a matter of political and ethical choice as to what extent the activities of individuals are constrained by bounding such activities with rules and regulations. In the end, an over-emphasis on the bureaucratization of schools, of the need to control the actions of individuals, is a judgement not only on the philosophy of education espoused, but also on ourselves. As Schubert (1990) has said, at the heart of such issues:

> ... lies the question of our faith in human nature and its potential, and the amount of external or internal control needed for decision and action to be good and just.
>
> (p. 68)

As we shall see in the next chapter, if the degree of bureaucratization of a system is the acid test of our faith in human nature, the degree of conformity and dissent valued within a society is the litmus paper.

# Chapter 4

# Educating dissent

## INTRODUCTION

If the conservative tends to talk of duties, of what kinds of responsibilities a person has to an institution or society, the liberal tends to talk of rights, of what an individual should be allowed to do within them. Yet clearly, whether one is talking about the management of society or of a school, there needs to be a balance between the two. For example, an effective exercise of citizenship will depend upon a duty to uphold the law of the land, and be involved in its administration, to participate in the political process, to taxes, and possibly to undergo a period of military service. But it will also involve the possession of such rights as freedom of thought, conscience and expression, the right to participate in the control of power, and the right to remedy the abrogation of these rights. Moreover, democratic citizenship will never be realized by the prosecution of only one side of the debate. It can never be just a list of duties, for that way lies political absolutism. Similarly, it can never be just a list of rights, for that way lies the disintegration of society.

The expression of duties and rights will clearly be different, moving along a continuum from conformity through to dissent. And as with duties and rights, conformity and dissent also have Janus faces. Both can be hero or villain, depending on the situation, the need, and the perception of the spectator. Conformity is, in many cases, indispensable. In any situation where a group must function together, each person must know the set of norms which prescribe the rules of conduct and the procedures of that group. Cohen and Manion (1981, p. 316) give the colourful example of the Bedouin Arab who, on approaching a strange encampment, indicates his whereabouts and peaceful intentions by kicking sand high in the air, and then touching noses three times with all male inhabitants. Conformity, then, is adaptive; we, as much as the Arab nomad, could not function without it. And it is at least partly because of this need to create predictability in interactions that societies create norms and the ensuing conformity to them. Parents begin this process, schools continue it, and the institutions of adulthood confirm it. The concept of conformity should therefore be viewed with few if any pejorative connotations. It is the extent and the inflexibility of the practice that can produce problems.

Similarly, dissent has a place in any society where it is not automatically accepted that those in authority have the monopoly on correct decisions, or where it is believed that people must learn precisely the same thing in order to be educated. Where the situation is otherwise, it is imperative that members of society not only are given the ability, but also believe that they have the ability, to make real changes, both to the structure of society and to themselves. The ability to dissent from official decisions, prescriptions or orders is essential for healthy personal and societal functioning. The question again is one of balance. Too much dissent would produce anarchy; too much conformity would produce dictatorship. Part of the function of educational policy, then, and of the organization and management of schools, must concern the judgement of where this balance lies, the assessment of present balance, and then the remedying of any perceived imbalance.

Important questions for schools, therefore, are: how conformist are people? how capable are they of dissent?

## EXPERIENCES OF CONFORMITY

There are several by now classic experiments which can be drawn on to help in this. An understanding of how norms are created and why people conform to them was suggested by Sherif (1935). He found that an individual placed in a darkened room will believe that a stationary light actually moves. He also found that there will be great variance between individuals as to the perceived amount of this movement. However, when these individuals were placed in the same room together, Sherif found that their judgements about this movement tended to converge. This suggests two things: firstly, that members of groups use other members' judgements to help make their own; and secondly, that judgements at variance with the group norm are eliminated. This is clearly neither good nor bad: in ambiguous situations people use each other's judgements to determine what is the case, and sensibly tend to conclude that the opinion favoured by the majority is more likely to be correct than the idiosyncratic judgement. Conformity in this situation probably makes good survival sense. But it does tend to exclude the individual's judgement.

This experiment, however, only shows conformity with regard to ambiguous perceptual phenomena, and whilst interesting, it is hardly life-threatening. Irving Janis (1972), however, has observed similar conformity of group opinions in much more serious situations. Taking the evidence of transcripts and observations of US presidential advisory committees from the 1950s onwards, Janis has shown how like-minded individuals can come to be remarkably impervious to alternative opinions, indeed intolerant of them. The formulation of major decisions in a non-critical atmosphere happened, for example, over policy towards the Chinese in the Korean War, and in the Bay of Pigs fiasco in Cuba, and seems to have been instrumental in taking the US deeper and deeper into the Vietnam War. Janis called this effect 'groupthink', and in so doing warns us of consensuses of opinion which are too certain of themselves. There must be, he argues, at least one devil's advocate in every group. The need for encouragement of some dissent could not be clearer.

Indeed, it is remarkable how conformist people can be. The elimination of individual judgement is also seen in situations which are clearly not ambiguous, where individuals come to refuse to believe the evidence of their senses. In the experiment by Asch (1951), subjects were shown lines of varying length and asked to match these lines against other target lines. Asch engineered the situation so that the subjects heard the opinions of other individuals first. These other individuals were in fact collaborating with Asch, and had earlier been instructed to express judgements which were clearly wrong. Subjects had no difficulty in matching the lines when they were not faced with this pressure. Where they were faced by people giving obviously wrong judgements, over one-third gave the same incorrect answer. They either refused to believe the evidence of their senses, or meekly went along with the group even though they knew the group was wrong. This situation, then, differs substantially from the Sherif experiment: with the Sherif experiment there was no possible validation of judgement; in the Asch experiment there clearly was, and yet a substantial minority of subjects still conformed.

Again, one might ask whether this really matters. Judging the length of lines is hardly going to affect anyone's well-being. Is there evidence that people will go against their better judgement, where to do so would harm another person, simply because of over-conformity?

Consider, then, the following experience. You see an advert in a local paper. It is from the Department of Psychology at the local university. You have never participated in a psychology experiment before, and think that it might be rather interesting. The advert says that it should not take more than a couple of hours of your time, and on top of that you will be paid a small sum for taking part. You decide to go along.

On arriving, you are given the promised payment, and introduced to another individual who will participate in the same experiment. You are to test his memory on a series of paired words. You are also told that if he fails to remember the words correctly, you are to administer a small electric shock to him, and to gradually increase these if he continues to get the pairs wrong. You raise your eyebrows at this, but he does not seem to mind, so you agree. He goes into the room next door, and you see him being strapped into his chair. You move to your seat in front of an array of controls, and the experiment begins.

At first there is no problem, as he gets his first pairs right. However, when the subject begins to get his paired words wrong, you increase the voltage. At first there is no sound, but then, at 75 volts, there is a grunt of pain from the other room. At 120 volts, the subject states that the shocks are painful. At 150 volts the subject asks to be taken out. Whenever you ask the experimenter whether you should continue or not, he simply tells you to continue. If you ask him whether the shocks are harmful, he replies that although the shocks may be painful, there is no permanent tissue damage. If you show real unwillingness to continue, the experimenter says that the experiment requires that you continue, or that it is absolutely essential that you continue, or that you have no other choice, you *must* go on. You can see from the array of controls in front of you that you could continue shocking the subject up to a maximum of 450 volts. When would *you* refuse to continue?

When Stanley Milgram (1974) asked a body of psychiatrists to predict what percentage of his volunteers would continue shocking up to the maximum voltage, they predicted no more than 2 per cent. Milgram's results are chilling – 65 per cent of his subjects continued shocking up to a maximum in the situation described. The general public did little better than the psychiatrists. When Kelman and Hamilton (1989) asked them to predict what most people would do, 17 per cent said they would continue shocking to a maximum, but only 3 per cent said they themselves would. People have a very optimistic view of themselves: the Milgram paradigm suggests that in this case it is very wide of the actual truth.

One reaction to the Milgram experiment is to suggest that the volunteers were not duped at all: that they knew that this was a 'put-up' job from the start. (Indeed, it was: the subject being shocked was a professional actor who was putting on a performance. The only subject in the experiment was the individual delivering the shocks.) The evidence, however, does not support the interpretation that the volunteers knew all along. Firstly, the film Milgram made of this[1] shows people clearly in a high degree of distress, wanting to refuse, but finding themselves unable to do so. Secondly, in one situation (Milgram, 1974, p. 97), a volunteer who managed to refuse to continue physically pushed a co-participant who wished to shock the victim into a corner and threatened him with violence if he tried to continue – hardly the response of a man who thinks the situation is a fake. Finally, in one variation of the experiment (Milgram, 1974, pp. 59–62), Milgram has the experimenter leave the room on a prextext, but with the instruction that he could be contacted by phone should the volunteer need help. In this situation, the number of volunteers who continued to shock to a maximum was very close to the percentage predicted by the psychiatrists – around 2 per cent. Clearly, the psychiatrists, general public and the respondents had all failed to take into account one vital element of the situation – the degree to which people will conform to the orders of a perceived authority, in this case a professional psychologist. They had been so intent, one must assume, upon looking at the functioning of individuals, upon the aggressive or destructive instincts people may be attributed with, that they had failed to take into account a far more potent paradigm – that of the influence of social norms, of the unthinking obedience by individuals to society's authority structures and figures. What Milgram's experiments suggest is that people may not want to inflict harm, but may do so because of the influence of the people and the institutional structures around them. One needs to look beyond psychological theory to take on board the pressures stemming from the institutions in which people are socialized and earn their living. The school is one such organization and Milgram's paradigm testifies to one aspect of such an organization – the awe with which the expert is perceived in our society. The Milgram authority, like the teacher, is a seemingly innocuous professional, with few or no powers of punishment, and yet few people in the experiment found the inner strength to go against him. This, I think, has important implications for the image of teachers, and where we treat them as all-knowing, and unquestionable, we instil this kind of awe. A different form of perception needs to be generated.

This failure to realize the influence that a professional authority can have over the pupil – and then the layperson – is alarming, and doubly so because in other situations the layperson seems perfectly well aware of the power of authority. This is graphically illustrated in an infamous non-experimental situation, the My Lai massacre in Vietnam on 16 March 1968. In this action, Charlie Company of the US Army, under the command of Second Lieutenant William L. Calley Jr, slaughtered virtually an entire village of old people and children. There were some who refused the order: James Joseph Dursi testified that when ordered to shoot, he just stood there shouting 'I can't! I can't!', though he did nothing to actually prevent others from killing the inhabitants. Only those removed from direct orders seemed able to go further than this. Chief Warrant Officer Hugh Thomson, Calley's inferior in rank, but not in his line of command, saw the carnage from his helicopter, landed and shielded what survivors he could find. He ordered his own men to train their guns on Calley's men and open fire if they tried to kill any more people. But these were the exception: the vast majority of Charlie Company participated in the massacre.

Calley was the only man to be convicted, and yet the basis of his defence was that of *respondeat superior* – that he was neither morally nor legally culpable because he had only been doing his duty and following orders. Certainly, whilst My

Lai was an atrocity, it was one of a series of atrocities in a particularly savage war. Calley, it could be argued, was only continuing what he had seen going on around him and had been tacitly condoned by his superiors.

American public opinion at the time appeared to side heavily with Calley. In their survey of responses to crimes of obedience, Kelman and Hamilton (1989, chapter 7) found that 62 per cent of the population thought that most people would follow the instructions of William Calley at My Lai and shoot innocent women and children. A significant minority (34 per cent) also said that they would do the same thing themselves. Public opinion seemed to have had its eventual effect. Calley was initially sentenced to life imprisonment, which was then reduced to twenty years, and then again to ten. In all he served three years of the sentence, but spent this time under house arrest in his apartment, where he received visits from his girlfriend.

The difference in perceptions of obedience in the Milgram dilemma and in the My Lai dilemma seems to lie in the nature of the authority. The Milgram authority is a seemingly innocuous professional man, with few or no powers of punishment, and with few or no demands on the volunteer in terms of duty, and it is probably the hidden nature of this authority which fooled so many people in the Milgram experiment. It seems, therefore, particularly important to note that authority in terms of expertise is precisely part of the hidden curriculum of the school.

The My Lai situation is much more obviously powerful, for it is a military situation, in which, throughout training, there is a deliberate attempt to get soldiers to obey without question. Indeed, the US Army is one of the few bodies in the Western world which uses the word 'indoctrination' in a purely functionai, non-pejorative sense (White, 1972, p. 120). Moreover, being part of the military is generally seen as being part of a body carrying out a patriotic duty, and for many this will be perceived as the carrying out of orders precisely due to this duty. Finally, there is a clear and powerful threat of retribution if orders are not carried out. All of this adds up to a situation which many can recognize much more easily and to which many can respond with a great deal more certainty. However, both the Milgram and the My Lai responses are worrying, if for different reasons. The My Lai responses send clear messages about the dangers of indoctrination, of misguided loyalty, of the power of the threats of punishment. The Milgram paradigm, on the other hand, suggests a situation just as dangerous, for it has its effect much more quietly. It is clearly necessary to attempt to unpick these causes of over-conformity, to identify the threads of dissent.

## THE MODES OF CONFORMITY

Some of these causes were suggested in the Asch experiment referred to above – did people conform because they really believed that the others were right, or did they conform because they felt the group pressure and did not wish to appear foolish? A more detailed analysis of possible responses was made by Kelman (1958), who suggests that there are in fact three bases for obedience to authority. This is based upon whether people are rule-, role- or value-following individuals. Applying this to the My Lai massacre, it would mean that those who did not really believe in what Calley did, but believed that anyone else in his position would have been punished if they did not follow orders, would be rule followers – paying lip-service through fear of punishment, ignoring the order when they could. The key word for the rule follower, then, is *compliance*. Role followers, on the other hand, are essentially those who believe that they have a duty to fulfil, and that it is part of that duty to carry out such acts. Their role as a military person, their role as an American soldier, would lead them to commit such acts. There would be no fear from them of punishment, but they would feel duty-bound to perform the action. The key word here, then, would be *identification*. Of those who said that they believed that Calley was guilty, and that they would not commit such an act, the key feature is a focus not on punishment to oneself, nor upon the conception of one's duty, but upon the consequences to the victim. With this change in perspective comes the understanding that an act has to be justified against one's own value scheme – that leaving this decision to an outside body is simply not good enough. The key word here, then, is *internalization* – the notion that an act must be consonant with one's personal overriding values. It is only by placing an act within this context that the cognitive framework is then available within which an order can be properly assessed. Only then is it possible to decide whether this order should be followed or not. It is precisely because Calley failed to see the massacre at My Lai in this light that he was able to perpetrate such an action.

It is interesting to note that Kelman's formulation of compliance, identification and internalization almost exactly corresponds with that of the extremely influential developmental psychologist Lawrence Kohlberg (1981). His formulation of an ascending five- or six-stage, three-level hierarchy of moral developmental thinking (see Figure 4.1) is doubly interesting in that its first formulation was in 1958 – when Kohlberg was only just completing his doctoral thesis. Here, it seems, is a case of two thinkers pursuing two parallel but unconnected typologies, which suggest essentially the same process of thinking. It also, I think, adds an extra perspective on notions of people remaining at stages 3 and 4 in the Kohlbergian levels. The background to Kelman's typology suggests that role-oriented individuals are as liable to commit crimes of obedience as rule-oriented ones. Indeed, they may be even more so, for rule-oriented individuals will refuse orders whenever they feel they are not being observed and so will not be punished, whilst role-oriented individuals will continue precisely because they have an image in front of them of what their duty is. Of course, both Kohlberg and Kelman, by placing value-oriented individuals at the top of a moral hierarchy, assume that these individuals hold values which reject violence to others. Those who accept a code which explicitly incorporates violence to another party (like the Nazi party, the National Front, etc.) are probably even more dangerous than rule- and role-oriented people.

It is also extremely significant in the context of this article to note that Kohlberg's work increasingly moved from the study of moral-reasoning processes in individuals to the study of institutional effects, and in particular to the proposals for a particular form of school which would facilitate rather than hinder the development of autonomous, and in some cases dissenting, opinions – that of the 'just community school' (Power *et al.*, 1989). This is an institution wherein the pupils play a major part in the structuring of rules and procedures, and where the ethos is one which actively encourages them to express opinions which may dissent from those of the teachers, but which are valuable precisely because they are expressions of personally formulated responses which lead to greater personal commitment to the institution. Kohlberg was by no means the first, and will not be the last, to point out that the normal structuring of schools does not encourage pupils to accept rules

A woman is dying because she is suffering from a very rare and dangerous disease. So far there has been no medicine which can cure the disease. However, now a scientist invents a drug which can cure the disease, but he wants a great deal of money for its use. The sick woman's husband, Heinz, tries to raise the money for the drug but can't find enough to pay the scientist. What ought Heinz to do? Why?

| Content | Reasoning which focuses on the life issue (Heinz should steal the drug) | Reasoning which focuses on the law issue (Heinz should not steal the drug) | Form |
|---|---|---|---|
| **Pre-conventional** | | | |
| Stage 1 | because if you kill someone you'll be in jail for a long time and for stealing you aren't punished much. | because if he does he will be caught, locked up, etc. | People see rules as dependent on power and external compulsion |
| Stage 2 | if he thinks his wife would help if he were dying. | because if you commit a crime you have to go to jail long enough to make up for it; because if you steal you only have to pay back the person. | People see rules as instrumental to reward and satisfaction of needs |
| **Conventional** | | | |
| Stage 3 | because he tried to be decent but now feels he has no choice; or because he would have the best of intentions. | in order to leave a good impression on the community; so or that others won't get the wrong impression. | Rules are seen as ways of obtaining social approval |
| Stage 4 | because he is obligated by his marital responsibility, wedding vows, covenant of marriage, etc. | because respect for the law will be destroyed if citizens feel they may break the law anytime they disagree with it. | People hold the views that authority knows best, that 'doing one's duty' is most praiseworthy |
| **Post-conventional** | | | |
| Stage 5 | because that is part of the implicit social contract which all human beings have with one another; because responsibility to others is one of the basic principles that life is founded upon, etc. | because if individuals are to live together in society, there must be some common agreement; or because laws represent a necessary structure of social agreement. | Moral rules are seen as there to maintain a social order but on a kind of 'social contract' basis |
| Stage 6 | | | Behaviour is defined by ethical principles chosen in terms of universality, consistency and comprehensiveness – justice being the overriding consideration |

**Figure 4.1** Kohlbergian stages of justice reasoning.

through their ownership, but through threat of reprisal. This clearly leads to nothing more than rule-following, and disobedience when unsupervised. The paradox of educating for dissent is that it eventually produces a much higher level of commitment than educating for conformity, because of the degree of participation permitted.

## DISSENT AND BUREAUCRACY

Dissent and bureaucracy make poor companions. Dissent implies flexibility in decision-making, for it must allow for change and indeed welcome it as part of the productive process. It also implies an intimacy in interactions, for dissent can only be productive where people understand the need for it, and trust people's motives for it as well. It implies an intimacy precisely because where education is seen as a process of aiding the learner rather than one of direction, then dissent is always a possibility. As John Macquarrie (1972, p. 205) has put it,

> ... teaching is seen as a mode of being with, a positive mode of solicitude in which one leaps ahead of the other so as to open his possibilities for him, but never leaps in for the other, for this would be really to deprive him of his possibilities.

Organizations which would foster such attitudes must incorporate into their structures such flexibility and personalness. Poor soil for their growth, then, would be the form of organization most prevalent in the Western world today – that of the bureaucracy, for bureaucracy, by its very nature, values the predictable and the universal, dislikes change, and finds the personal at best an irrelevance, at worst an impediment.

It should perhaps be pointed out again that the total elimination of bureaucracy in schools is not being advocated, even if that were possible. It is clearly the case that bureaucratic procedures are needed in any organization which requires some degree of predictability, continuity and reliability, and this includes the school. Indeed, the growth in the bureaucratization of schools on both sides of the Atlantic can be traced precisely to these needs (e.g. Katz, 1975; Armytage, 1970). However, as with the concepts of conformity and dissent, the issue is not one of total acceptance or rejection, but one of degree, and this chapter is suggesting a present imbalance. So the question does need to be asked: what are the factors within bureaucratic functioning which facilitate conformity and discourage dissent?

Kelman and Hamilton (1989, pp. 16–19) suggest that there are three elements within bureaucratic structures which need to be noted for their tendency to produce over-compliance, and, in so doing, denigrate the personal and the dissenting. These they describe as authorization, routinization and dehumanization. Authorization is where people say 'It wasn't my fault, I was only obeying orders'. It is the escape clause that people may find in any hierarchical, duty-defined organization, for such structures in effect absolve the individual from responsibility, making them feel only a functionary within a much larger body. Pusey (1976), in his analysis of the bureaucratization of Tasmanian education, shows how teachers use the system to transfer responsibility and blame to those higher up. They refuse to take responsibility or use their initiative and demand of the school principal exact clarification of roles and duties in order for them to be able to carry out no more than that which is demanded. He also shows that students in such a system adopt the same kind of approach to participation, demanding of teachers constant direction. As one social science teacher said to him,

> You suggest some fascinating research project to them – something which they could do by themselves and in their own way by using the library and resources of their own choosing. What do they do? They ask you to tell them what books to use, to tell them how much of it should be writing and how much of it should be pictures. They want to know how to set it out. They want you to set a deadline for its completion and to give them marks for it instead of comments.
>
> (Pusey, 1976, p. 67)

What the teacher fails to see, but Pusey brings out, is that the behaviour is a product of the system within which they work. The pupils will not change, and neither will the teachers, until the system is changed to a less stratified and hierarchical one. The result is a system which fails many and relationships which stimulate few. One might be inclined to observe the same general unwillingness to take initiatives – and the consequent impoverishment of relationships – in the reactions of teaching staff in the UK to the imposition of a specific number of teaching hours within the year – 1265 – and training 'Baker days' within them. The result has been a reduced commitment to the system, as witnessed in a dramatic tail-off in out-of-school activities, as teachers have reacted to the bureaucratizing of duties by working strictly within the limits imposed on them.

Related to the effects of authorization come those of routinization. Routinization, through the use of rules and regulations, prevents the general rule from being adapted to suit the individual case, simply because these decisions are pre-specified. Further, routinization allows the actor to focus on the details of the job, rather than on its overall meaning. This was part of Eichmann's excuse at his trial: he only attended to details and organization of trains and their timetables. By so doing, he, and anyone else in a bureaucracy, can almost completely avoid facing the ultimate consequences of their actions. Where, in schools, functions are increasingly made the object of specified criteria, from the exact specification of the roles and duties of a staff position to the detailed ordering of curricular objectives, the same distancing of teacher from teacher, of teacher from pupil, becomes not only possible but probable. Anderson (1968), in his examination of the Boston public school system, showed how the impersonality of bureaucratized schools, through their size and the degree of curricular and pedagogic specification, led to the distancing of teacher from student, preventing the formation of the kinds of genuine relationships which form an essential grounding for a true educational meeting, and for consequent individuation to take place.

The final aspect of bureaucracies which can lead to such atrocities is that of dehumanization. The detailed specification of roles and duties allows the bureaucrat, indeed encourages the bureaucrat, to view people as numbers rather than as people, as figures rather than as personalities or members of the human community. And psychologically distancing oneself from others is as effective a means of dehumanizing the victim as physically distancing oneself. In like manner it is far easier to issue commands which harm others if there is no picture of or any personal contact with that person. Bureaucracy allows this to happen. More than this, it actually structures situations so that they are more likely to happen. Is this, one might ask, precisely what happens when the results of a school are published to be compared with those of another as a means for parents to judge the better performance? The clear intention of such thinking is for the more successful school to survive, and the less successful to die. But what happens to the teachers at the less successful school who are trying their best? To the children who are not moved out? Are these really to be sacrificed? Only at the impersonal level could one contemplate such actions. Moving from the ideological to the personal perspective, from the rational to the caring, generates a new approach, in which one begins from the individual and moves outwards.

This is well illustrated in the example that Noddings (1984, p. 42) gives of the Roman commander Manlius, who, in order to remain consistent in the application of a harsh law he had made, executed his own son. Noddings does not argue that Manlius should have excused his son because he was his son (but continued executing others). Nor does she agree with what Manlius did. What she says is that if Manlius had started at the personal level, he would never have made such a rule in the first place. In other words, caring and the personalness of relationships must inform the construction of rules at the social level, just as they must be used in the application of such rules. Bureaucratic rules, limited to functional rationality, can lead to an amnesia of caring.

## THE SOCIALIZATION OF CONFORMITY AND DISSENT

If, then, the bureaucratic organization of schools can lead to over-conformity, are there other structures within schools which do the same thing? In this respect, Melvin Kohn's work (1977) is particularly significant because, though it deals with conformity based on the social class of the individual, his findings seem readily generalizable to the school. Kohn's work suggests, perhaps surprisingly, that social class is a more important determinant of values than are race, region, religion and nationality added together. His research suggests that the crucial determinant of this class-based influence on values is the nature of work that people perform. Working-class men have supervised, directed work: middle-class men have greater freedom and self-direction in their work, and this influences their valuation of what is important. The middle-class man values self-direction, the working-class man values conformity. As Kohn (1977, p. 164) says,

> Occupational experience helps structure men's view, not only of the occupational world, but of social reality in general.

These experiences at work translate, firstly, into parental expectations. Kohn reports that middle-class parents valued experiences for their children concerned with how and why things happen, displays of good sense and sound judgement, responsibility and self-reliance, the ability to face facts squarely, and the ability to do well under pressure. Working-class parents, on the other hand, were more concerned in their children with displays of good manners, neatness, obedience and acting (as they saw it) as children of their sex should. They were more rigidly conservative, less tolerant of nonconformity, less trustful, and more resistant to change.

This different emphasis in values was further translated into approaches to the discipline of their children. Middle-class parents interpreted behaviours in terms of intent, working-class parents in terms of immediate material consequences, and would discipline accordingly. Such variation is understandable if one considers that occupational opportunities channel working-class parents into viewing rules as inflexible: hence they punish simply for infringement of these rules. Middle-class parents, on the other hand, being more flexible and self-directed, view in terms of intentions. Both are a consequence, not of personality differences, but of job socialization.

A number of points can be made here. Firstly, it might be argued that because working-class work is generally more poorly paid than middle-class work, there is less freedom in choice of life-style for the working-class man – he is constantly faced by financial problems, and simply making ends meet. In such circumstances, sticking to the conservative, immediate, well-tried and trusted is much preferable to the novel, risky, untried and speculative. Only those with sufficient resources (the middle class) are in a position to try the untried. Only when the situation becomes really desperate – when they have nothing to lose – do the working class turn nonconformist and revolutionary. The paradox of this is that those who may need change the most are the least likely to bring it about unless the situation becomes really desperate, while those who are most in the position to change are the least likely to do so – they're doing very nicely, thank you.

Two further points relate to class-based conceptions of discipline. The first is that the different conceptions of the bases for discipline sound remarkably like Piaget's distinction (1977) between heteronomous and autonomous stages of moral development, and give one pause for thought as to just how developmental this process is, and how much of it relates to parental attitudes and social background. There has been enough cross-cultural research in this area over the last twenty years (e.g. Schmidt, 1973; Donaldson, 1978; Pool et al., 1985) to make this a genuine possibility.

The other point is a practical one for teachers. If schools propound values which are more consonant with middle-class than working-class values – in terms of things like personal judgement, self-reliance and autonomy – then clearly there will be more problems of communication with parents and children of a working-class background than with those of a middle-class background, for they will approach the problem of discipline with very different values and end-results in mind. Indeed, it is not possible to guarantee that the different sets of values will ever be effectively reconciled. One should at least, however, be aware of these different value sets and thus be prepared to discuss, argue and educate within this larger frame of understanding.

Perhaps the most important point arising out of Kohn's research for the educator is his finding that the crucial determinant of class-based values was the nature of the work that his subjects performed, these being exclusively working-class and middle-class men. It would not be stretching his findings too far to suggest that precisely this point could be made for children. After all, are not their two places of work the home and the school? The importance of the home has been made in the previous paragraph. Here it can be pointed out that the occupational experience of children helps to structure their experience of social reality just as much as it does that of their parents. What they experience at school in terms of the degree of autonomy allowed – in terms of both class and school management – will have profound effects upon their perception of what they themselves can do. The child is truly father of the man.

Much of Kohn's research is supported and expanded by two other sources. The first is the earlier writings of G. D. H. Cole. Cole suggested (1919, p. 34) that the greatest evil in society was not poverty but, as he called it, 'slavery'. The extension of the franchise had not resulted, he suggested, in the democratization of society at all. And why not? Because people had been 'trained to subservience' through the normal routine of their work. For Cole,

> . . . the industrial system . . . is in great measure the key to the paradox of political democracy. Why are the many nominally supreme but actually powerless? Largely because the circumstances of their lives do not accustom or fit them for power or responsibility. A servile system in industry inevitably reflects itself in political servility.
>
> (Cole, 1919, p. 35)

Whilst Cole's solution to this problem, a Guild Socialist system, cannot be the concern of this book, the implications of such a system for education are. Cole argues in the same tradition as Rousseau and J. S. Mill, and suggests that only by people being educated into participation at the local level could they come to appreciate the mechanics of participation or feel personally effective enough to do so at the national level. It does not strain the argument too far, I think, to suggest that participation in decision-making should not only occur at an institutionally smaller level, but should also be begun as early as possible. Schools fit the bill perfectly.

The second source of support for Kohn's work is that of Kelman and Hamilton (1989, chapter 9). They categorized respondents on a survey regarding the Calley massacre as either DRs (those who denied that Calley had any responsibility for My Lai) or ARs (those who asserted that he did). They then found that the DRs were more likely to have less education, less income, a poorer job, and be from the lower class or the petite bourgeoisie. ARs, not surprisingly, were likely to be quite the opposite – to have had more years in education, have a higher income and a more prestigious job, and be in the higher reaches of the middle class. Kelman and Hamilton point out that whilst this finding was statistically significant, it was not that dramatic – there was a large minority of ARs in the first group, just as there was a large minority of DRs in the second group. Moreover, they were quite certain that this is not a personality characteristic, but more a consequence of the position in society in which people find themselves. Thus they argue that DRs, through having less education, may lack the informational resources to know enough about a situation to change it, or the cognitive strategies to formulate a non-compliant alternative to the order given. Moreover, through having less prestigious occupations, they find themselves in jobs which are generally more directed than those of their AR counterparts, and are much more liable to sacking or firing. In such situations, they are much more likely to be socialized into an obedient compliance, either through the activities taken to supervise them, or through their own unwillingness to 'rock the boat'. And further, with little or no contact with powerful people, they will probably view authority as distant and impersonal, and therefore see themselves as incapable of contacting this authority or influencing the decisions.

The DRs' experiences may well parallel those of many children at school. What, one may ask, are the effects of schools structuring children's experiences? What happens when the curriculum offered does not examine alternative possibilities and epistemologies? What happens when attention is not directed to the purpose and fairness of school rules with a view to restructuring them? What if pupils and teachers are not actively invited to participate meaningfully in the discussion and implementation of change in school organization? The experience of most children is, I suggest, as directed, if not more so, than that of the average working-class adult. And the end-result is that most young people come out of schools having had a very similar socialization experience to that of working-class adults. Schools, then, can be the primary socializers of children in terms of rigidity, conservatism and compliance. This has important implications for their future political socialization. As one of my students put it in an examination reply,

> Can we seriously discuss the nature of democracy in a school which mimics the power structure of a benevolent one party state?

## CITIZENSHIP, EDUCATION AND DISSENT

However, remediation strategies do follow from the above. If people are to come to see dissent as an essential part of citizenship, then a number of things need to be done.

Firstly, citizens must be given access to multiple, multicultural and international, perspectives in order to demystify authority. Once it is clear that authority is but one voice (as Kelman and Hamilton (1989, p. 324) say, 'authorities also function as partisans'), then they are less inclined to accept without question the opinions or orders of authority. Therefore, in order to provide a multiplicity of perspectives for the teacher and child, there must be a move away from 'little England' or other parochial perspectives, and an increased emphasis on international views on different matters. This involves a comparative analysis not only of educational policies, but also of other institutions, and a general internationalizing of the curriculum. It will allow a broadening of vision, and the consequent realization that there are other ways of doing things besides those suggested by current authorities.

Through the development of multicultural and international perspectives in schools there would probably come a much greater appreciation of the subjectivity of knowledge. Pupils and teachers must come to a much clearer understanding of the fact that there is very little in the curriculum which can be taken as 'fact': most is at least arguable and open to different interpretations. The scenario must change from one of uncritical transmission to one of critical reflection by both teachers and pupils. The educational paradigm must move from what Rogers describes as the 'mug and jug approach' (1983), or Freire as the 'banking concept of education' (1972), to one in which both teachers and pupils see themselves as fellow travellers, albeit the teachers are more experienced and have travelled further. Downey and Kelly (1986, p. 124) argued that

> ... the oddest thing about the teacher's authority is that it must contain within it the seeds of its own destruction ...

Perhaps 'destruction' is too strong a word, for a relationship is still maintained, and so is an authority, but certainly this authority is changed to one of experienced consultant rather than possessor of truths, and in so doing inducts pupils into a journey of exploration, tolerance and possible dissent.

In the most general sense, there need to be structural changes within society so that authority is more dispersed, and more people have personal experience of it, or have personal contact with those who do exercise it. In this way, authority loses some of its mystique, and the person in the street can come to understand that authorities are human and fallible and make mistakes just as they do. This also weakens the effect of authorization in bureaucracies. It follows, therefore, that there must be a democratization of school structure to the extent that not only do teaching and non-teaching staff experience participation in the running of the school, but also pupils have some experience of it. Only in this way, by actually experiencing authority and understanding its process, can students learn to demystify the concept, to place it in proper perspective. Such a proposal is, of course, very far from current proposals, but is an essential reorientation of school structures if there is a genuine commitment to the democratic education of pupils for future citizenship. If they experience nothing but the effects of authority, and have no chance of actually exercising it, what sort of socialization are they being given for their future involvement in the political activities of the country? The provision of the exercise of authority by students, or the lack of such provision, is an acid test both of schools and those in authority.

Finally, there must be strenuous efforts to make people consider the consequences of their action. There must be an education away from the mere compliance with the implementation of rules and regulations, and a persuasion to the identification of numbers and figures with individuals, to the comprehension of the overall purpose and structure of the organization within which they work, and therefore the relating of their duties to a total design. A simple but effective way of doing this would be to reduce the organization's size, so that it becomes possible for functionaries to know the individuals with whom they are dealing. It follows, then, that in order for those within schools to fully understand their efforts on others, they must be able to identify these others, and this must mean a reduction in both school and class sizes, for it is in this way that individuals can meet and know each other on a face-to-face basis. In so doing we lessen the chance of individuals being treated as faceless units, and therefore being dehumanized. This aim may well clash with the economic aim of efficiencies of scale, but this again is an acid test of the desire to do something about this problem. If economic efficiency is given more emphasis, it should send a clear signal to people as to the real priorities of policy-makers.

This journey, whilst being radical for many, is not as radical as some might at first think: the same kind of recommendation has come from sources religious and spiritual. Look, for instance, at the maxims suggested by Derek Webster (1982, pp. 69–70) for guiding teachers in how to enhance in children a receptivity to awe.

All ten perform precisely the kind of function deemed necessary in this chapter, and I quote them in their entirety:

1. Inspect the focus with which children work, and offer a refocusing at greater depth.
2. Show a new facet to what children take for granted.
3. Use symbolic language to indicate what is 'beyond' children's accepted reality.
4. Encourage children's amazement by fostering a self-questioning about their own bodies.
5. Help children to see that there is mystery within reasoning and explanation. (The first uses thought which is an enigma to itself while the second usually becomes part of a further or wider questioning.)
6. Foster an astonishment at the world which sees no life as trivial, expendable or unimportant.
7. Keep alive in children the intensity of their childhood experiences preventing a complete withering away into what is commonplace.
8. Enhance that wonder at being which will not allow children to become totally accustomed to the laws which govern their conception of reality.
9. Stimulate a degree of unconformity among children so that their adjustment to life does not smother the tensions which create new viewpoints.
10. Provoke children to the insight that the meaning of life is only partially reconstructed.

## CONCLUSIONS

In the most general sense, such changes in national consciousness, school restructuring, teacher–pupil relationships and epistemological understanding are all crucial. They provoke within children a sense of wonder and awe at the world, which fosters personal growth, an appreciation of beauty, and a journey of the spirit. The changes also remind one of the partisan nature of any authority, and undermine absolutist claims that it alone is privileged in possessing timeless truths, which support its position, and which it is the duty of schools to impart. Such an approach also points to the dangers of a too-rigid adherence to national curricular prescriptions, for it deplores the rigidification and bureaucratization of knowledge, and urges a much more qualitative and modifiable approach.

The results of the Milgram experiments were not freaks, and the My Lai massacre was not an isolated incident.[2] The possibility of both lurks round the corner of all societies and organizations which insist on pursuing the unremitting inculcation of conformity, and the stigmatizing of dissent as the actions of an antisocial minority. The mechanics for such inculcation are to be found within the functioning of the major institutions of present-day society. An over-representation of conformity, and a diminution of dissent, leads from individual acts of the uncaring to those of violence, and from there to group victimization, and ultimately to genocide.

It is for members of each institution in society to explore its implications for their organization, and to formulate proposals to prevent it. The notion that dissent is, within limits, a necessary quality, an essential part of being an active citizen, should become part of the educational agenda. The education of dissent should be a compulsory element of any national curriculum.

## NOTES

[1] Milgram's film *Obedience* is distributed by the New York University Film Library.

[2] For a sobering account of the societal dimensions of this subject see Chalk and Jonassohn (1990).

# Chapter 5

# Educational management and the market-place

## INTRODUCTION

The last two chapters have, among other things, examined the effects of bureaucratic structures upon those working within and without them, and described some of the alienating and brutalizing effects that they can have. Clearly, their effects will be the more profound the more a government is alienating and brutalizing, and such effects apply to governments of both the left and the right. Fascism and Communism are alike in elevating perceived community needs above those of the individual. And it is by neglecting the individual and the particular that one loses the ability to appreciate an individual's rights and needs, to even see them as unique beings. Down this road, it has been suggested, lie prejudice, discrimination, violence and ultimately genocide. One needs to be suitably wary, then, of any political ideology which locates the rights of the individual behind those of the community, and instead perhaps look to one which recognizes the rights and liberties of the individual as the supreme virtues that a society must pursue, and which translates these into the organization and running of its institutions, including those related to education. Such a philosophy, it is claimed, is that of the new right, the new liberals. This movement – in the particular variation of free-market economics – has shown revived influence over the last ten to fifteen years in the policies of Western governments. As part of its approach, it attacks bureaucracies by undermining the very structures upon which they are formed. Bureaucracies are seen as much more sheltered, and hence more powerful in their effects in the public domain than in the private sector. In the private sector, it is argued, because firms are in competition with one another, and must produce the most efficient service if they are to offer prices which undercut their competitors, they tend to make sure that their organizational structures are as streamlined and efficient as possible. If one believes, as free-marketeers do, that schools have been typical examples of state-run institutions which have been sheltered from the winds of competition, and thus have developed bureaucratic machines neither efficient nor responsive to consumer demands, then the solutions are fairly clear: decentralize control, and pass the running of them to those directly affected. One then moves along a path from state-run to privatized education.

Paradoxically, this philosophy of free-market economics is almost Marxist in its ramifications, for in the Western world over the last ten to fifteen years it has had the most profound effects not only on economic policy, but also upon personal, social and political philosophies. As Marx argued that economic relationships are the root cause of the structuring of social relationships within society, so free-marketeers have proposed precisely the same thing, though beginning with different values and arriving at different conclusions. Its major thinkers have in different ways all linked their exposition of economic theory to a conception of the good society, suggesting that the creation of the good society is only possible through particular economic policies. The influence of this philosophy, then, has transcended pure economic theory, and touched, and continues to touch, all aspects of the functioning of society, including that of education. Evaluation of it, therefore, cannot remain in the domain of pure economics, for whatever success or failure it has there, it might still be approved or criticized – and ultimately accepted or rejected – for the effects it has in other areas.

How far one moves along this path will, of course, depend upon the particular group one chooses within this general theory. One can, I think, identify three main groups which, though all radical in a political sense, still differ in degree. The first, and most radical, is represented in the anarcho-libertarian views of someone like Murray Rothbard (1978), who would entirely dismantle the apparatus of state, arguing that state intervention inevitably involves aggression against either a person or their property. As no person, in Rothbard's thesis, may be aggressive to another, this must mean that the state should be prevented from interfering in anyone's life. Educationally, this would mean that each family would, unhindered, choose the form of education they feel is best suited to their needs. Such arguments follow on the thoughts of writers like Ivan Illich (1973) and Everett Reimer (1971), who argue that education has been confused with schooling, the state providing the latter but seldom the former, which should be better conceptualized as life-long, rather than the 'sentence' children are given in their youth. It incidentally also shows that it is simplistic to assign the designations right or left wing to the arguments of this movement.

A fairly obvious objection to the anarcho-libertarian thesis is that there would seem to be some need for a body to prevent more powerful individuals from being aggressive towards others. Thus, slightly further down the road would be a second group of new right theorists, the 'minimalist state' thinkers like Robert Nozick (1974, p. x), who argues that

> ... a minimal state limited to the narrow functions of protection against force, theft, fraud, enforcements of contracts, and so on, is justified ...

but believes that

> ... any more extensive state will violate person's rights not to be forced to do certain things, and is unjustified.

Compulsory state education, then, would be anathema, but a position of ensuring that each child received a minimum education of a privatized variety would be acceptable to minimalist sensibilities.

A third group would accept the reality of the state, but believe that its influence in present times is too dominant, and should be reduced as far as is consonant with providing a basic level of material security for citizens; government should not be given the task of increasing the material equality between them. This group, what one might call the mainstream new liberals, has been the most influential on government policy, and comprises thinkers like Friedrich Hayek, Milton Friedman, and the public choice school (see Green (1987) for a good exposition). The role of the government, then, is to provide as much freedom as possible for individuals, and leave the free market to decide upon the distribution of rewards between them. However, this does not reduce the state to minimalist functions, for as Hayek (1979, p. 41) has said,

> Far from advocating such a minimalist state, we find it unquestionable that in an advanced society government ought to use its power of raising funds by taxation to provide a number of services which for various reasons cannot be provided, or cannot be provided adequately, by the market.

Whichever approach one takes, it is clear that the effects upon education will be profound. All will be advocating much greater parental involvement, much greater personal choice, much greater influence of the free market upon educational structures. However, as the first and second groups have had only marginal effects upon educational policy, this and the two following chapters will concentrate attention upon the third group, and in particular on the two most influential writers within it, Hayek and Friedman.

This chapter, then, will review the key tenets of the market-place philosophy, locate them within an overall conception of the good society, and then translate this philosophy into educational-management practice. The next two will ask whether such a philosophy is valid in its theoretical claims, or in its practical consequences.

However, before looking in more detail at the implementation of this philosophy in society in general, and education in particular, it is important to set the scene, and explain the socio-political and economic context in which the philosophy of free-market economics has found itself. This will involve a brief description of the British social and political situation over the last few decades.

## THE DECLINE OF SOCIAL DEMOCRATIC CONSENSUS

It is hardly surprising to find that the high tide of social democratic enthusiasm in Britain was during and immediately after the Second World War. It was, after all, a time shortly after the economic recession and high unemployment of the 1930s, when people had come to believe that unfettered free markets increased the poverty of the lowest members of society, and in so doing reduced substantially their freedom to act. The Second World War was a time when a common threat and a common good could easily be perceived, when it was clear that all had to pull together if all were to survive, and when government seemed to have shown itself capable of organizing and managing the resources of the nation. As Sir Keith Joseph said:

> The Second World War brought about a swing of the pendulum in which it came to be believed that government could do almost everything for everybody without infringing freedom of opportunity.
>
> (Joseph, 1976, p. 28)

In such conditions, a form of morality which saw the good of all as being identical with the good of the individual was a very possible one. It was also possible for people to believe that this pulling together was something rather more: as people of all

71

classes had pulled together, so there should be a more equal distribution of the nation's wealth. Thus Richard Titmuss (1987, p. 126) could see a genuine union of ethics and politics, with an ultimate goal being to 'universalise humanistic ethics and the social rights of citizenship'.

It was from such motives that the 1944 Education Act was substantially formed. It is not that surprising that two major educational innovations should come at the end of two world wars. H. A. L. Fisher on the 1919 Education Act had said that

> ... every just mind begins to realise that the boundaries of citizenship are not determined by wealth, and that the same logic which leads us to desire an extension of the franchise point also to an extension of education.
>
> (Wardle, 1976, p. 35)

The same kind of impetus can also be traced from the 1944 Act: a just reward for all who fought an external enemy, a reward which the government could provide, and one which would cohere the citizenship of the country. Whilst the tripartite system which the Act embodies has come to be seen by many as a typical example of middle-class monopolization, because proportionately so many of their children went to grammar schools, this view has the benefit of hindsight. Certainly, the Labour party of the time were enthusiastic supporters, seeing the Act as one of real social democracy, of increased sponsored mobility for working-class children. As Manny Shinwell wrote in praise of the grammar school in 1958,

> ... We are afraid to tackle the public schools to which wealthy people send their sons, but at the same time we are ready to throw overboard the grammar schools, which are for many working class boys the stepping-stones to universities and a useful career. I would rather abandon Eton, Winchester, Harrow and all the rest of them than sacrifice the advantage of the grammar school.
>
> (Chitty, 1989, p. 30)

Indeed, comprehensive reorganization was sold by the Labour party not on the grounds of replacing an unfair system of allocation, but on the grounds of providing more of the same. As Hugh Gaitskell, the leader of the Labour party, put it,

> ... It would be nearer the truth to describe our proposals as 'a grammar-school education for all'.
>
> (Chitty, 1989, p. 36)

Thus, both these pieces of educational legislation – the tripartite system and comprehensive reorganization – can be seen as embodying the principal tenets of social democracy: the people of a nation pulling together, a more equal distribution of the nation's wealth, and the acceptability of governmental involvement in social engineering. Such legislation, then, represents a view of the possibility of social consensus which, as we shall see, free-marketeers would have little truck with.

However, it is fair to say that the social and ethical sides of social democratic thinking were displaced by economic arguments: state power during the war had habituated people to the idea of state intervention in the economy, and it was because of this acceptance that ideologues like Keynes and Beveridge could argue for the use of state power for economic management, in terms of public ownership for the sustaining of full employment, and income tax and compulsory insurance for welfare-service provision.

Even those on the right of the political spectrum in Great Britain came to subscribe to welfare-state economics. The experiences of major recessions and very high levels of unemployment in the 1930s, and the loss of the general election in 1945, had convinced most in the Conservative party that they would not gain power again in the foreseeable future on a political platform which passively accepted so many people out of work. It was hardly surprising, then, that there grew a consensus in British politics, derived from both ethical and pragmatic reasons, for the need for increased government intervention. It was therefore also to be expected that Keynesian economic solutions would be readily adopted by all major political parties. Macro-economic management, then, would become a major function, if not *the* major function, of government. As Keynes wrote,

> ... the central controls necessary to secure full employment will ... involve a large extension of the traditional functions of government.
>
> (Hoover and Plant, 1989, p. 20)

The major thrust of social democratic thinking was thus that economic growth could be accelerated and maintained, and greater efficiency achieved, by state planning and intervention. However, by placing such emphasis on the economic arguments, such a strategy left itself open to the possibility that if it ran into trouble economically, it would have little in the way of ethical arguments to fall back on. This has proved to be the case. Jordan (1989, pp. 134–5), for instance, has pointed out that appeals against cuts in local government provision have been made on the grounds of protecting 'jobs and services', and hardly at all on the (ethical) grounds that such cuts would weaken the social relations within the community. By tying itself so closely into a production and consumption model, social democratic theory thus became extremely vulnerable to attacks on precisely this ground.

Cracks in the Keynesian edifice became really pronounced with the advent of the 1970s. When the rise in oil prices hit Western economies, and recession started to settle in, traditional Keynesian remedies seemed to make little difference, indeed seemed even to exacerbate the problem. Pouring money into the economy actually seemed to increase inflation. Moreover, those systems and institutions within the economy which had money poured into them were in effect protected from the real world of competition, and so inefficient and wasteful practices within them were institutionalized and rigidified. This then cumulatively stored up trouble for the future. It was the acceptance of this scenario by the Labour government in the mid-1970s which led to the adoption in 1976 of the monetarist economic remedies prescribed by the IMF. Indeed, as Riddell says,

> If there was a Thatcher experiment, it was launched by Denis Healey.
>
> (Gamble, 1988, p. 201)

The same sorts of critique of welfare-state education policy also began with the Labour government of the day. Chitty (1989) has argued persuasively that much of the legislation of the Thatcher government can be directly traced back to the initiatives instituted by the Callaghan government. Thus there came the 'Great Debate', initiated by Callaghan's Ruskin College speech of 1976. The Green Paper of Shirley Williams came the following year, repeating many of the criticisms, and suggesting the need to investigate the possibility of a core element of the curriculum to be provided by all schools, and that work in schools should be made more relevant to needs of industry. Both these themes would be repeated in one form or another time and again, and would usher in a change of climate which would see the acceptance of an increasingly interventionist, dominant and dominating role for the government in education over both the teachers and the LEAs. The Green Paper put this change in perception of the role of government in this way:

> It would not be compatible with the duty of the Secretaries of State to promote the education of the people of England and Wales, or with their accountability to Parliament, to abdicate from leadership on educational issues which have become a matter of lively public concern.
>
> (DES, 1977, para. 2.19)

Two things become clear from this. The first is that if there has been a change from welfare-state thinking to free-market and monetarist thinking, it did not occur as a great divide between two governments: it began in the last few years of the Labour government, and was taken over and continued by the Conservatives when they took office. The second thing is that Conservative policies in the 1980s and 1990s are not purely free-market policies. There is a paradoxical mixture of a free-market liberalism and centralist autocracy, which makes the moral claims of Thatcherite government ultimately contradictory. This issue will be addressed in much greater detail in the next two chapters.

If social democratic economic claims were seen as shaky, so were social democratic moral claims. By claiming a large interventionist role for the state in economic affairs, not only were all the problems of bureaucratization increased, but also such governments implicitly claimed the same kind of interventionist stance in other affairs, with the increasing bureaucratization of them as well. By creating a welfare state, they seemed to many to be saying not only that the responsibility for caring for others had moved from the individual to the state, but also that judgement on when and how to care had moved as well – the state knew best. Clearly, then, the message was that individual choice must be restricted on the basis of decisions made by those in authority, and then translated through a bureaucratic apparatus. Many found this morally repugnant, a more civilized variant of the 'big brothers' they had just spent a war fighting.

The first systematic attack was made as early as 1944 by Friedrich Hayek in *The Road to Serfdom*. In this book, Hayek developed the argument that Fascism and Communism were actually not very different, for they both strove to centralize the tasks of government, to locate power and control in the hands of only a few. Hayek suggested that this was logically imprudent, ethically unhealthy, and politically disastrous, and that the social democracies, who were at war fighting such regimes, were in fact proceeding down the same road, if at a slower pace. Hayek (1944, p. 10) argued that such governments

> ... have progressively abandoned that freedom in economic affairs without which personal and political freedom has never existed in the past.

By instituting welfare-state legislation, they were interfering with the freedom of the individual, and trading off liberty for a desired greater equality. And yet, because of the severely restricted understanding of human beings, due to each person's inherently subjective grasp of reality, the more that one attempted to understand and control situations beyond one's own local situation, the more likely were things to be misunderstood, and misapplied. Social-welfare legislation, by its very nature, cannot succeed, suggests Hayek, because individuals can never know enough to engineer social change. What will happen instead, he argues, is that, firstly, such engineering must encroach on individual liberties, and secondly, by interfering in the normal market process, the efficiencies of this system will be disrupted, such that more intervention will be required to offset the problems caused, leading to a vicious circle of governmental interventionism and reduced personal liberties. The end-result is clear. Where, he says,

> ... the same representative body lays down the rules of just conduct and directs government, [this] necessarily leads to a gradual transformation of the spontaneous order of free society into a totalitarian system conducted in the service of some coalition of organised interests.
>
> (Hayek, 1973, p. 2)

and further,

> This would have to go on until government literally controlled every circumstance which would affect any person's wellbeing.
>
> (Hayek, 1976, p. 85)

Totalitarianism, then, is just around the corner of all social democratic policies.

Milton Friedman takes a similar line, arguing like Hayek for the indissoluble link between economic and individual freedom. He states (Friedman, 1962, p. 195) that the heart of liberal philosophy is a belief in the need and right of individuals to make the most of their capacities unhindered by governments or other individuals, and further (1962, p. 9) that he personally knows of no example

> ... of a society that has been marked by a large measure of political freedom and that has not also used something comparable to a free market to organize the bulk of economic activity.

He is quick to point out, however, that one must distinguish between equality of rights and opportunity on the one hand, and material equality or equality of outcome on the other. The former is the aim of a liberal society, the latter is the aim of one engaged in social engineering, which, like Hayek, he says can only take a society down the path to totalitarianism.

Much of Friedman's work, like Hayek's, was published at precisely the time when it would have least impact in official circles, and they and thinkers of like mind have had to wait for some considerable time before their ideas have gained the official ear.[1] Throughout this time, however, they have argued that social democratic policies continued to infringe on personal liberties and locate yet more control and power with the state. An educational example of this would be the 1944 Education Act's provisions for a parent's choice of school. It states:

> ... the Secretary of State and the local education authorities shall have regard to the general principle that so far as is compatible with the provision of efficient instruction and training, and the avoidance of unreasonable public expenditure, pupils are to be educated in accordance with the wishes of their parents.
>
> (Maclure, 1988, p. 30)

This is the politest possible way of saying that, in the final analysis, the location of children in school will be decided by government, whether central or local. Attention will be paid to the parent, but the whip hand rests not with the consumer but with the provider. The 1980 Education Act (no. 2) said much the same thing: whilst section 33 of this Act required that local authorities consult school governors annually over admission arrangements, the authorities were in effect given the final say in which children should go to which schools, and the provision of efficient education and efficient resource use were the first considerations.

Thus, while many might say that the activities of social democratic governments in the social engineering of a more prosperous and equal society were generally praiseworthy, there were voices which strongly disagreed, arguing that the end-result for society would be catastrophic. The welfare state increasingly placed expenditure and planning in the hands of the providers and not the consumers, and more and more, it seemed to critics, the aims of welfare-state institutions, most notably education and health, were determined by those running the institutions, and thus were directed to the satisfaction of *their* ends rather than those of the consumer. This, it was argued, was the root cause of increased bureaucracy in state welfare provision, and the inevitable destruction of democratic institutions. It would also so demotivate individuals working within these bureaucracies that they would cease to give of their best, and the whole economy would stagnate, thus inflicting damage on precisely that source from which income redistribution was to be taken.

To summarize, then, social democracy was perceived to have weaknesses on both economic and moral fronts. On the first, it could be exposed in its ambition simply by its record. On the second, whilst suggesting that part of its impetus was ethical in origin, it appeared to flout the ethical principles of individual liberty, personal responsibility and self-reliance. The market-place philosophy claimed to have better answers on both these fronts.

## THE NEW LIBERALISM AND THE MARKET-PLACE PHILOSOPHY

It would be unfair, as some have done, to characterize free-market economics as the philosophy of the greedy and the competitive (Loney, 1986). Whilst it might bring out these tendencies in some individuals, it is very clear that its theoreticians have very much the opposite in mind. Indeed, the concept of a just society is, they argue, inextricably tied to the functioning of free markets in at least two ways. Firstly, as Heater (1990, p. 267) points out, capitalist economic organization, as it fostered qualities of personal initiative and social fluidity, undermined medieval institutions and social structures, and was therefore 'a necessary precondition for the emergence of a true citizen status'.

Secondly, a just society – which Hayek (1960, p. 11) defined in the negative sense as that 'state in which a man is not subject to coercion by the arbitrary will of another' – can only be achieved when each person is allowed to pursue his own ends in his own way. How else, without resorting to a free market, he asks, can a society achieve this? In the free market, the theory goes, the freedom to pursue one's own interest is paramount, but this pursuit has the spin-off of producing benefit for all other members of the market-place as well. As each person tries to match what he or she has to offer to what others wish to buy, so the buyers benefit as well. Greater variety will be created, greater efforts to satisfy others' needs will be attempted, greater freedom for individual decision-making will be needed, and greater responsibility for the direction of one's own life will be the result. Interest solely in the good of oneself, then, leads to the good of all others in the market-place. The key insight, expressed as early as 1705 by Bernard Mandeville, was most famously formulated by Adam Smith:

> It is not from the benevolence of the butcher, the brewer or the baker that we expect our dinner, but from their regard to their own self-interest. We address ourselves not to their humanity but their self-love, and never talk to them of our necessities but of their advantages.
>
> (Smith, 1976, p. 16)

Both parties to an exchange, he argued, can benefit, and no external force or compulsion is needed to induce co-ordination between them, because their transactions are of a voluntary nature. That is why an individual who intends only to benefit himself is led by an 'invisible hand to promote an end which was no part of his intention' (Smith, 1976, p. 16).

And the role of government in all of this? Clearly, if the market, through the invisible hand, determines the nature of transactions to the mutual advantage of each participant, governmental activity can be – should be – restricted. It is restricted – prohibited even – from direct interference in the functioning of the market. This, though, does not actually eliminate the need for government. As Friedman says (1962, p. 15)

> ... government is essential both as a forum for determining the 'rules of the game' and as an umpire to interpret and enforce the rules decided on.

But crucially, the use of state power for economic management, in terms of things like the use of public ownership for sustaining full employment, and the imposition of income tax and compulsory insurance for welfare-service provision, is excluded. Friedman goes so far as to argue (Friedman and Friedman, 1980, p. 5) that whilst in the free market the 'invisible hand' operates to sustain co-operation and mutual benefit, an individual who attempts to promote the public interest by government intervention is led by another 'invisible hand' to promote private and parochial interests, because the use of government necessitates the creation of a bureaucracy, which then promotes its own perpetuation, and therefore services its own interests rather than the ones it was originally set up to pursue.

The free-market philosophy, then, envisages a society returning to a belief in the absolute liberty of the individual, located in a market-place unconstrained by the deadening hand of bureaucracy. In this kind of market, self-interest of buyer and seller is the cornerstone, but the benefit is seen to reach all, precisely because of this self-interest. All members will try increasingly hard to match what they have to offer to what other people wish to buy. It unleashes large measures of individual freedom, initiative, motivation and personal responsibility. From economic freedom, then, stems personal and political freedom, a move away from interventionist government towards genuine political and economic liberalism. Such an approach deals remarkably well, it is claimed, with questions of motivation, efficiency, freedom and justice.

It deals with questions of motivation through its espousal of supply-side economics which in effect suggests that a major demotivator in the welfare state has been the high levels of taxes on the rich needed to finance welfare schemes. The cutting of such levels of taxation will, it is claimed, motivate people to work longer and harder because they will be able to see directly the fruits of their labours – cash in their hands. For the poor, it is claimed, the welfare state has similarly acted as a demotivator to work, simply because the level of support has been so high that it made little or no sense to work for a wage which could be equalled or surpassed by governmental handouts. The answer, then, must be to cut subsidies, so that people will see a reason for trying to find work. As George Gilder (1982, p. 73) has put it,

> What the poor need most of all in order to succeed is the spur to their poverty.

The free-market philosophy also claims to deal with efficiency, because those most affected are those who make the decisions, not some bureaucrat distanced from the issue. Harris (1980, p. 29) argues that

> Even the best are unequal to the task of spending half the national income and supervising how much of the other half is deployed. They are unable to bring under control the once obedient servant of government that has grown since the war like a malignant Topsy.

What is needed, then, is a dissolution of governmental bureaucratic management, and the return of such activities to those directly involved and affected by them.

Thirdly, such an approach claims to deal with freedom, for it demonstrates the superiority of the economic market over the political market. The political market

... offers the citizen ... one vote every three or four years between two or three parties, offering a massive package of policies and promises without any indication of their cost ...

(Harris, 1980, p. 15)

The economic market, in contrast, allows for the possibility of

... consumers voting every day with their pennies and pounds and choosing between the widest range of goods and services offered by competing producers, each with a powerful interest to cater for changing individual preferences. The structure of relative prices that spontaneously emerges serves as an information network that is not available in any other economic order ...

(Harris, 1980, p. 15)

Finally, the approach deals, it claims, with justice, because it returns the concept to its original meaning, a negative concept in which each is free to pursue his own interests without the coercion of others. The more recent, and for free-market thinkers incorrect, definition of justice – social justice – assumes that a society is only just on the basis of its record in redistributing wealth. Equality, rather than liberty, becomes the catchword, and yet, it is argued, this pursuit of equality inevitably involves the coercive appropriation of someone's property or wealth in order to redistribute it to others. This, being coercive, cannot be just, and reduces the amount of liberty in that society. The market, on the other hand, as Hayek (1976, p. 70) says,

... allocates command over goods and services to particular people; this can be neither just nor unjust, because the results are not intended or foreseen, and depend on a multitude of circumstances ...

This approach, it is claimed, does not exclude the capacity for care and compassion; it only relocates it at a level – a personal level – where people can judge how and when to perform most appropriately in this manner. Thus Friedman (1962, p. 12) argues that

As liberals, we take freedom of the individual, or perhaps the family, as our ultimate goal in judging social arrangements.

Indeed, in many respects, the family acts as a fulcrum for the other concepts in free-market social and moral ideology, for it is the status of the family which free-marketeers feel has been downgraded by social democratic policies. As Patrick Minford (1984, p. 7) argues,

The provision of direct social services is regarded by many as something that the family should undertake. When the state provides these services, there is serious concern that families feel morally justified in abandoning their responsibilities to the state.

This connection between the family, society and morality was brought out even more strikingly by Sir Keith Joseph in a speech at Edgbaston in 1974:

> The socialist method would give away from the family and its members the responsibilities which give it cohesion. Parents are being divested of their duty to provide their family economically, of their responsibility for education, health, upbringing, morality, advice and guidance, of saving for old age, for housing. When you take responsibility away from people, you make them irresponsible.
>
> (Joseph, 1974)

The connection between morality and the economy should now be apparent. The greater the governmental intervention, the greater the governmental spending, and the less that responsibility is left with parents, the greater the moral decline. The answer, then, is clear: reduce government spending, and allow the family, rather than the government, to be the director of choices. As Sir Keith put it, parents should be free to choose

> ... in spending their money on better education and health, for their children instead of on a new car, leisure, pleasure ...
>
> (Joseph, 1974)

Perhaps, then, the individual is not the core unit of society, but rather the family is. Having said this, it is a fairly unusual view of the family, and of society in which it is placed. As Friedman (1962, p. 13) says,

> In its simplest form, such a society consists of a number of independent households – a collection of Robinson Crusoes, as it were. Each household uses the resources it controls to produce goods and services that it exchanges for goods and services produced by other households, on terms mutually acceptable to the two parties to the bargain.

## EDUCATIONAL IMPLICATIONS

The message for schools is clear. It is increased government interference which has produced a corporatism which has allowed the producers – the teachers – to gain a stranglehold over what goes on in the schools. Little wonder, then, the free-marketeer would argue, that the 'golden age' of teacher control in education occurred at precisely the same time as the major social democratic legislation in the same area. Such legislation allowed them to increase their influence upon policy-making, and has increasingly distanced the consumer from the process.

Now, however, a new vision of society is at hand. The mainspring for society is located within the free market, and society is conceived as composed of consumers and producers. Societal institutions like schools are now defined in economic terms, and it is from such terms that the relationship towards, between and within such institutions will tend to follow. In educational terms, this is normally taken to mean that the parent is the consumer, and schools and teachers are producers. Rather than schools working together under the general direction of local authorities in an interdependent and co-operative relationship, market theory ideally envisages schools as working in competition with one another as independent institutions, offering wares which consumers can decide to buy or not as their preferences take them. In such a way does the customer achieve greater choice, and in such a way is the school motivated to improve its product, for, in order to survive, it must find out what consumers want, and supply these wants. The whip must move from the provider to the consumer. Only in this way, by competing for bottoms on seats, can schools develop an efficiency and an attractiveness which will increase their quality, improve their output, and provide a greater freedom for the consumer. Competition through the free market is therefore seen as the way to produce a successful educational service in a freer society.

This is the reason why major reforms in the UK in the 1980s have attempted to enhance this process. Four will be mentioned here: open enrolment, grant-maintained schools, the publication of attainment targets, and local management of schools.

*Open enrolment* is the measure designed to counteract the policy, described above, of vesting ultimate power for the placement of pupils with the local authority. The concept of open enrolment means that maintained schools must accept a full complement of pupils at least up to their 'standard number', usually that number admitted in 1979 (a high-water mark of student numbers), unless the figure in 1988 was higher, in which case this latter figure is the one to be adopted.

The rationale behind the move was clearly explained in the Conservative election manifesto of May 1987:

> Schools will be required to enrol up to the school's agreed physical capacity instead of artificially restricting pupil numbers, as can happen today. Popular schools, which have earned parental effort by offering good education, will then be able to expand beyond present physical numbers.
>
> (Maclure, 1988, pp. 28–9)

Clearly this, in true market fashion, invites direct competition between schools, for parents can vote with their feet: those schools that they do not like, they need not send their children to. In this way, the more successful schools grow larger, and, through per capita funding, become even more successful, whilst the less attractive lose pupils and funding, and in effect get their just deserts. The market, rather than the local authority, now decides.

*Opting out* is the term popularly used to describe what maintained secondary schools, and maintained primary schools with over 300 children, may do if they wish to separate themselves from the control and inspection and help of local authorities, and instead be directly financed by the DES. Whilst it has been suggested that one of the reasons for the creation of such schools was the desire to break the stranglehold of what are perceived to be 'loony left' local authorities, the more substantial reason follows the same kind of ideological logic as with open enrolment. They provide, along with those schools which decide to remain with local authority control, private schools, City Technology Colleges, and voluntary-aided schools, a greater variety from which parents may choose. They thus introduce a strong competitive element into interschool management, the idea being that the greater choice available to parents will pressurize schools into raising their standards, and make them much more parent/consumer-oriented.

*The publication of results*: under the legislation of 1988, children in England and Wales are tested in a number of the National Curriculum subjects, and these results are published to provide a composite picture of the school's standards over any one year. Clearly one of the reasons for this testing is to ensure that one of the central ideas of the National Curriculum is fulfilled – that all children in state schools have access to the same breadth and variety of curriculum, and are not impeded by the limited interest or expertise of particular teachers. It sends a clear message to schools that if they are not very strong in certain areas, then they will have to improve the provision of those subjects very quickly. The first reason, then, was a simple way of making sure that curricular provision was broadened and deepened.

The other reason was that publication of results would provide parents with the information to make choices between schools. Clearly, if a market situation is to operate, then consumers must have information about the goods they are to buy if that choice is to be made on rational grounds. Publication of results provides, it is argued, just such information for parents, and therefore increases the likelihood of parents making such choices, and of schools upping their standards to attract or retain parents. It is thus a significant move in the creation of a market system within education.

*Local management of schools (LMS)* essentially compels local authorities to distribute funds to secondary and primary schools with more than 200 pupils by means of a per capita formula which should be weighted to take account of 'any other factors affecting the needs of individual schools which are subject to variation from school to school' (Maclure, 1988, pp. 28–9). The governing bodies of such schools are now responsible for expenditure on staffing, books, equipment, heating and lighting, cleaning and rates. The responsibility for selecting headteachers and other staff, for their promotion or dismissal, moves to being that of the governing body as well. The local authority's role is therefore considerably circumscribed, but it remains responsible, among other things, for home-to-school transport, the advising and inspecting of schools, and the administration of pay, tax and superannuation.

The most obvious intention of LMS is to make schools more efficient by having those who are most aware of the needs of individual schools, the head and the governing body, take much greater control over how money is spent within the school. The idea, of course, is that through such savings, finances can be spread onto other desirable projects, thus improving the efficiency and quality of the education that the children in that school receive. This, again, is an illustration of the market in action, for response to customers is seen to be much more accurate if made by those who are nearest to them.

It is significant to note here that the most direct translation of the market philosophy into education has not yet been attempted on a widespread basis. This would be the introduction of a voucher system of education, first proposed by Milton Friedman (Friedman, 1962; Friedman and Friedman, 1980), in which parents received a voucher for the education of their child to spend at the school of their choice. Strongly advocated by some right-wing theoreticians, this proposal has had a mixed reception in government circles, alternately being vigorously investigated, and then dropped as a serious policy proposition (Green, 1987, pp. 154–63). Its trials in the field have also been mixed (Levinson, 1976), and it has also become increasingly clear that it is not one proposal, but a variety (LaNoue, 1972). However, in its simplest form, it does seem, at a stroke, to take choice and decision-making away from the provider, and pass them directly to the consumer. By thus passing decision-making from provider to consumer, it changes parents' perceptions from seeing themselves as recipients of 'free' education to customers who pay for it. The change in perception, it is argued, will inevitably lead to a much more acute assessment by parents of the system, and a consequent much higher quality of service.

Further, as Stuart Maclure (1988, p. 163) says, the mechanism for instituting such a reform is very simple, as it could be done

> ... by giving parents vouchers equivalent in value to the cost of their children's education in existing schools. They could then use these vouchers to 'buy' education from the school of their choice. Schools would cease to be 'maintained' by public authorities. Instead they would depend for funds on the fees they could charge, to be met, wholly or partly, from the vouchers.

Moreover, it need not be an end-point, but rather

> The education voucher would be a half-way house to the eventual policy of leaving income with taxpayers to use for education. It could gradually be replaced by lower taxes, perhaps over 20 years, as the readiness of parents to buy education was strengthened by increasing knowledge of its benefits.
>
> (Seldon, 1977, p. 68)

Maclure suggests that the legislation up until the present time has been passed precisely to accustom the public in this country to the ideas of the voucher system. There may well be truth in this and, indeed, it may have already achieved much of such an intention: it was, after all, an idea which was unthinkable at the start of the 1980s, and yet can be (and is) discussed as a genuine possibility at the present time. Certainly the variety of schools now on offer to parents – private, local authority, grant-maintained, those with devolved budgets, grammar, secondary modern, technical, comprehensive, City Technology Colleges, and voluntary-aided – can be seen as part of an overall strategy to provide a much increased parental choice in type of school, the logical culmination of which would be the provision of a voucher to spend at the type of school to which they would prefer their children to go.

## CONCLUSION

There can be little doubt that the theory of the free market has had a major effect upon the thinking and practice of many people. Whilst the philosophy is much more ingrained in the American psyche, it has come as something of a culture shock to most people in the UK. There is little doubt, though, that the legislative programme of the Conservative party during the 1980s and early 1990s has changed the perception of the way in which many of the institutions in society function. This chapter, then, has looked at the underlying philosophy of the theory of the free market, and then upon its impact upon educational structures and management in the UK. Clearly, though, it is not without its critics. The next chapter will look at the problems with this approach, both at a theoretical level, and at the level of educational practice.

## NOTE
[1] See Graham and Clark (1986) for a good description of this.

# Chapter 6

## Free-market assumptions and implications

### INTRODUCTION

In the last chapter, the approach of free-market thinkers to the structuring of society, and in particular to the restructuring of education, was examined. The next two chapters will examine the assumptions of the theory, as well as the consequences of such a view for both society and education. This will begin by asking if such a view of economic functioning is an accurate one, before moving on to question whether its assumptions about human nature are valid. It will conclude with an examination of the implications of this view for society in the wider context. The next chapter will concentrate upon the consequences of such an ideology for the education system, and in particular the management of schools.

### FREE-MARKET ECONOMICS AS A VIEW OF ECONOMIC FUNCTIONING

Whilst this book is primarily concerned with ethical evaluations of influential theories on educational-management practice, it must be appropriate here to enquire as to the validity of the theory from an economic point of view, for its validity at this primary level will almost certainly have consequences at other levels as well.

It is perhaps appropriate to begin by pointing out that there are few or no players in the market-place who actually desire the state of affairs present within it: no player, that is, actually enjoys being at the mercy of the vagaries and uncertainties of market conditions. At any moment, another seller may come along, undercut your price, and leave you and your family hungry. Each seller is, out of self-interest, going to attempt to control actions within the market, and this is precisely what is attempted in the real world. The simplest and most powerful way of controlling such uncertainties, as a seller, then, is to make sure there are few or no other sellers within the market – to achieve a monopoly of that product. In this way, by controlling the supply of a needed good, prices are determined by the seller, and not by competition. Indeed, one need not have a total monopoly of a product, as long as there is a private agreement between producers not to break ranks and attempt to undercut one another. Oligopoly, then, works as well as monopoly (some would say better, for it presents the veneer of competition to the consumer). Whilst competition does exist for many products, it should be noted that it is through monopoly or oligopoly that well over 50 per cent of trading in the Western world is performed – from oil, to weapons, to soap powder. Large corporations not only control the market within which many goods are sold, but, and again out of self-interest, increasingly reach back to control other areas which lead to uncertainty, including the production of raw materials for the finished goods, and other bodies which might attempt to control their trade, such as governments.

An inevitable consequence of such practice is that as free-market practice declines, so one necessarily moves from a vision of pure economics (which free-marketeers would claim is value-free) into the realm of politics and social and foreign policy. The large corporations, then, cannot avoid spending a large part of their time being involved in matters which deal with social and political values. To assert, as some free-marketeers do, that the practice of economics by businesses is value-free becomes increasingly remote from the truth the larger that business becomes.

Moreover, not only do large corporations benefit by controlling the market, but they also benefit from their sheer size in being protected from adverse market conditions. So, when governments espouse free-market theories and attempt to arrest inflation by high interest rates, it is the large corporations who are the last to suffer. They can, because of their size, cut back on sales, production and employees, rather than increasing prices and passing these on to the consumer. They also have sufficient financial reserves of their own to be able to avoid for some considerable time having to rely on banks and the high interest rates being charged. What is happening to smaller companies in the meantime? They are the first to go to the wall, for they have considerably less room for cutbacks, and have to rely on the banks for finance. The result is that the assumption by governments of free-market functioning (and the consequent use of monetary and fiscal measures such as high interest rates) hits the small businesses first, as well as those other members of society in the weakest position – the young, the unskilled, and minority groups. Large corporations may not enjoy such times, but they are invariably the last to suffer. It is the rest of the 'market' – those who are much more subject to free-market pressures – who are the first to suffer.

So whilst free markets may exist in theory, they exist only partially in practice, and just as importantly, only then for most of the time with governmental interference in the monopolistic tendencies of companies. Clearly, such tendencies – against the free market, towards monopoly, and governmental interference – should all be noted when considering the role of the free market in education.

## THE MARKET-PLACE MENTALITY AS A GIVEN OF HUMAN NATURE

If doubt is cast upon fundamental existential assumptions of free-market economics, then perhaps questions should also be raised about two other assumptions basic to the philosophy.

The first is that the market, and hence competition between people, is natural to the human condition. The most natural form of human existence, it is claimed, is one where people compete in selling their goods or expertise, and use their rewards to select among goods or expertise for the services they require. It is in providing the conditions for this fair competition that governments have a function, and it is in the exercise of individual choice within, and as a result of, these markets that the liberty of the individual acquires its most essential meaning.

The second assumption is that humanity is composed of individuals who are basically selfish. This assumption is not put forward to denigrate humankind, merely to point out that people are biologically constituted to try to survive in a world which owes them nothing. They must seek their own destiny, must fend for themselves if they are to survive and prosper. The market, then, merely gives expression to a basic urge, and it is because of these two 'givens' of human nature that the free market is such a worthy form of organization.

However, both of these assumptions need to be questioned. It can be argued that market-place institutions, instead of providing a structure for natural inclinations, in fact produce the conditions under which the mentality occurs. The erosion of altruism in the community, and the promotion of self-interest, of a view of other human beings as impersonal units in a game of economic self-betterment, would then all be seen as products of a particular, engineered, social structure, and not the initial conditions which lead one to adopt the market as the most natural choice.

Evidence for this point of view comes from the examination of other cultures. A good example is that described by Graves and Graves (1983) – the inhabitants of Aitutaki in the Cook Islands. Graves and Graves argue that both current major psychological theories regarding the development of prosocial behaviour in children – the social-reinforcement and cognitive developmental viewpoints – spring from a cultural ethos in Western society of 'self-contained individualism', where human beings are seen as being self-centred and egocentric until they are properly socalized. As they say, the predominant view is that

> ... individuals have to learn altruistic behaviour because human beings
> are innately motivated by self-interest and are by nature utilitarian.
>
> (Graves and Graves, 1983, p. 245)

Instead, they argue that both altruistic and egocentric tendencies exist as potentialities in human beings from birth, and that the portrayal of these behaviours will depend upon the environment within which the child is reared. On Aitutaki, for example, a fisherman who in the past caught a large amount of fish would 'store the surplus in his neighbour's belly', for, there being no refrigerators, the fish would simply rot after he and his family had eaten their fill. This act placed a social obligation on the neighbour to return the favour, and in so doing fostered social skills of co-operation and negotiation. No altruism *per se* is involved – the good of the individual coincides with the good of the community, supporting the Aristotelian view that one becomes generous by performing the act of generosity. Altruism, then, may well arise for many people simply as a consequence of the act of giving. It is a fine philosophical point, but it may well be that the better society is the one where individuals do not have to try to be good, but where goodness occurs without effort. This runs counter to most modern Kantian conceptions of morality, but may well be the most realizable. Rather than placing difficulties in the citizen's or student's way by asking them to live in a society which encourages egocentric and competitive behaviour, and then asking them to resist such behaviour, might it not be better to attempt to design schools – and ultimately society – where such difficulties do not occur?

On Aitutaki, this pattern can be perceived in other activities as well. The lengthy and tedious business of thatching roofs needed a communal effort for it to be completed in a short time. The business of tilling, planting, hoeing and reaping was a communal effort for much the same reasons. However, the introduction of labour-saving devices has brought about a dramatic change in social relations. Refrigerators mean that fish can be stored indefinitely, and links of mutual obligation are severed. Metal sheet roofing has the same effect, eliminating the need for communal thatching. Tractor hire means that the individual farmer can generally do the job himself, or at least with only the help of his immediate family. People can now afford to quarrel with their neighbours, for they no longer need them in the same way as they did in the past. Crucially, then, the social conditions which produced the need for social skills of co-operation and negotiation have been unwittingly destroyed by the introduction of other social factors. The question remains: if the people of Aitutaki could have foreseen the social consequences of the introduction of these new labour-saving devices, would they still have adopted them? The price seems to have been a high one.

One possible criticism of the above argument would be that the example chosen of such a balmy Eden is interesting, but hardly applicable to a modern, complex, industrialized society like our own. There is some force to this. Whilst the example at least shows that other forms of social organization are not only possible, but equally as 'natural', there is clearly a need to examine the implications of such a philosophy for Western society as it exists at the present time. So it is with these questions about free-market assumptions in mind that we move to a consideration of the implications of this theory for society in a wider context.

## FREE-MARKET THEORY AS A VIEW OF THE WORLD

It has already been mentioned that the works of the free-market thinkers, and the works of Marx, Freud and Lorenz, can give rise to similar feelings. It is not only that the world is seen through different lenses when we read them; more profoundly, there is also the feeling that, interesting though this perspective may be, there may be something fundamentally distorting about the view. Let us take two examples, the role of the family, and the status of the child.

The role of the family was commented upon in the previous chapter, when it was pointed out how, in free-market theory, it becomes the focal point for care and concern, but also how each household is 'a collection of Robinson Crusoes' (Friedman, 1962, p. 13), using its resources to produce goods and services which it can exchange with other households. A number of things should be noted about this description. Firstly, there is here a clearly atomistic view of society, each family having their own little desert island from which they sail out to exchange goods with families on other desert islands. A more conventional picture, however, might be rather more incorporative, in which families, having a similarity and empathic concern for each other, do not view themselves, and are indeed not viewed by others, in this isolated manner. The glue for the fabric of society is supplied by this similarity and empathy. Clearly, this is not the case for Friedman or other free-marketeers. The glue for them is supplied by the economic transactions between families, and it is the relationships created by such dealings which join people together. Friedman goes on to include within the notion of the family the function of the breadwinner, and then gives this function pride of place. By so doing, the 'family' can now be defined in terms of goods and services produced and exchanged by its breadwinner. It is then only a short step to a description of the role of the breadwinner in the society at large – in the free market. As with a Marxist analysis, economics intrudes into everything.

A similar point can be made about Friedman's description of the status of children. Is he going to talk of care, of rights, of developmental capabilities?

> ... children are at one and the same time consumer goods and potentially responsible members of society. The freedom of individuals to use their economic resources as they want includes the freedom to use them to have children – to buy, as it were, the services of children as a particular form of consumption ...
>
> (Friedman, 1962, p. 33)

There is something repugnant about viewing children as 'consumer goods', and their 'services' as a 'particular form of consumption' by adults. A basic problem with the philosophy, then, is that it finds it hard to see people except as means to an end, the end being that of consumption. It tends to cheapen the quality of human relationships. In practical terms, it also ensures that the 'consumer' in policy matters is almost inevitably the parent (with some reference to business and industry), but almost never the child.[1]

Perhaps the major reason for this strange view of people stems from the fact that morality plays a curiously limited role in a free-market society. As citizenship is about competition in the market-place, morality ceases to have any real connection with it. With social democracy, citizenship and morality are explicitly joined through the notion of social engineering for a better society. With free-market theory there is no social engineering, save that everything will be done to facilitate the move towards a market society, in which any restrictions upon individual competition and self-interest are abolished. As Hoover and Plant (1989, p. 51) put it,

> In the individualist conservative view, the basis of evaluation of anyone should be what other people are prepared to pay for their goods and services. In this sense, moral merit or desert does not matter. What matters is the result of a person's endeavours and whether others are prepared to pay for it. This is the only criterion of value applicable in a free society.

Such an attitude effectively limits the application of morality, putting the market-place off-limits to moral responsibility. Friedman (1962, p. 133) states quite clearly that there is only one social responsibility of business:

> – to use its resources and engage in activities designed to increase its profits so long as it stays within the rules of the game ...

and he goes on:

> If businessmen do have a social responsibility other than making maximum profits for stockholders, how are they to know what it is? Can self-selected private individuals decide what the social interest is?

Much of this argument, as we have seen, stems from Hayek's subjectivist epistemology – that because we are personally so limited in what we can understand, it not only makes little sense to attempt to devise strategies of a societal scope, but it is also positively dangerous. Social engineering will be unpredictable in its ramifications, simply because we understand so little about society. It is a dangerous conceit of social scientists, says Hayek, for them to believe that they can adequately describe societal functioning, and then prescribe remedial strategies through forms of social engineering.

There is much in Hayek's argument which can be accepted. This book began with the assertion that we *are* constrained by our own subjectivities, and should be mindful of the implications of such a conclusion. We do need to be cautious about proposing solutions based on an overconfidence in our own abilities. Yet his ultimate conclusions do not necessarily follow. There is something arbitrary and dogmatic about an approach which rules out of court *all* attempts at social engineering, no matter how limited. Karl Popper, a close friend and associate of Hayek, in his monumental work *The Open Society and its Enemies* (1966), starts from the same premises as Hayek, and argues that the philosophical underpinnings of totalitarian states of the twentieth century can be traced back to the thought of those writers who advocated the importance of the societal over the individual, and of the possibility of large-scale social engineering. However, unlike Hayek, he comes to the conclusion that 'piecemeal social engineering', where small steps only are taken so that any negative effects can be quickly counteracted, is not only possible but ethically desirable. He does not, as Hayek does, rule out of court societal action simply on a subjectivist principle. Indeed, the present writer has argued elsewhere (1990) that subjectivism of judgement does not mean a relativism of judgement – there are degrees of subjectivity, and it is possible to argue for the greater validity of one judgement in contrast to another. This, then, does not rule out by simple fiat societal engineering, but rather urges, as Popper does, for a more tentative and limited approach, which appreciates one's own and others' fallibilities and limitations. Such an approach leads to a more tolerant and, dare one say, more moral society. One need not opt out of moral involvement: rather, prescriptions need to be more guarded and tentative.

Indeed, it might be argued that free-marketeers do not actually practise what they preach. For example, if one knew of a society where children did not have equal access to educational opportunities, would it not be incumbent on free-marketeers to attempt to bring this equal access about? If they did not, then they would be guilty of a conservative and protective attitude to the existence of non-market conditions. If they did attempt to redress such conditions, however, it seems that they would be involved in some form of social engineering. They might of course reply that this was not really social engineering at all, but only ensuring that the market is allowed to function properly. All that are being addressed, then, are the procedural rules of the society, and there is no real experimentation at a social level. The problem with this argument, however, is that social issues *are* being addressed, and outcomes socially engineered to achieve a desired end state, the perfect free market. Whether they like it or not, they appear to be engaged in the same process as any other set of social scientists.

Whilst it is not being suggested that one person has the complete answer to society's ills, there clearly are cases of injustice and unfairness which people must attempt to redress if they wish to live in a fairer society. Hayek, Friedman and other free-market writers sometimes give the impression that the free market allows one to opt out of such responsibilities. However, opting out of one's responsibilities is abnegation – and hence neglect – under any system, for a healthy society needs active, committed participants, and cannot survive by the setting up of a system which then free-wheels. Such a point of view is all the more remarkable considering that one of the inspirations for Friedman and Hayek, John Stuart Mill, came to exactly the opposite conclusion. Where, he argued, the pursuit of wealth is the main focus of a society, it tends to

> fasten his attention and interests exclusively on himself, and upon his family as an appendage of himself; —making him indifferent to the public ... and in his inordinate regard for his personal comforts, selfish and cowardly.
> (Mill, 1963, p. 230)

An excellent example of this moral abnegation is given by Friedman when he discusses the case of a grocery store about to hire a clerk, but situated in an anti-black area. Friedman (1962, p. 111) argues that

> When the owner of the store hires white clerks in preference to Negroes ... he may not be expressing any preference or prejudice or taste of his own. He may simply be transmitting the tastes of the community. He is, as it were, producing the services for the consumers that the consumers are willing to pay for.

What is patently lacking in this is a sense of injustice, of moral outrage. What we get instead is an initial observation that the owner may go out of business if he hires the black clerk, followed by the remark that he is merely delivering what the customer wants. And if his customers like to dress up in white hoods and robes, and hang or burn the odd negro, should he sell the noose and the kindling? Societies are made by the involvement of people in their running, not by the simple institution of rules. This is the clear danger with Hayek's insistence on governmental intervention being limited to the institution of procedural rules only. He fails to see that whilst these are certainly required, moral involvement by its members, and by its authorities, is required as well. Free-market thinking finds great difficulty in dealing with these matters. Many issues transcend the free-market code, and need, for non-market reasons, active citizen intervention and active government interference in a market situation. Indeed, whilst it has already been agreed that the emergence of the present form of citizenship required the existence of a capitalist economy, in order to undermine rigid feudal hierarchies and deferential behaviours, yet clearly, as Heater argues (1990, p. 267), although capitalism and modern citizenship 'emerged in double harness, the yoke chafed for both'. The reason is easy to see. Capitalism generates economic inequalities, and encourages personal acquisitiveness: citizenship demands equal status and dignity for all, which results not only in the acceptance of the notion of formal political citizenship, but also in the demand for egalitarian measures to make such political citizenship translatable into reality. Clearly, the two practices are going to make uneasy bedfellows.

So whilst it may be true that the seller does his best to make himself and his product appealing to the consumer, this does not begin to deal with deeper ethical issues. If the ultimate aim of free-market theory is to sell a product, then this can just as well involve deception as honesty. Both of these – deception and honesty – become second-order principles, vehicles in the business of buying and selling, and precisely because the ultimate values are those of buying, rather than those of engendering personal, social and spiritual growth, they cheapen human contacts, reducing these relationships to means to ends, rather than as ends in themselves.

Further, and precisely because honesty, trust, truthfulness and other virtues are now little more than second-order principles, when businessmen *can* get away with something, then clearly they will. There is no background moral injunction against malpractice, merely governmental restrictions – Hayek's procedural rules – to be worked round.

Morality, as one would normally think of it, ceases, under free-market theory, to have a real role in the public sphere, and becomes linked solely to the part of the private sphere where people consciously adopt responsibilities towards others – the family. Hence one finds within the philosophy an endorsement of the duties of marriage and family life, of responsibility for one's children and parents, and a concomitant move away from state involvement in such relationships, with moves away from child allowances, the persistent doubt over the future of a national health service for any but the most basic cases, and the running down of public care for the elderly, and the pursuance of a setting up of privately run 'granny farms'.

Significant consequences flow from such a philosophy. One is that a dogmatic adherence by governments to intervention in people's lives only on the basis of procedural rules may well result in the kinds of bureaucratic abuses against which its advocates so strongly inveigh. For just as those within bureaucracies, in theory at least, are obliged to follow rules without being permitted to modify these rules to suit the particular case, so the mechanical implementation of procedural rules could very likely lead to the same kinds of unthinking, uncaring abuses.

Further, because morality is now restricted to the private sphere, the sphere of morality is larger for the poor than it is for the rich, simply because the rich are in a better position to offload their responsibilities by hiring others to do their duties for them. Care of children can be bought through nannies and boarding schools, care of elderly parents through private nurses or nursing homes. The poor, who have not got the money for such things, must bear this burden themselves.

Another consequence is that society, in the sense of a large number of people with generally agreed values, ceases to exist. As Margaret Thatcher said,

> There is no such thing as society. There are individual men and women and there are families.

> (Thatcher, 1987)

Whilst Mrs Thatcher has since withdrawn this remark, it should not be seen as either a misquotation or an aberration, but rather as following clearly from all of the above. If society consists, as such a philosophy suggests, of the market-place and the home, then relationships are restricted to producers, consumers and private moral beings (with perhaps the odd private, charitable association who do such things because they derive pleasure from such interests). The philosophy lacks a concept of society because its members lack any common interest in its good.

Perhaps, though, this is not quite right. The market-place philosophy does have a vision of the good society, and this is a society of production, consumption and ownership. And from this vision, two further interesting consequences flow.

Firstly, because the philosophy of the market-place is dictated by the language of economics, focus is maintained upon economic concepts. Economic growth – the output of all the things produced, consumed, used, or invested – becomes not just an aim in life, but *the* aim in life. The Gross National Product (GNP) – the value of everything that is produced and sold by a country in the course of one year – becomes not just a value, but *the* value. The result is that other aims and values cease to be regarded as worthwhile. It becomes an unquestioned assumption that economic growth and the pursuit of a larger GNP are the only things to be considered. Other, less measurable, assets, which may be non-economic or uneconomic, are given scant regard. The quality of life becomes tied to economic goals instead of to things like the search for individual fulfilment, time for leisure, an absence of pollution, or the development of a genuinely democratic and accountable form of government. The idea that one could have a lower per capita GNP but higher standard of well-being is simply not available to such an ideology.

Secondly, though the theory is only partly economic in origin (at least in Hayek's case being also linked to a subjectivist epistemology), its vision is tied to economics, and it does tend to see people in terms of buying, selling and consuming. Increasingly its advocates find it difficult to imagine that other spheres of activity may be non-economic in nature. Notions of sympathy for others not within one's immediate family circle, of human rights, of care for the environment for non-profit-making ends, are moved beyond its scope, and its understanding of human nature. Educationally, the possibility of a disinterested pursuit of knowledge, or personal, social and political development in a non-material sense, are concepts given little or no attention, because they do not fit economic preconceptions of what human beings are. Schools involved in such activities, organized and managed to pursue such aims, tend to be categorized as inefficient, unproductive, and finally irrational. Management and organization must therefore be adjusted to make them more (rationally) oriented to real (consumer) needs.

Now, precisely because free-market economics tends to look at everything through such lenses, the consequent pauperization of moral concepts in the public sphere infects concepts in the private sphere as well, and reduces their richness and depth. One can take two such concepts: the meaning of co-operation, and the meaning of altruism. To begin with, look at the assumptions which Friedman (1980, p. 222) makes about the basis of co-operation between members of the free market:

> ... competition does not protect the consumer because businessmen are more soft-hearted than the bureaucrats or because they are more altruistic or generous, or even because they are more competent, but only because it is in the self-interest of the businessman to serve the consumer.

This essentially is Adam Smith's key insight, that both parties to an exchange cooperate when both sides benefit. However, it is important to point out that this form of co-operation – where people agree within a competitive environment upon an exchange of goods (which we shall call 'competitive co-operation') – is very different from one where two people work for the same end ('non-competitive co-operation'). In the latter, the situation is inherently stable, for there is no friction between them, and their aims are in accord. 'Competitive co-operation', however, is inherently unstable because such co-operation is hardly ever voluntary, for one person in a transaction is nearly always in a more advantageous position, and can thus drive a harder bargain. This means that co-operation is grudging at best. Further, in such a situation of unequal co-operation, competition is as much a part of the process as co-operation, as each party works towards either monopoly or monopsony, getting the best price. If one takes all of these factors into account, it becomes clear very quickly that the normal 'free-market' situation is characterized not by stability, co-operation and satisfaction, but by instability, competition and dissatisfaction. Smith's and Friedman's Utopia begins to look much less attractive.

Another key concept in free-market theory is that of self-interest. Clearly, it is closely linked to that of individual economic and political freedom, but it has to be defended against charges that a society cannot be built around individuals who care for none but themselves, their businesses and their families. Friedman, however, does not place his definition of self-interest quite there. He says

> Self-interest is not myopic selfishness. It is whatever it is that interests the participants, whatever they value, whatever goals they pursue. The scientist seeking to advance the frontiers of his discipline, the missionary seeking to convert infidels to the true faith, the philanthropist seeking to bring comfort to the needy – all are pursuing their interests, as they see them, as they judge them by their own values.
>
> (Friedman and Friedman, 1980, p. 27)

Friedman is trying to extricate himself from the charge of proposing a society of selfish individuals by arguing that whatever we do, we do it out of self-interest. Altruism, philanthropy, caring for others, are basically not other-regarding, but self-regarding. We do them because it makes us feel good. By making this crucial assumption, Friedman is asserting that the free market does no more than simply reflect real human nature. But is he justifed in conflating self-regarding and other-regarding behaviour? The very fact that we can talk of a social worker who helps others because it makes him feel good, and one who does it out of pure compassion, and a desire to help others, suggests that the two are separable. If they are separable, then it is a dangerous and limiting assumption to assert that people are basically self-regarding, for, if implemented, it would prevent people from developing altruism, and thus limit and cheapen human nature and society.

One further criticism of free-market approaches needs to be made here. If one of the principal assets of this philosophy perceived by its champions is that of greater freedom for the individual, then one of the principal problems with social democracy is perceived to be the drive towards greater equality. This, it is claimed, is not only economically inefficient, but is also morally reprehensible. And yet both of these claims can be questioned.

Firstly, egalitarian strategies can actually enhance economic efficiency because greater equality of opportunity will increase the number of people in a given society who can enter sections of the job market which otherwise would be closed to them. By so allowing a greater choice of applicants, one is encouraging the employment of the most talented, and thereby increasing the efficiency of the economy. Indeed, it could be argued that forms of positive discrimination may in the long run be justified not only on moral grounds but also on economic grounds.

Secondly, few would argue against the notion that both freedom of choice and equality of opportunity are morally desirable, and that both should be pursued in the creation of a better society. However, one individual's freedom can and does affect another's, and any society needs to address the problem of balancing individual freedoms. Whilst, as free-marketeers argue, government intervention can lead to the diminution of individual liberty, so can the free-market alternative. The free-market course, then, could only be acceptable where each individual *genuinely* has the same opportunity as everyone else to compete in the market. Free-market theories begin from the assumption that measures to introduce free-market mechanisms will take place within the existing structures of society. If this is the case, ingrained injustices within society, such as discrimination on the basis of class, race and sex, will work against such groups and ensure that equal access to the market will not happen. Until governments intervene to redress such injustices, and unless they continue to be redressed even within a free-market ethos, mechanisms will continue to work which will disadvantage particular groups and thereby invalidate the claims of free-marketeers. Pure free-market theory, then, could only work in a perfect world. Until this happens it must be used in conjunction with other competing theories.

A final point emphasizes this conclusion. Whilst the free market may have a place in any society, yet its aspirations need to be kept in check, precisely because it encourages the forms of behaviour and attitude which would lead to the destruction of the very principle upon which such behaviours and attitudes are founded. Take a simple example given by Hoover and Plant (1989, p. 226). If one lives in an area in which there is a corner shop and a supermarket, then, for any one individual, the existence of both would be beneficial, the former for convenience, the latter for economy. And yet the consequence of pursuing the 'rational' choice of using the latter for all major purchases, and the former only on the odd occasion, is to drive the corner shop out of existence – an unforeseen and unintended consequence of rational behaviour in the market, a consequence which none wanted and none would choose. Precisely the same kind of problem will probably be seen with open enrolment in schools. By instituting such a policy to increase choice of schools, we may force a school out of existence, and thereby actually reduce choice. If such are the consequences of unfettered free-market choice, then the long-term rational strategy would seem to be one which takes into account the short-term rational strategies of individuals, but balances these against other (social) costs. This, it would seem, inevitably means a greater involvement by government than free-marketeers would wish, but one which is nevertheless essential. Some notion of social values, of the common good, is necessary if one is to create an environment within which the market itself can flourish.

What is emerging from this discussion is that free-market writers seem to find it difficult to imagine that there are other reasons for doing things besides monetary gain. As Freud tends to interpret everything in terms of early sexual development, as Skinner tends to explain everything in terms of operant conditioning processes, so they tend to explain everything in terms of personal profit. Look at a question which Friedman asks in a rhetorical fashion, rhetorical because he cannot see that there could be any plausible answer to it:

> If your income will be the same whether you work hard or not, why should
> you work hard? Why should you make the effort to search out the buyer
> who values most highly what you have to sell if you will not get any benefit
> from doing so?
>
> (Friedman and Friedman, 1980, p. 23)

This clearly assumes that the only reason for working is money. Friedman has obviously not read a writer like J. A. C. Brown (1984), who argues that 'economic man' is a man of fiction, not fact. What does this economic man look like? He bears an uncanny resemblance to a Friedmanite hero:

> Economic man ... is a rational creature who uses his reason primarily to
> calculate exactly how much satisfaction he may obtain from the smallest
> amount of effort, or when necessary, how much discomfort he can avoid.
> 'Satisfaction' does not mean pride in one's job, the feeling of having
> accomplished something or even regard to others; it refers only to money.
>
> (Brown, 1984, p. 30)

Leaving aside the very questionable assumption that all occupations are about buying and selling, such a myopic viewpoint fails to understand that many jobs are done because they are inherently interesting, and people work hard at them – are workaholics – precisely because of the nature of the job, and not because of the financial rewards attached to it. Does Milton Friedman work so hard purely because of the money? I very much doubt it. There is the excitement of ideas, the cut and thrust of debate, the pleasure at creation and execution of a personal project. Many of these things are non-quantifiable in an economic sense, and yet are of profound value to society. Schools which pursue these aims are performing a valuable service. How will they fare with a free-market philosophy? The next chapter deals with this question.

## NOTE

[1] And yet, as Chapter 10 of this book will argue, there are solid ethical and practical reasons for conceptualizing the child as a consumer of education, for, after all, it is children who attend school.

# Chapter 7

# Bifurcations, contradictions and educational practice

## INTRODUCTION

The last two chapters have given descriptions of the free-market approach, and then examined some of its major assumptions before moving on to examine some of the problems of translation into societal practice. It is now time to examine its translation into educational practice. However, one is immediately faced with the problem that the policies in the UK over the last decade have not been all of a piece, and are at times almost contradictory in their aims. This is important for three reasons. The first is that where policies contradict one another, they may either cancel each other out, or cause considerable confusion and distress. Secondly, this is a feature, it will be argued, of the composition of power groupings within the Conservative Party at the present time, and these tensions are bound to be seen in future policy formulations. It is therefore most important to be aware of how the present legislative pot-pourri came into being, and how it is likely to change in the future. Lastly, it is very likely that these major policies, whilst being modified by future governments, will be kept in a similar form to the one they have at present. So even a change in the colour of government will not necessarily make the position easier for the management of schools. For all these reasons, a brief description of these tensions is necessary before moving onto an examination of their translation into legislative fact.

## THE BIFURCATION OF CONSERVATIVE POLICIES

Whilst it is undoubtedly the case that both the UK and the US have seen the rise to ascendancy over the last twenty years of market-place economics, and the consequent championing of the individual, of initiative, and freedom of choice, this has, curiously, paradoxically, and contradictorily, travelled the political road with another very different animal. It is one of the difficulties of political analysis to locate ideological points of view, and this is particularly the case here. So far I have designated this movement as 'free market', occasionally as the 'new liberals', and infrequently as the 'new right'. Whilst these sufficed when discussion of policy was at a theoretical level only, *practical* politics have the tendency to embrace several, and sometimes conflicting, ideologies. Indeed, for the voter, one of the most confusing things is that political parties, traditionally described as 'left' or right', may well have large elements of both within their fold, as David Green (1987, p. 2) says,

> Fascism ... is ... described as 'right-wing' because it is 'not socialist', yet liberalism is the absolute antithesis of Fascism. And communism, which ranks as left-wing, comes very close to Fascism in its suppression of political dissent ...

Indeed, if liberalism is the antithesis of ideologies which place the state and its authority above that of the individual, then it is indeed surprising to find that both camps are to be found in the present Conservative party in the UK. Traditional conservatism, as embodies in the writings of people like Roger Scruton, dislikes liberalism as much as it does socialism:

> The value of liberty is not absolute, but stands subject to another and higher value, the authority of established government.
>
> (Scruton, 1984, p. 19)

It rejects the freedom of liberals as much as it does the social justice of socialists, and offers instead the values of authority, allegiance and tradition:

> The state has the authority, the responsibility, and the despotism of parenthood.
>
> (Scruton, 1984, p. 111)

The result for the conservative, then, is that it is

> possible for the conservative as it is for the socialist to be, should the need arise, 'totalitarian'.
>
> (Scruton, 1984, p. 33)

This second group, then, values order rather than liberty, tradition rather than entrepreneurship, constraint rather than freedom. It is most publicly seen in politicized forms of Christian evangelism such as the American 'moral majority' movement, or in the calls in Britain for a return to 'Victorian values'. It is also why many in the Conservative party have looked (and do look) down their noses at Margaret Thatcher, John Major and exemplars of their creed. These exemplars tend to be (like Thatcher and Major) self-made men and women, whilst the traditional order favours the man or woman of background and inherited money. It is why Thatcherism has been, and 'Majorism' probably will be, more radical in many ways than either the traditional wing of the Conservative party (misleadingly called the 'Wets') or the 'acceptable' side of the Labour party. Both of these, it could be argued, have in their different ways espoused the concept of *noblesse oblige*, and a wish to conserve: one inherited wealth and property, the other the gains and privileges of the welfare state. Indeed, this similarity was noted by Milton Friedman, when he commented on the 'affinity between aristocracy and socialism', and that the welfare state 'owes more to the Tory principles of the nineteenth century than to the ideas of Karl Marx and Friedrich Engels' (Hoover and Plant, 1989, p. 71). Free-market economics, in its most ideological form, would open all activities to the wind of competition and the market, and thus opposes both of these factions. Whether one admires the politics or not, it is something to wonder at that such an ideology has withstood and had such an effect upon the deeply entrenched beliefs of both these forces.

Government policy over the last decade, then, has been a curious hybrid of traditional conservatism and and the new thinking. It is a mistake to think that it is only one of these. As Hoover and Plant (1989, p. 12) point out,

The phrase 'New Right' has been applied variously to the movement from moral traditionalism and to the advocacy of the free market ... What the phrase conceals is the sense in which the belief in moral restraint is finally inconsistent with a programme of unrestrained economic liberty.

The point is that there is clearly a fundamental divide on morality here, for the new liberal conservative must, to remain logically consistent, espouse a relativistic vision of personal values and morality, for it is a central tenet of his or her belief system that each person be allowed to pursue his or her own good, 'good' being defined by that person. The traditionalist, on the other hand, is very much an objectivist, advocating certain fundamental and unquestionable values. Logically, the two are incompatible, and yet, practically speaking, they have coexisted within the same party, and indeed sometimes within the same person, with few if any of their critics picking up this total incompatibility. Such is the world of politics.

A number of examples of this contradiction can be seen in policy and practice over the last few years. A first example would be the views expressed on the question of the dependency culture supposedly created by the welfare state. Conservative critics argue that it is not just that principles of self-reliance and personal responsibility are diminished by the existence of a welfare state, but also that welfare does something just as bad – it creates dependency among its members. Because the state acts as the major provider in society, it is therefore claimed that people lose the ability to work and think for themselves. The poor actually get poorer in a welfare state precisely because they are conditioned to lose their initiative. As the American Enterprise Institute put it,

> ... the most disturbing element among a fraction of the contemporary poor is an inability to seize opportunity even when it is available and while others around them are seizing it.
>
> (Hoover and Plant, 1989, p. 71)

Free-market theorists argue that staying out of poverty is relatively simple and does not involve welfarism; it involves nothing more than completing education, getting married and staying married, and getting employed and staying employed, even if the pay is initially not that attractive. It is, they argue, in the creation of attitudes and dispositions that welfarism and the market-place differ most significantly; the former creates dependency and eventual penury, the latter initiative and a fulfilling life.

The contradiction in the argument lies in the fact that free-marketeers reject notions of public morality and conceptions of social justice, simply because it is argued that there can be no agreement about what such things might amount to. People seek their own ends, which are by the nature of things inherently different. This being the case, the state should not attempt to interfere. However, the dependency argument, by asserting that it is possible to describe a set of moral characteristics which people in society ought to pursue, and others which people ought to be persuaded to drop, precisely violates this principle.

A second example of the contradiction within conservative policy is that both US and UK governments have, and in true free-market fashion, either completely abnegated responsibility for some special issues, or expressed only limited interest in them. These issues have included environmental concerns, job safety and nuclear power. However, in clear paternalistic, Victorian fashion, they have given firm moral directions for other areas, notably sexual morality, pornography, and the family.

It should give the reader pause for thought when it is realized, firstly, that those issues upon which commitment is expressed are precisely those which do not involve an egalitarian redistribution of assets, and secondly, that the poor will be regulated in their behaviour by dependency theory, but the rich will not. Indeed, when one sees the contradictory practices of the free market and conservative paternalism embedded within policies of the same government, one might be inclined to question the extent to which such theories are espoused for their intellectual legitimacy, and to what extent they are espoused because they provide a rationale for the pecuniary advantage of sectional interests.

A final educational example stems from the UK. Perhaps the clearest indication of this tension between free-market and paternalistic tendencies lies at the heart of the major educational reform act of the last 40 years – the 1988 Education Act. Within it are very explicit examples of free-market thinking – the local management of schools, the expansion of consumer choice through the creation of new categories of schools from which to choose, and the clearer information to consumers to allow for this choice. On the other hand, perhaps *the* major reform in the act, the National Curriculum, in many ways contradicts free-market thinking, because it limits consumers' freedom of choice. Governing bodies, parents and children may not choose and design their own curriculum, except within the constraints created by central government. Central government has very much determined what kind of curriculum the consumer will have. A free-market approach, on the other hand, would have left such things to the consumer to decide. Whilst it could be fairly argued that instituting a national curriculum allows for greater consumer choice in that it prevents the provider – the teaching profession – from dictating what the consumer will have, true free-market thinking would have ensured that the provider could not do such things, and would have pursued policies which directly enabled the consumers to institute the curriculum they wanted. The 1988 Act does little more than move the locus of control from one body (the teachers and the LEAs) to another (the DES), and still leaves the consumer without any real say in the matter. The 1988 Act, then, is a very good illustration of this bifurcation of conservative policies, and of the contradictions that result in practice.

## EDUCATIONAL IMPLICATIONS

Mindful, then, of these problems, it is time to ask what effects free-market thinking has had upon the education system in the UK. Three examples of current legislation will be used:

(a) open enrolment;
(b) opting out;
(c) local management of schools.

## (a) Open enrolment

The concept of *open enrolment* means that maintained schools must accept a full complement of pupils at least up to their 'standard number', usually that number admitted in 1979, unless the figure in 1988 was higher, in which case this latter figure is the one to be adopted. It is argued that two very beneficial consequences follow. Firstly, it reduces the paternalism inherent in the system, and enables parents to have a much better chance of choosing the school they really want their child to go to, for it prevents artificial limits being placed on schools' capacities by LEAs or schools themselves. It also means that parents can now be much more comfortable in taking their child away from a school they do not like. When this becomes a possibility, it is argued, so schools must of necessity pay increasing attention to the wishes of parents. No longer do parents see themselves as recipients of state aid, but as purchasers of goods. The changed perception, it has been argued, will have dramatic, and beneficial, effects upon education. Secondly, if each school is placed in a market situation, market forces will decide the fate of that school. This again is seen as advantageous, because it is believed that the free market is the most efficient means of allocating resources and responding to consumer wishes. Open enrolment, then, fulfils complementary aims of liberty and efficiency.

The impact of open enrolment will be seen both within and between schools. It probably has implications for the organization of individual schools and the classrooms within them, as it is possible that there will be relatively more overloaded or underloaded classes, as parents move their children from school to school. Similarly, it will have an impact at the interschool level, where, as the number of pupils in a school determines the extent of its finances, it is argued that each school will do its very best to retain the pupils it has and entice others away from neighbouring schools. The move, then, is designed to institute competition between schools. In so doing, one must assume, some schools will get bigger, and some will get smaller, and the losers may eventually go to the wall. This is one means, then, through which schools can be induced to maintain and improve their standards and service.

These are the principal claims for open enrolment. There seems to be good reason to believe that parents will examine the qualities of each school more closely when their child is about to start school. Whether they will also be more inclined to move their child if they become dissatisfied is a matter which can only be determined once the legislation is fully translated into practice. It seems possible, however, that parents will only move their child if things do not improve at a particular school after they have sought redress from the school itself. Much, then, depends upon the schools' relationships with the parents, and in this respect much has changed in the last decade as schools have realized how important a partnership is with parents in improving children's educational performances, and so have taken steps to improve their communications with parents (e.g. Wolfendale, 1989; Docking, 1990). What may well happen is that the very good schools or the very bad schools – those so good or so bad that parents are strongly motivated to get their children in or move them out – are most affected by the legislation, whilst those in the middle band – the good, reliable schools, and the vast majority – are affected rather less so. However, where pupil numbers only just support teacher numbers, even a small drop in intake may mean the loss of one teaching job. Open enrolment, then, combined with the local management of schools (see below), will probably induce most schools to keep a warier eye on numbers than has been the case in the past.

Other questions about open enrolment have been voiced at both practical and theoretical levels. In terms of the efficiency claims of free-marketeers, one needs to understand why the 1944 Education Act stated that

> ... the Secretary of State and the local education authorities shall have regard to the general principle that so far as is compatible with the provision of efficient instruction and training, and the avoidance of unreasonable public expenditure, pupils are to be educated in accordance with the wishes of their parents.
>
> (Haviland, 1988, p. 170)

The Education Act (no. 2) 1980 said much the same thing: whilst section 33 of this Act required that local authorities consult school governors annually over admission arrangements, the authorities were in effect given the final say over the schools to which children should go. The provision of efficient education and efficient resource use were first considerations. It could be argued that they had to be. This previous legislation was an attempt at a balance between conflicting rights and needs: the rights of parents, and the needs of local authorities to make sense of changing demographic trends. Thus, when demographic trends took a downturn in the 1970s, local authorities were left with the uncomfortable task of organizing educational provision with too few pupils and too many schools. They could (as they did) close down and amalgamate schools, but such a procedure can only be taken so far. There is bound to come a time when trends will begin to move upwards, and then places must be available. So another solution, and one adopted by authorities, was to have deliberately low admission limits to schools. If schools were kept below capacity, children could then be accommodated, when trends rose, with little disruption and little loss of efficiency. The alternative was, when pupil numbers increased, and if closing and amalgamating was rigidly adhered to, to embark on a costly building programme.

It might, then, be fairer to see LEAs as attempting to make sense of an otherwise impossible position. The introduction of open enrolment has torn a large hole in this policy, and has made planning for future contingencies extremely difficult. This, then, would seem to be a good example of where social democratic policies may turn out to be more efficient than those of the free market.

Moreover, it could be argued that in some cases the free-market policy of open enrolment may actually do little or nothing for future parental choice. This can be seen if one looks at one set of possible consequences. If parents in an area with three choices of school, A, B and C, move their children to schools A and B, there may come a time when school C is no longer economically viable, and may have to close. Parents will then, as a direct consequence of open enrolment, have their choice limited to two. Similarly, if there is an increase in student numbers, the policy of open enrolment may well lead to an inability to supply schools, except by increasing the allowable intake, or by embarking on a costly building programme.

Far better, it might be argued, is a managed system where school C is helped or coerced to pull its socks up, but not threatened with closure. Indeed, a curious and neglected fact is that DES Circular 3/87, a document published only a matter of months before the open-enrolment proposals, was extremely clear in its endorsement of the need for forward planning in order to deal with falling school rolls and to increase efficiency and cost-effectiveness. Certainly, in terms of actual parental objections to the scheme, it seems to have worked remarkably well. Nottinghamshire County Council, for example, in their submission to Kenneth Baker (Haviland, 1988, p. 170) point out that in 1987, 99.88 per cent of parents were satisfied with the existing system; whilst the Conservative Association, in a similar submission, stated that

> ... the vast majority of LEAs manage to meet the first choice of nearly all
> parents, with a success rate of over 90 per cent the norm. In many LEAs
> the figure is well over 90 per cent.
>
> (Haviland, 1988, p. 183)

Further, not only might variety of choice actually be restricted, through school extinction, and as a consequence of open enrolment, but choice may also be limited through pressure on schools to provide the standard and the popular. Some of the most innovative ideas in education have been produced precisely through an ability to depart from the norm, to persevere in a policy of apparent radicalism. The poor standard of commercial TV in the US is strong evidence that the need to respond immediately to popular taste is not conducive to high-quality materials, and tends to result in little more than the safe, the tried and trusted, and the bland. These are the kinds of worries voiced by those concerned with the future financing of the BBC, and much the same kind of thing could happen to schools if they do not have the financial independence to explore new ideas, but must constantly respond to transitory and populist demands.

Another consequence of the combination of populist opinion and the abnegation of responsibility for social consequences is the very likely possibility of racial ghettos being created through the policy of open enrolment. There has been a deafening silence from the DES since the publication of the Swann Report (DES, 1985) and its appeal for positive moves by educational institutions and the state actively to pursue a policy of racial integration and harmonization. This, however, runs counter to market-place philosophy, where the only logical policy can be one of no policy. Thus, instead of authorities taking a lead in attempting to heal racial divides and ethnic tensions, they sit on the sidelines and let events take their course. Open enrolment opens up the real possibility of all-white, all-black and all-Muslim schools, ensuring that suspicion and distrust is furthered through there being no contact between the groups. Any socially responsible government, it could be argued, would want to prevent such cultural separatism, but in this respect the philosophy of the market-place dictates a precise absence of responsibility.

Free-marketeers would argue in their defence that the use of managed systems, complaints of lack of educational innovation, and the worries over the creation of racial ghettos, are all cases of paternalism. The first involves the movement of choice and decision from parents to the LEA, and such movement inevitably involves a loss of responsibility and freedom for the individual parent, and a changed perception of themselves from buyer to recipient. The second and third, it could be argued, are both simply reflections of parental choice, and any attempt at change could be described as elitist, for if parents do not want innovation or racial mixing for their children – some might say want their children to be used as guinea-pigs – then schools should not have the right to use them in this way.

It has to be accepted, I think, that there are genuine points made here. Lack of parental involvement *can* lead to abuse of the system; it can lead to unchecked experimentation which is damaging to children; and it can lead to policies like the forced desegregation by bussing in the US in the 1970s which did as much harm as good. But against this, one must place the arguments of organizational efficiency, of the constant need to improve and experiment, and of the social benefit of increasing multicultural understanding. Clearly there has to be a balance between control and parental choice, which can be achieved only through dialogue and education of all those involved. Dispensing with one side of the equation, as doctrinaire free-market thinking appears to do, seems neither rational nor necessary.

It might also be remarked here that the adoption of such free-market policies leads to other, less tangible, but still very damaging consequences. Competition in this form leads to a zero-sum game, where for one to win, another must lose. This *might* provide some form of motivation for work within schools, for the threat of closure is undoubtedly an incentive to work better. But the adoption of such an approach is a curious one in the light of current business approaches. It is very reminiscent of what McGregor (1960) called the Theory X approach to management, which assumes that people can be induced to work by the expectation of gain for success or the expectation of loss for failure. More typical in modern business literature is a theory of management which assumes that individuals can derive satisfaction from doing an effective job *per se*. They become ego-involved with their jobs, emotionally committed to doing them well, and take pride from evidence that they are effective in furthering the objectives of education (Vroom and Deci, 1985). This surely ties in much better with a philosophy which sees education as being a process of human development and interpersonal relationships, the pursuit of knowledge as a good in its own right. The market-place philosophy, however, tends to see education as a means to a market utilitarian end. One has, I suggest, at bottom the clash of two fundamentally opposed ideas of human existence, and one of them clearly has had the legislative whip hand over the past decade.

## (b) Opting out

This describes the process by which maintained secondary schools, and maintained primary schools with over 300 children, can become grant-maintained schools, directly financed by the DES, rather than being controlled, inspected and aided by their local authority. The rationale for this procedure has much the same kind of logic as with open enrolment. Such schools, it is argued, contribute to the greater variety of educational institutions from which parents may choose. By increasing parents' range of choice, they further competition between schools. And by so doing, it is argued, local authorities and schools are pressured to listen more to what parents want, and to raise their standards to attract their children.

There is clearly a genuine attraction in this proposal for parents who dislike the educational policies of their local authority, and can see no recourse by staying within their control. Parents who disagreed with an educational, political, religious or racial policy of an authority could then take their children beyond its influence. Opting out thereby increases individuals' freedom of movement and choice, and promotes involvement and responsibility within the parent body, and accountability and motivation within the local authority and teaching body.

The approach does, however, have its problems. A first is that the very concept of allowing a (transient) body of parents to decide upon the future status of a school, and of the education of future children within it (with no present legislative provision for opting back in in the future), suggests that opting out is an increased choice and freedom for some parents bought at the probable freedom of choice of a future majority of others. As the Association of Metropolitan Authorities argued in its submission to Kenneth Baker,

> ... the choice will be exercised by a particular group of parents at a particular time and will bind future generations of parents and children to a given form of education and type of school.
>
> (Haviland, 1988, p. 121)

A second problem is that, like open enrolment, competition has its indirect effects. Interschool competition, and the zero-sum game played through it, will do little or nothing for the professional and personal development of staff. Indeed, instead of increasing motivation, it will probably reduce motivation to a carrot-and-stick variety.

In terms of the inter-management of local authority schools, it becomes more than likely that opting out will, as with open enrolment, drastically reduce a local authority's ability to plan for student demographic changes. Of course, if, as Simon (1988) suggests, much of the 1988 Act was designed to do little more than weaken local power and centralize it at the DES, then the creation of grant-maintained schools becomes more understandable.

A final result of opting out stems from the fact that, should applications outweigh places, it is the governors who decide which pupils to accept and which to reject. In this instance, governors may well apply selective criteria, which could be in terms of academic achievement, or the financial standing of parents. The 1988 Act says nothing more than that the governors must act in accordance with their Articles of Government and the law of the land, and that the character of the school must remain unchanged. But one must ask who is to judge what a present character is, whether the character remains unchanged, and what would be done if it did. Selective criteria may be used in such a way as to circumvent these restrictions, and if this were to be the case, such criteria would not just affect the school, but, because schools have an interdependent relationship, would affect the intakes of other schools in the vicinity as well. The likelihood is that if a school acquired a good academic reputation, opted out, and set selection requirements, it would cream off not only the more academically able pupils, but because of this, the better teachers as well, and would present real problems for other neighbouring schools. In this respect the research by Rutter *et al.* (1979) is well worth noting. Their research showed that school intake needs a reasonable balance of children likely to achieve examination success if an ethos of a positive kind is to be produced. If the 'better' children are creamed off, and the majority of pupils fail to succeed in examinations, an ethos which runs counter to the school values will be produced. An initial balanced intake is therefore crucial, something very difficult to achieve if opting out and selection procedures have become possible.

## (c) Local management of schools (LMS)

The 1988 Education Act, section 38(3)(b), essentially compelled local authorities to distribute funds to secondary and primary schools with more than 200 pupils by means of a per capita formula which was weighted to take account of 'any other factors affecting the needs of individual schools which are subject to variation from school to school'. The governing bodies of such schools are now responsible for expenditure on staffing, books and equipment, heating and lighting, cleaning and rates. The responsibility for selecting headteachers and other staff, for their promotion or dismissal, has moved to being that of the governing body as well. The local authorities' role has therefore been considerably circumscribed, but they remain responsible, among other things, for home-to-school transport, the advising and inspecting of schools, and the administration of pay, tax and superannuation.

There are a number of very praiseworthy intentions behind the introduction of LMS. Firstly, it reflects the common-sense belief that those closest to expenditure will be the most able and the most motivated to use most efficiently the resources at their disposal. This will be particularly true if they know that they have a specific budget to work within, and if they also know that any savings they make can be used on other targeted projects. Savings and efficiencies, then, are seen to be of direct benefit to the school, and not simply absorbed back into local authority coffers. This is a variation on the theme of the problems with large bureaucracies, that those distanced from a situation apply procedures and formulae which may be unsuitable to the particular instance. LMS, because it is expedited by those closest to the expenditure, will motivate people to make the best use of what they have to dispose of. Such thinking seems both sound and sensible.

Another intention is a standard one of free-market theorists – to increase the involvement and responsibility of parents in the running of the school, and thereby to increase the effectiveness of the school in responding to the needs of the local community. LMS, it is claimed, therefore has a prominent role to play in the democratization of education, for it involves the whole community – teachers, parents and governors – in the running of the school to a degree not seen before.

However, it should be noted that whilst many commentators agree with the general principle of financial delegation as a means of more accurate targeting of resources, several have raised severe doubts about the actual efficiency of the move, as economies of scale will almost certainly be lost. The Association of County Councils (Haviland, 1988, p. 140) points out that

> ... central government's emphasis on 'value for money' can sometimes only be satisfied if there is a capacity to enter into contracts covering a number of institutions or even the whole of an LEA area. Block purchasing arrangements for fuel, food and even books and arrangements for such work as grounds maintenance to a number of establishments all provide examples of the potential economies of scale ...

Similarly, the Association of Metropolitan Authorities (Haviland, 1988, p. 145), argued that there are increased auditing requirements if individual school accounts are to be closed individually. Indeed, contrary to the suggestion that devolution of finance is a sure-fire way of ensuring more efficient management, they suggest that 'delegation is not a cheap way of running schools . . .'.

Further, there is considerable anxiety over the research into such implementation. The Society of Local Authority Chief Executives puts the matter succinctly:

> The general impression given is that a number of authorities have successfully introduced schemes for the devolution of financial resources to schools. This is not the case. Those few authorities that have introduced schemes similar to what which the Government is proposing have done so only in pilot schools.

> (Haviland, 1988, p. 158)

So there is initial concern about both efficiency and implementation. There is also doubt about its real aims. Some of the less persuaded observers have argued that far from being a democratic move, this is a rather neat way, by obscuring actual DES funding, of shifting the blame for shortcomings for inadequate financing from central government to the schools themselves.

Further, if one of the major aims of LMS is to devolve responsibility and create greater financial freedom, then it is important to notice two ironies. The first is that the scope for redirection of spending will be as little as two or three per cent (see, for example, the comments made by the National Union of Teachers, and the Advisory Centre for Education, in Haviland (1988), pp. 154, 164). The second is that all local authority plans for financial delegation must be approved by the Secretary of State. If not, they can be rejected or amended, or one of his own devising instituted. It is certainly arguable whether this really is greater financial freedom, or simply a shift of implementation from local authority to school – with the Secretary of State holding the reins.

Three other aspects of LMS should also be noted, two possible consequences, the other an underlying aim. The first consequence for the intra-management of schools could well be an attempt by governors to provide education on the cheap. With something like 70 per cent of a school's budget being spent in terms of teachers' salaries, a governing body will be strongly impelled to employ young, cheaper teachers, rather than the older, more experienced, and hence more expensive ones. In crude financial terms, this might make some kind of sense, but then one should really ask the question, will the education of the children in the school suffer in the long term by employing an imbalance of the young and the inexperienced? Governors are certainly at liberty to spend money on the older teachers, but situations do occur where financial constraints are tightened to such an extent that the school has little option in this matter. If this is the case, then talk of increased financial freedom is spurious, and merely a smokescreen for reducing financial support.

The second possible consequence directly follows from this. There already exist examples of schools which have had to 'let teachers go' in order to balance their books. This, under LMS, is the responsibility of the governing body, and yet it will in practical terms almost certainly devolve to the head, as the person who really knows what is going on in the school. This fact will not be lost on teachers, either, and so one can envisage for the first time genuine tensions between head and staff, as staff become aware of who will fire the bullet, and as heads understand that staff know that it is they who will do the firing. The consequences for participative forms of management, and relationships in general, are not good.

The final, and equally important, question, is whether a society is desired which dispenses with the talents of people purely because they become too experienced. If, however, the argument is used that the market will decide, this really deserves the same reply – that the market is *not* deciding, simply because schools will not be in a position to buy who they want. Much of this boils down to the criticism in the previous chapter of the new liberals' advocacy of the primacy of negative liberty. This version of liberty suggests that government activity should be restricted to doing no more than prevent others from infringing on a person's choice of action. The problem with this is the same as that with private schooling and medicine – freedom is only there for those who can afford it. In like manner, schools may well find themselves in a position where they cannot afford the teachers they want, and if this is the case, then again, free-market theory is being used as a spurious argument to support a cost-cutting exercise.

## FROM COMPETITION TO PARTNERSHIP

The influence of new liberal thinking upon education was not welcomed when it arrived, but it has been, and continues to be, a refreshing and challenging one. If, at times, responses by educationalists have been more knee-jerk than considered, legislative implementation has led them, willingly or not, to consider the realities of the situation. The assessment of this is by no means all bad. Indeed, in the context of the ethics of education proposed in this book, the new liberal thinking has much to offer.

As we have seen, one of the reasons why the approach has gained such ground in the Western world over the last couple of decades is that it has been seen as an antidote to excessive bureaucracies. It clearly can lessen the degree of alienation which people may feel when confronted with large impersonal organizations, for the educational reforms derived from this approach are designed to engage people at the grass roots level, in activities which directly affect them. It can therefore give new meaning to these activities, as well as to the lives of people engaged in them. To take the case of LMS, by having this function at a level where expenditure has direct consequences for those who execute it, it provides a motivation, an involvement, a personalization, and a meaning which is most unlikely to be found when such actions fail to have such direct effects. Whilst the economies-of-scale argument noted above is an important one to consider, the arguments for relocating the level of execution to those actually engaged and affected by the process are strong and convincing ones. It is also to be expected that the personalization of these processes will also reduce the other negative structuring effects of bureaucratization upon individuals mentioned previously – the authorization, routinization and dehumanization. Where people literally rub shoulders with those in authority, they are less likely to be fearful of the concept of authority, and can recognize that that person can also be wrong. Where routines are designed at the local level, their meaning is less likely to be lost, and they are less likely to be kept simply because they have always been that way.

And where, because of the scale of the operation, each affected individual can be identified as an individual, there is much less likelihood of people treating others as numbers rather than as people. All of this, a direct consequence of a free-market approach, is much to the good.

There are, however, two major caveats which must be made about the existing state of affairs. The first concerns the bifurcation of policies and legislation at the present time. Where there are these incompatible tendencies – the one towards centralization, the other towards localization of control – there are bound to be conflicting messages which schools will receive. How this will translate into practice is difficult to say. Three possibilities will be raised here. One possibility is that different areas of school-management policy – financial management, enrolment of pupils, local authority control, curriculum management and assessment of pupils – remain fairly static in the degree to which they are centrally or locally controlled, and fail to affect one another. If this were the case, then, for example, the curriculum might be very centralized in terms of control, enrolment of pupils might be very locally managed, and the two might fail to conflict.

Whilst it is possible that some areas may fail to conflict, it is highly unlikely that they will remain static in their degree of control. A second scenario, then, is one where these areas of management policy move up and down the scale between local and central control, as different governments and different ministers place emphasis upon one or other end of the spectrum, this depending on their political affiliations and the pressures placed upon them. This has already happened in a number of cases in the UK. As pointed out above, LMS is hardly as locally controlled as might at first have been envisaged, for much of the expenditure of schools is taken up with essentials, leaving little room for local experimentation. At the other end of the scale, the more rigid prescriptions of the National Curriculum in terms of statutory teaching and testing have been, and continue to be, progressively watered down because they fail to match, among other things, the reality of the number of children in a classroom, and the hours a teacher has to teach. There is a distinct possibility, then, that the more extreme examples of central and local control will move towards a mixed form.

A third scenario is not necessarily in conflict with the second, but envisages a situation such that with a spectrum of policies, different schools will pick up and run with one particular end of the control spectrum, depending upon the educational philosophies of head, staff, governing body and parents. This scenario refers back both to the first chapter, where it was argued that the educational philosophies of a management team will interact with more general management approaches dictated from elsewhere, and also to the work of Lipsky (1981), who argued that 'street-level bureaucrats' can and do undermine high-level policies from below to make their professional lives bearable and workable.

What this points to, I suggest, is the uncomfortable conclusion for both policy-makers and commentators that legislation almost never has precisely the effect that is intended, and has less of the intended effect the less that those implementing it were not consulted, and, therefore, do not feel they 'own' it. Crystal-ball gazing is a hazardous occupation, and particularly so in matters of educational policy.

If the first caveat on the introduction of free-market policies has been the difficulty of predicting their likely effects, a second caveat is perhaps more conceptual. It is that, despite all of the attractive things which a free-market approach claims to do, it has to be asked whether it fundamentally misconceives the roles of the people engaged in the educational process.

To appreciate this, it is useful to examine the description that Docking (1990) gives of the possible position that parents may play in the organization of schools. He suggests three:

1. parents as problems;
2. parents as customers;
3. parents as partners.

The first position is the classic one where a school has a large notice outside the school indicating that parents must stay outside the playground until the end of the school day, and then children will come to them. It suggests that they be viewed as uninterested in their child's progress, or as 'pushy', and if so then as intruders on the teacher–child relationship. In either case, they are perceived as lacking anything of use to the educational endeavour. The teacher is the expert, and does not need laypeople sticking their noses into things they don't understand. Whilst such attitudes still persist in some areas, it is very clearly the case that teachers have increasingly come to realize the immense amount of help which parents can give, not only in terms of help within the school, but also in terms of insight into the nature of the child, providing a much-needed co-ordinated response to the child's needs.

The second is the one typified by the free-market philosophy. A succinct example of this outlook is that found in *Whose Schools?* by the Hillgate Group. As they say, a school's survival

> ... should depend on their ability to satisfy their customers. And their principal customers are parents, who should therefore be free to place their custom where they wish, in order that educational institutions should be shaped, controlled, and nourished by their demand.
>
> (Hillgate Group, 1986, p. 7)

The problem with this approach is that it is inherently confrontational, with dialogue between interested bodies being seen in terms of rights. What happens is that, as with the market, each person is defined as separate and self-interested; and yet what is educationally much more valuable for the child is a relationship between interested parties which sees them as partners, who do not compete against one another, or attempt to sell their wares, but who are on the same side. Defining parents as customers unduly restricts their role, and hence the function of the school, because it fails to see that parents have a complementary role to play to that of the teacher. They are not on different sides, as the second model suggests, but are partners in the same enterprise.

This therefore takes us into the third model, where parents are seen as partners. Such a perception has profound ramifications for relationships. If, using the second model, you wished to explain a particular teaching strategy to a parent, it could only be because you were trying to sell your approach to them, for by informing them, you ensure that they will continue to patronize your school, and you will stay financially viable. Fundamentally, I suggest, this is a relationship which can never rise above the manipulative. A partnership model involves a deeper, more meaningful, and fuller set of human relationships, for here there is two-way dialogue, and both parties are involved in informing and educating each other for the same purpose – the benefit of the child and themselves. Whilst the free-market model moves some way beyond the alienation of bureaucratic procedures, it fails truly to attain the best educational relationships because it conceptualizes interested parties as being in competition, whilst, for the best educational experience, the relationship must be one of partnership.

## CONCLUSION

The free-market model, to its credit, moves the management of education from the bureaucratic and the alienated through to the personal and the motivated, and in so doing breathes new commitment into the system. However, it must ultimately fail to match educational management to true educational experiences, because it can only see relationships in terms of the confrontational. If a child, if a school, if an education system is to really succeed, the watchword must not be competition, but partnership. If it is to combine the ethical with the effective, school management must learn from the insights of the free market, but must move beyond this ideology, and instead cultivate procedures and relationships which retain the local and the personal, but bed these instead in a collaborative exercise. Only by doing this can it achieve its ultimate function, that of a community, building empowering structures, and facilitating the development of relationships which can be practised before being implemented in the larger society.

# Chapter 8

# Education and business management

## INTRODUCTION

Much of this book so far has examined the influences upon educational management from a variety of social, political and industrial perspectives. Without doubt, the most constant and influential of these sources has been the business community. It is time, then, that the transfer of business theory to educational management was examined. Where these borrowings are valid, they increase an understanding of educational management, and the ability to cope with it. Where they are insensitive and undiscriminating, however, they may distort a proper conception of education, and produce a version of school management which destroys morale by undermining good educational practice. This chapter, therefore, will attempt to do a number of things. Firstly, it will briefly ask why education has turned to business practices for much of its management theory. Then it will examine ways in which schools may differ from other organizations. In the light of these, it will then review possible borrowings, and so indicate those which merit direct transfer, those which can only be treated as analogies, and, finally, those which ought to have little or no place in educational thinking.

It was argued in Chapter 2 that education has, for four main reasons, increasingly turned to business for its management theory. Briefly, these were:

1. because organizations have many things in common – some of their characteristics, such as deciding on key tasks and how these should be accomplished, are universal to all organizations;
2. because education has had so little management theory of its own;
3. because, in the present socio-political ethos of free-market economics, those in government have attempted to apply their own perspectives to non-business institutions;
4. because, in an era of financial belt-tightening, there is a generally perceived need for all divisions of the public sector to be efficient in the same manner as businesses have to be.

However, it still has to be asked: are schools the same as other organizations? Handy and Aitken (1986) have suggested that there are at least four ways in which schools differ from other organizations.

Firstly, there is still a common perception in schools that teachers don't have the time for management. Theirs is such a heavy work schedule that this is a matter which must be secondary to considerations of teaching *per se*. Allied to this belief is a lack of interest in the subject – the 'we are teachers, not managers' syndrome – which probably stems, in part at least, from the lack of time, but also from the simple belief that management isn't really important. As Handy quite rightly points out, such an attitude does not make management go away – it merely makes some types more likely than others. Thus it may lead to the autocrat founding a dictatorship, or to a situation of teacher autonomy which looks little better than anarchy. Lack of interest, then, is no excuse, though lack of time may well be. However, education is not alone in thinking it never has enough time to do what it ought to do. At the most, this difference is one of degree rather than of kind.

The second difference is what Handy and Aitken (1986, p. 34) call the 'pile of purposes' argument. Business purposes are seen as being few and simple, whilst educational purposes are seen as many, varied and conflicting. There may well be some truth in this, in that schools have to satisfy a variety of taskmasters, some or all of whom may be in conflict with one another. These purposes may be more varied than those of business, for a business, despite its varied outputs and approaches, will at the end of the day usually be judged on whether it made a profit. This criterion may be waived for a number of years – while, for example, reinvestment is going on. However, even this reinvestment is for the purpose of future profitability, and while there may be qualitative judgements as to when profitability should be seen again, this quantitative criterion remains. The criterion of profitability may also be modified by other, possibly ethical, impulses. Traidcraft (UK), for instance, trades on the underlying principle of helping Third World countries, and practising Christian values. Businesses dealing with ethical investments will deliberately eschew investing in companies who have dealings with oppressive régimes, even if this means not maximizing possible profits. And finally, companies like Rowntree or Marks and Spencer have had a well-known reputation for the treatment of their employees and the environment in which they work. Profit maximization is not, then, necessarily the only end, though loss minimization is, for any business, the bottom line; but for most, it will be the major determinant.

Education, on the other hand, has rather more criteria than even these businesses, and even within one criterion, finds enormous difficulties in assessing whether that criterion has been reached. You want an articulate, enterprising, flexible, sensitive individual as an educational end-product? When does someone become this? There is no cut-off point, even if we all think we can tell such people when we see them. The judgement is necessarily subjective, and this is one of education's enduring difficulties and attractions. We all know how important its products are, but no one has yet found, or ever will find, a way of standardizing the product, or of verifying that a certain standard has been reached – unless, of course, one describes such products in such a simplistic, behavioural way that many of the higher qualitative attainments are ignored. Perhaps, then, the 'pile of purposes' is not quite the right description. Perhaps it is the 'questioning of quality' which is the real problem.

Handy's third difference is that of 'role-switching'. By this he means that within education there appears to be an assumption that the good teacher makes a good headteacher, a good manager. The good sales representative does not always make a good sales manager, and is not automatically promoted, so why does this kind of thing happen in education? I think the answer is that it does not, much, any more. It may have been the way in a previous era, but it would not apply very much today. This may well be one of the benefits of a borrowing from business theory. There is a clear awareness that untrained 'role-switching' is not a good thing, though there is a common-sense appreciation of the fact that someone who has been a good teacher is more likely to be able to influence and help other members of staff, and appreciate their difficulties and problems, than someone who last encountered a classroom when in short trousers or gymslip.

The final difference is simply stated as 'the children'. Where do they fit into conventional management theory? Are they workers? Are they clients? Are they products? They appear to be all and none. This problem refers us back once again to the 'pile of purposes' problem, but also points to the fact that schools cannot be classified as 'usual business institutions' and must be appreciated in the light of who participates in their running, and what they aim to achieve. If schools are organizations designed primarily to enhance the personal, social and political development of their inhabitants, then they certainly do not conform to any business notions of the purpose of an organization. The problem with the classification of the children, then, points once again to the fact that schools are unusual beasts, and must be appreciated for that very idiosyncrasy.

These, then, are the four differences which Handy points out, and yet there is a fifth, and perhaps even more important, difference which cannot normally be seen by asking how schools are different. It is more generally perceived by changing the object under examination, by looking at the theoretical development of industrial sociology. A survey of this literature clearly indicates that much of it has been designed primarily for the use of industrial management in the improvement of workers' productivity. Thus it might be the case that key thinkers in this area became influential as much because their ideas resonated with the needs of management at that time, as for any particular academic merit of the work as such. The researchers, moreover, were not completely academically independent. Whether it was Taylor improving the production of pig-iron at Bethlehem Steel, the 'Human Relations' group at Western Electric, or members of the Tavistock Institute in British coal mines, they came to the research from a particular value position, that of the management, because it was the management who employed them. To what extent, one must ask, is such a theoretical or value orientation applicable to an educational situation? To what extent does a 'management and workers' perspective fit a school? And even where researchers have not been actively employed by a particular company, the research is still imbued with theoretical assumptions about the importance of the approach taken which still need to be highlighted and questioned for their appropriateness. These are questions which need raising and answering if unwanted theoretical perspectives are not to be employed in education.

If these remarks are true, then much of the business literature needs to be examined extremely carefully, for if it is not, any non-critical transfer will almost certainly incorporate the kinds of problems mentioned above. Education, then, must not become the inhabitant of a Procrustian bed of business theory, its inhabitants to be unnaturally altered to fit a particular theory. The only real way of making sure this does not happen is to look at the fit between the bed and its occupants. In other words, what are the business analogies which increasingly work their way into the educational management literature? There appear to be nine:

(a) Management is an essential part of any organization.
(b) Education is to be consumer-led.
(c) There is to be a standardization of product.
(d) There is to be increased efficiency in financing.
(e) There is to be greater accountability.
(f) The standard approach is to be management by objectives.
(g) Education is to be oriented primarily at the job market.
(h) Management will be essentially hierarchical in nature.
(i) The way to improve performance is through competition.

Each will be dealt with in turn.

## (a) Management is an essential part of any organization

A certain amount has been said about this already. The climate has undoubtedly changed in education; one has only to look at the number of management courses now on offer to teachers, at the importance given to the consideration of management strategies, at the number of books published in this area, to appreciate that the development of educational management has become a national priority area. There can be little doubt that this emphasis is a 'good thing': as noted above, the denial of the importance of management does not make it go away; it simply makes it more likely that unintended, or bad, forms of management proliferate. The major caveat, of course, comes in the form of asking what *intentional* forms of management are suggested to the senior management of schools. It is with this question that the bulk of this book is concerned.

## (b) Education is to be consumer-led

ilosophy was expressed so well by Drucker (1968, pp. 67, 74) that I can do no quote him:

is our business is not determined by the producer, but by the
... the question can therefore be answered only by looking at
s ... from the point of view of the customer and the market
customer considers value is so complicated that it can only
y the customer himself. Management should not even try to
should always go to the customer in a systematic quest for

er of things to be said about this. It should be pointed out many businesses, particularly the larger ones, would simply statement. Too much time, effort and money is invested into cars, televisions and computers for these investments to be at the ory popular taste. Companies will do their level best to control the re that the consumer comes to believe that a particular product is ey have wanted all along. Advertising is the essential mechanism for used, at least in part, to convince a public that they need to buy a ar product to make them more comfortable, sexier, or better smelling, to ve more prestige, or because Mr Jones next door has got one. It is therefore simply not true that all businesses believe Peter Drucker's slogan. If they did, they would not be able to plan for – and control – the future, and they would probably go out of business.

Moreover, it is worth pointing out that, once again, this piece of advice is meant only for a business audience. It would have the same caveat as mentioned above. Yet it is undoubtedly the case that these are the lenses through which education is increasingly viewed. Thus, in educational terms, one can see its effect in Great Britain in the increasing influence of governing bodies over the running of schools, in the rights of parents to opt out of LEA control, on open admission policies to school, and in the increasing popularity of an educational-voucher scheme, whereby parents 'spend' the voucher at the type of school which they most desire their children to attend.

Thus, there are 'consumers', just as there are 'producers', 'products' and 'raw materials'. However, there are two questions here, both of which challenge the philosophy behind the phraseology. Firstly, it must be asked whether the analogy of 'consumer' fits the role of any of the above bodies snugly, or instead distorts their real roles. Do we really 'consume' education? 'Consume' suggests a simple, undirectional activity: food is taken down from the shelf, is bitten, chewed, swallowed, and all is gone. Education, though, is not like that. It does not have a prepacked shape, except in the most superficial and unhelpful sense, for it changes people even as they are 'consuming'. An educational relationship changes all the people engaged in the activity, both teacher and taught, and not only will an educational experience be different from one person to the next, but it will also be different for the same person at different times during the course. New perceptions, new understandings, and new visions will radically affect the way in which material is approached, delivered and comprehended. It is an interpersonal and social experience which is different each time it is encountered. To liken it to a consumer experience is to misdescribe it radically, and, possibly, to ensure that a cheapened prepackaged version is all that can be seen and offered.

Secondly, who, after all, are these 'consumers'? Even in its entrepreneurial sense, there are problems with the term. Does it mean the person who pays for the product, or the person who uses it? This may seem a matter of little moment, and the distinction may be glossed over precisely because of this, but in educational terms it is of considerable importance. For education changes the person who uses it, and what education consists of will determine what sort of person will develop. So are the consumers the parents (because they raise the children and pay through their taxes for the schools)? Are the consumers the children (because they are the ones actually involved in the activity)? Or is the consumer the country's industrial base (because it will need a future workforce)?

By ignoring this question – who is the consumer? – or by assuming there is a simple answer to it, one ignores many other questions. Thus, by interpreting the parent as consumer, we give more choice to one section of the population, but fail to recognize rights that a substantial number of children may be capable of utilizing, and therefore deserve to have. This issue will be taken further in Chapter 10. However, by interpreting the child as consumer, education may be limited to a diet of their present interests, which will be dictated at least in part by parents' understandings and by media advertising. By interpreting industry as the consumer, a healthy business and industrial base may be created, but education may well be impoverished, and ultimately society, if its other functions are ignored. These other functions might include: education's role in cultural transmission, a view of the child as being at the centre of the process, and the use of education as a means of social reconstruction. By ignoring the first, we pauperize our conception of the world. By disregarding the second, we alienate the child from the teaching process and from those in positions of authority. And by paying no attention to the third, we rigidify and institutionalize faults and failings in society as it stands at present, and store up trouble for the future.

A final and important point is to question whether consumerism should dictate the kind of education provided. For a start, the confusion noted above over who precisely is the consumer should lead one to be cautious when assigning this right to any one interested group. There are going to be different 'pulls' for what education is perceived to be needed, and it is both sensible and ethical to allow sufficient flexibility in the system for different interested parties to be able to affect policy and direction. This point applies, moreover, not just to different 'consumer' groups, but also to producers and providers.

This disagreement over the ultimate purposes of education points to the richness and unpredictability of the educational process, which is not always reflected in popular taste and passing fashions. It would be well, then, for policy-makers to set an agenda which, whilst responding to such tastes and fashions, also paid attention to less temporary concerns. Doing this means recognizing the importance of, and then incorporating within policy, the expertise and interests of theoreticians, practitioners and consumers. It is sometimes said that new Secretaries of State arrive at the DES with an ideological agenda, but then turn 'native', the ideology becoming more and more diluted. It might be more accurate to argue that such ideology may find great difficulty when confronted by a deeper understanding of the meaning and purpose of education, and of the practicalities of implementation. A simplistic ideology of consumerism may well be a case in point.

## (c) There is to be a standardization of process and product

An advocate of standardization might well argue that one of its undoubted benefits is that objectives can be clearly stated and evaluated. 'I intend to sell twenty tractors this month.' It does not take much effort to see whether, at the end of the month, twenty tractors have been sold, and to check before selling that the product comes up to scratch. If the construction, paintwork or performance is poor, the product will not be sold. One tractor should be like another. Standardization facilitates not only the control of the process, but also the evaluation of performance.

However, standardization is problematical not only in educational terms, but also in business terms. Davis (1990) points out that business analogies actually derive from two separate camps. The first is that of manufacturing industry and of a Taylorian scientific/rational view of management. Such a view sees the school as a machine, running smoothly, uniformly onward, its parts interchangeable, its products predictable. The parts of this machine are of course human beings, pupils and teachers, but they become viewed as cogs in the machine, to be moulded and adapted to its running via the educational process. The influence of the machine metaphor is extensive. One often, for instance, reads in educational management literature of teachers as 'human resources' to be developed, rather than of them as resourceful humans to be valued and credited with the ability to make professional judgements. How much does the introduction of standardization tend to introduce a de-skilling element into the pedagogic exercise, turning the teacher into a technician rather than a professional? It is from this camp that the argument for twenty identical tractors would come.

The other camp is that of business and commerce, which more probably involves the satisfaction of a customer by personal service. This will usually vary with the personalities of the parties involved, and one method may well be as good as another in achieving ultimate goals. Standardization, then, would be precisely the wrong method to adopt. This would clearly suggest that the business/commerce view is much more akin to that of education than the manufacturing camp. Just as with customer service, numerous reviews of teaching methods have concluded that there is no one standard method of teaching which always produces the best results (e.g. Wragg, 1987, pp. 4–8). This may be awkward for those who want a nice, simple means of evaluation, but it does suggest a commerce rather than a manufacturing approach. Evaluation should be tailored to fit the practice, not the other way round.

There are, however, arguments for educational standardization, and from both ends of the political spectrum as well. Denis Lawton (1983) saw the standardization of the curriculum through a national curriculum as the natural complement to a comprehensive system of schooling: if you give children equal opportunities by providing the same kinds of school, you should provide them with access to similar curricula as well. Kenneth Baker (Baker, 1986) saw a national curriculum as the means to upgrading the parochial and limiting educational menu given to children in schools where teachers do not themselves feel competent to provide more. They may not feel competent at present, but the imposition of a national curriculum means that they are going to have to become so.

Both arguments have their merit, though one can still entertain misgivings; clearly, the more that one standardizes what is to be taught, when it is to be taught, and how it is to be taught, the more one takes away from the teacher these judgements, the more one de-skills him or her, the less satisfactory will be the individual service to the pupil. Neither does such a proposal address the question of who decides what a national curriculum should consist of. This is a value-laden political decision simply because what one puts onto, and omits from, the curriculum agenda shapes the minds of future generations. The danger with too much concentration on curricular standardization is that one does not pay sufficient attention to who is going to do the standardizing, and for what reasons. Problems of value cannot be omitted from the educational exercise.

What, finally, of the standardization of product? A first question must be what this 'product' is. Are pupils products? With a machine metaphor, perhaps. But do we have to accept either the metaphor, or that children (or any human beings) must be viewed as such? Do we want children to be standardized? Given standardized opportunities, perhaps. But from a practical point of view, because of children's different interests and endowments, one must expect different results from these equal opportunities. And from an ethical point of view, one might even argue that such differentiation is a good thing in itself, as it provides a social and cultural variety which enriches society.

The conclusion must be that the argument is in many ways a replay of the earlier argument between bureaucracy and the individualization of treatment. At its best, standardization might aim for equality and fairness in overall system provision; at its worst, it destroys individual motivation and initiative. Clearly, straightforward analogies from industry supporting standardization are not possible, not only because they are only drawn from part of that world, but also because they fail to appreciate the necessity of the individuation of the education process. One needs to be very cautious indeed in any translation.

## (d) There is to be an increased efficiency in financing

It seems commonsensical to argue that efficiency is to be recommended, because lack of efficiency means wasted resources, and wasted resources mean not getting the results you could. Whilst the argument can be accepted at this level, there are still problems which give real pause for thought.

Firstly, and as argued in Chapter 2, notions of efficiency can be connected with the simplistic and limited vision of a rationalist/scientific management view of human nature and the world, wherein it is believed that one can plan down to the last detail the way in which events will take place, and that people and efficiency can be viewed in a similar manner. This, however, is simply not true. Not only is it a strong criticism of scientific management that it will demotivate the people involved in the process, but also it is in the nature of things that there are so many variables to control that the unexpected is just about always more likely to happen than the expected. Efficiency, then, is not quite the simple achievable concept which it is sometimes proposed to be, and the prosecution of it in a simplistic way often results in gross inefficiencies.

Moreover, we should ask questions about the meaning of 'efficient' – efficient in sheer monetary terms, in temporal terms, in terms of the amount of labour expended, or in terms of suffering incurred? Some of these may amount to the same thing, but there is no necessary guarantee – one form of efficiency may well clash with another, and it is only when such questions are asked and answered that one can begin to choose between the alternatives on offer. As Fay (1975, p. 50) points out,

> ... the point here is that whatever one gives will reflect a judgement as to that set of factors which a policy scientist thinks the most important in situations of this type, a judgement that cannot be scientifically made for it involves reference to the *values* of the scientist.

Thus, even if a project does look on paper as if it is more economically efficient, this does not begin to deal with the question of whether economic efficiency is the crucial criterion one wishes to employ in making the decision. Efficiency is not a neutral word, but describes a preferred state of affairs, which may conflict with other states of affairs. It is a preference which can be questioned, for, as Rizvi (1989, p. 214) argues,

> the idea of ... efficiency is a goal, the preference for which over other goals, such as mass participation, has to be argued for in specifically moral and political terms.

Take the example of deciding to build a bridge: it might be uneconomic, and yet so improve the quality of life of those living near it as to be deemed worth the investment. The same goes for staging expensive or inexpensive courses, building costly or cheap schools – the question of quality, and of the values behind one's ultimate decision, will always intrude. The crucial point is that 'efficiency' should be a negotiable value, not a concept beyond discussion.

## (e) There is to be greater accountability

There are a variety of possible meanings of the term 'accountability' which will affect ultimate evaluations. The analysis by Barton *et al.* (1986) is useful in that it has many transferences to and from the educational sector. They suggest that there are at least three modes of accountability:

1. moral accountability – to clients;
2. professional accountability – responsibility to oneself and colleagues;
3. contractual accountability – to employers.

All three of these seem to apply equally well to business and industry as to education. A fourth mode might be suggested, however, which would be peculiar to education. This would be

4. intellectual accountability – a perception by the teacher that he or she is under a discipline imposed by the intellectual criteria and structure of the subject which he or she teaches.

This final mode of accountability may provoke tension with other modes – particularly the moral and contractual modes – that business and industry does not have to worry about. Thus, where a simplified and distorted version of a subject is urged on teachers for utilitarian, economic purposes, the teacher may feel compelled to resist this. There may be an allegiance to the pursuit of truth through a particular area of the curriculum which is seen as overriding the demands of simple economic necessity. Where politicians and businessmen fail to see this, conflict and declining teacher morale are likely results.

Related to this is the *model* of accountability which might be employed. Lawton's (1983) models of 'bureaucratic' and 'democratic' accountability reflect his observation that the relationship between government and teachers has changed from one of 'partnership' to one of 'accountability' (p. 12), where 'accountability' means precisely the bureacratic, hierarchical model, in which only the pupils in the school are accountable to the teachers. The 'democratic' model, on the other hand, views most parties in the educational enterprise as accountable to each other.

Indeed, the 'bureaucratic' form of accountability is an expression of only one form of organizational management, and it should be clear from Chapter 3 of this book, as well as from the work of Handy and other management writers with widely differing approaches (e.g. Peters and Waterman, 1982; Drucker, 1968; Greenfield, 1985), that bureaucracy, line management and hierarchy are *not* the only, or even the most successful, forms of management strategy in business. There is, therefore, a strong case for suggesting that not only are there other models of organization available to education, but also the bureaucratic form is inappropriate, fixating as it does on hierarchy, roles, predictability and standardization.

This form of accountability also incorporates within it another aspect of the limited rationality seen in the preceding accounts of standardization and efficiency. It tends to prescribe a kind of rationality which Gareth Morgan (1985) describes as 'functional' or 'instrumental' rationality, a rationality which is limited to an ability to perceive the application of rules, and a consequent ability to apply and obey them. This kind of rationality is very different from 'substantial' rationality, where people are encouraged to develop not only a facility for conforming to directives, but also a talent for evaluating the appropriateness of those actions, and acting accordingly. The consequences of the adoption of one or the other form of rationality are profound:

> Whereas bureaucratic rationality is mechanical, substantial rationality is reflective and self-organizing. Mechanistic organization discourages initiative, encouraging people to obey orders and keep their place rather than to take an interest in, challenge, and question what they are doing. People in a bureaucracy who question the wisdom of conventional practice are viewed more often than not as troublemakers. Therefore apathy often reigns, as people learn to feel powerless about problems . . .
>
> (Morgan, 1985, p. 37)

Those designing accountability strategies in education which have this bureaucratic air may be more interested in control than in accountability *per se*. It is instructive in this sense to look at what de Tocqueville said on this issue:

> It (the power in the land) covers the surface of society with a network of small complicated rules, minute and uniform, through which the most original minds and the most energetic characters cannot penetrate, to rise above the crowd. The will of man is not shattered, but softened, bent and guided: men are seldom forced by it to act, but they are constantly restrained from acting: such a power does not destroy, but it prevents existence; it does not tyrannize but it compresses, enervates, extinguishes, and stupifies a people, till each nation is reduced to nothing better than a flock of timid and industrious animals, of which the government is the shepherd.
>
> (de Tocqueville, 1961, vol. II, pp. 381–2)

Whichever is the reason for their institutionalization, present educational models of accountability may well be inadequately conceptualized.

## (f) The standard approach is to be management by objectives

This, as we saw in Chapter 2, has a long history in business and industrial management, stretching from Taylor to Drucker, and then in education through Bobbitt, Tyler and Bloom. It has not always had an easy time, and has received various revisions on the way, perhaps most notably at the curricular level in the distinction between 'instructional' and 'expressive' objectives suggested by Eisner

(1986). However, the general notion has been adopted enthusiastically by educational theorists, the LEAs and the DES. There seem to be four major arguments used in its favour.

Firstly, it is argued that it makes no sense to plan and organize if we do not know where we are going. Aims and objectives provide one with the logical tools with which to decide where we want to go and how we are going to get there. Any other method must surely be fuzzy, imprecise and badly co-ordinated. The argument that teachers do not use them is not seen as an argument against aims and objectives, but as an argument against current styles of educational planning, or the lack of it.

Secondly, knowing where we want to go, and how we want to get there, we are able to specify in advance materials and resources required, predict possible outcomes and hence be able to evaluate them. Thus education becomes more clear and precise in what it is trying to do, more accurate in its achievements, and therefore more respected, not only by the academic community, but also by the community at large.

Thirdly, schools are built and funded by society as a whole; they cannot and should not be looked upon as the preserve of the teaching profession. This being the case, the public has a right to know how the billions spent on education are being spent, what they are being spent on, and whether the promises given for the spending of this money are fulfilled. The public, then, has a right to know if it is getting value for money.

Lastly, just as it is more clear and more precise to specify in advance what one is going to do, it is also the only real way of being sure that such clarity and precision are rewarded, that specific proposals do work. It is the only way, then, of ensuring that evaluation is possible. And without proper evaluation, practices can never be improved.

The arguments seem compelling, and indeed the approach has come to exert such a grip upon education that it is reaching the status of being seen as non-problematical, natural and obvious. Yet there are problems with it which managers and teachers need to consider carefully.

Firstly, such objectives assume limited and predictable outcomes, and yet, because human learning tends to be diverted from specified courses within actual lessons by different interests and people's different selectivity, it can make stating aims and objectives for the end of a lesson difficult, useless, or downright dangerous, in that it may constrict natural interest.

Secondly, the appropriateness of applying an aims-and-objectives approach differs depending on:

(a) the subject areas one addresses;
(b) the level within those subject areas with which one is primarily concerned; and
(c) the use of teaching style employed.

Thus (a) it might be argued that some subjects, like maths, science and language, are at certain levels capable of considerable predictability in the specification of what must be learned, whilst other areas, like music, art or literary criticism, are valued precisely because they lead to more unpredictable outcomes. However, (b) all subjects, at their most sophisticated levels, demand an artistic, individual and creative appreciation, one where a simple aims-and-objectives approach would be not only inadequate but positively destructive. Finally, (c) no matter what the level at which a subject is approached, the problem of *how* the material is to be learned will make too accurate a specification of aims and objectives counter-productive.

Thirdly, objectives stated in behavioural and content terms may be used as clear measures of evaluation. But many important, desired educational outcomes – the higher qualitative outcomes, involving appreciation and judgement – are less amenable, and may suffer from neglect if a too-rigid view of aims and objectives is adopted.

Finally, and perhaps most importantly, as Eisner (1986) has pointed out, the whole aims-and-objectives movement may be incorrect for education in psychological terms. Thus, a central argument of the aims-and-objectives approach is the logical point that educational objectives must be stated prior to an educational activity if one is to achieve the best results. And yet, psychologically, this simply may not work: much of the best teaching comes from broad descriptions of areas to be examined, and the investigation of these areas only then leads to the discovery of objectives as the activity proceeds. Pre-specification of objectives may be a rational procedure which does not work because it does not take account of the interest-based, discovery, and motivational-based nature of much learning.

What becomes clear from a brief review of these arguments is that there is an initial common-sense plausibility to an aims-and-objectives approach, which is increasingly conditioned by an appreciation of the educational exercise, and of the use of a limited notion of rationality. Of course, if one sees education in a different way, as the simple transmission of cultural inheritances, or as the training of individuals for places in an industrial market-place, then the matter is really not problematical at all. Aims and objectives as a means of teaching pass on the nod. They are ineluctably linked to the educational ideology one espouses. There can be little doubt that at the present time, an ideology which draws its principal inspiration from business increasingly predominates. Little wonder then that aims and objectives are sold to teachers so enthusiastically and so uncritically.

## (g) Education is to be oriented primarily at the job market

It is not surprising that a philosophy which is borrowed from business and industry should see its principal focus within education as the furthering of the connection with business and industry. Moreover, when a philosophy is implemented at governmental level by people the majority of whom learnt their understanding of life within this environment, it is not surprising that they should picture education as feeding this goal. Finally, in an age when Britain is seen as being in desperate, almost cut-throat, competition with industrial neighbours like Germany, Japan, and the US, it becomes an article of faith that to maintain present standards of living, education must increasingly focus upon training the youth of the country to compete in such markets. This demand is, of course, nothing new. One has only to look at what W. E. Forster, the architect of the 1870 Education Act, said to see the same kind of motivation:

Upon this speedy provision of education depends also our national power.

> Civilised communities throughout the world are massing themselves together, each mass being measured by its force; and if we are to hold our position among men of our own race, or among the nations of the world, we must make up the smallness of our numbers by increasing the intellectual force of the individual.
>
> (Wardle, 1976, p. 33)

A number of factors, therefore, come together to provide the motive force for making education the handmaiden of the job market. For those with economic blinkers, such concentration makes good sense, but for those who take a wider view of the purposes of education, this appears narrow and damaging, even, in the long term, to the economic good health of the country. For, as seen in Chapter 1, it is possible to argue for the ultimate purposes of education from, in brief, four different standpoints.

The first, the *GNP code*, and the one which appears to be the motive force in much educational decision-making at the present time, values knowledge which is conducive to the furtherance of the national economic well-being. It sees the child as a being to be trained to fit into this economic machine. Initiative and activity are encouraged only as far as these dovetail with ultimate occupational destinations. The teacher, therefore, is seen as a trainer, a constructor, a transmitter, a lower-order member of a hierarchy which begins at governmental levels and proceeds through the headteacher, to the teacher, and then to the child.

The second, the *cultural-transmission code*, values knowledge which is perceived as part of that country's cultural heritage. It sees the child as essentially a passive imbiber, one of many to be graded in their understanding and internalization of such knowledge. The teacher, therefore, is seen as a guardian, a transmitter of appropriate values, and again the situation is seen as essentially a hierarchical one. These two codes are similiar in many ways, and yet they differ crucially in what is regarded as valuable, for relevance to the prevailing economic situation is seen as the crucial criterion in the first case, but serves little or no purpose in the second.

The third, the *child-centred code*, sees the curriculum as based on each individual child's experiences and interests, each being active, involved, unique constructors of their own reality. It sees education as the antithesis of transmission, but as an open-ended activity in which the processes of exploration and discovery are seen as being vastly more important than the end-product. The teacher, in this situation, becomes a facilitator, a constructor of beneficial situations for the child, but in no way is a transmitter, for he or she must at all times be ready for the movement from one area of interest to another.

The last, the *social-reconstruction code*, sees schools as being essentially concerned with pressing social issues which need to be resolved, and therefore the curriculum takes the form of being topic- or problem-based. In this situation, children are active and critical, and gain their educational identity through interaction with others in social groups, in which each is seen as a necessary contributor. The teacher in such a situation is a facilitator, a constructor, a selector of relevant problems, issues and materials, but also a guardian of what is to be retained from the past. Here there is a mixture of democracy and guidance; the pupils have the right and duty to analyse and criticize, the teacher to act as guide and mentor.

Such sketches do not begin to do justice to the complexity and richness of argument which may be contained within such educational ideologies, and tend to present them as straw men too easily knocked down. However, if they at the very least convey the profound ideological gulfs which exist between those who hold conflicting views, these descriptions go some way to suggest that there is truth in each of them, but none must have the stage to itself. And where the danger is that education is oriented primarily to the job market, and is thus in the grip of a thoroughgoing economic code, the dangers for a nation's cultural heritage, for the interests and excitement of the child's learning, for the rational and critical development of a nation's customs and institutions, are all too clear to see. If in the past there has been too little emphasis on the GNP code (though the quotation by Forster shows that the awareness seems to have been around for a long time), then at the moment there appears to be too much.

## (h) Management will be essentially hierarchical in nature

This may seem a curious statement to make, for after all much of the latest educational management literature suggests a type of management which stresses self-development, professionalism, consultation and democracy. How can one talk of hierarchy when the suggestions from the DES for practice within schools seem to be for just the opposite?

But here, surely, is the problem. Suggestions for more democracy in schools tend to come from those above, and only for within the school situation. Heads are asked to implement change in a democratic way by a government that is instructing them as to the type of change in a hierarchical manner. One has only to look at the powers that the Secretary of State for Education created for himself in the 1980s – well over a hundred new powers in the 1988 Education Act alone (Simon, 1988) – to realize that flat forms of management are fine as long as they remain at the bottom of the educational hierarchy.

What appears to be happening is that some of the more progressive forms of business management are being advocated for internal school organization. The writings of people like Peters and Waterman (1982) are advocated as indicators of good practice within the school. But when it comes to the management of schools by those outside them, such progressive attitudes tend to disappear, and more repressive forms raise their heads, with only cosmetic attempts at consultation. A clear example of this in the UK was over the 1988 Education Act, when interested parties were informed that a series of 'consultation' papers, covering the main proposed measures of the Act, were to be issued at the end of July, 1987. The problem with this was that responses were to be returned to the DES by the end of September of that year. This was an impossibly short time in which to consult on proposals so important and far-reaching – the 1919 and 1944 Acts had two *years* rather than two months of consultation. It is also of interest to note in this context that the consultation exercise took place at precisely that time of the year when interested bodies were on holiday and so least able to respond. How would you describe the management style of a headteacher who pushed through such fundamental reforms in his or her school during the school holidays?

There can be little doubt in anybody's mind just what would happen if the style of management conducive to self-development, professionalism, consultation and democracy produced school staffs which fundamentally disagreed with the DES on matters of teaching styles, on curriculum emphasis, on evaluation and accountability. Such a style, I would argue, is only acceptable within strict limits set down within a hierarchical model. Such a style may be appealing to those who do not look beyond the school, and who do not question what is happening to education on a national scale. For those who do, present trends are characterized more by autocracy and manipulation than by devolution and a respect for professionalism.

## (i) The way to improve performance is through competition

Few people would deny that competition can and does act as a strong motivator, providing enjoyment, fulfilment and better service. Indeed, those within the business world would probably see competition between firms as the essential motive force for the way firms are organized and run. There is, therefore, strong support for the idea that competition between firms is valuable in giving customers the best value for money, and in making firms strive for an advantage in selling their wares or services. However, there *are* myths about the effectiveness of competition which need to be dealt with. An initial problem within business is that of the idea of competition *within* firms. Whilst competition between firms is probably the core component of a free-market economy, there is much less to be said for competition within them. Certainly, some businesses have worked on the idea not only of competition with their business rivals as the spur to success, but also of competition between individuals within the same firm as the key to improved individual performance. Harold Geneen's tenure at AT&T is a classic example of such a philosophy. However, what evidence there is suggests that internal competition becomes more easily destructive than constructive. For example, Belbin's (1981) work in identifying the characteristics of people who make the best teams in business showed that those teams which really could act like teams, who could co-operate together, rather than competing with each other, did most successfully. Interestingly, his experiences in forming such teams, and in then running exercises with them, led him to the conclusion that co-operation, valuable as it was, was alien to most individuals. Their initial reaction was to compete, not just with other teams, but with those within their own team. Rather than ascribing this to some 'natural' competitive instinct (which previous evidence in Chapter 6 has shown to be incorrect), Belbin argues that the basis for this destructive competitiveness lies in early formative experiences, particularly in schooling. As he says,

> Overconcentration on becoming top boy in the class provides an unconscious training in anti-teamwork.
>
> (Belbin, 1981, p. 13)

Thus, even at the business level, competition and co-operation need to be balanced if a company is to be successful. At the educational level this problem is translated into the fact that it is very much a matter of value judgement as to exactly what constitutes a 'company'. The entire strategy throughout education in the UK of setting targets and developing budgets was specifically designed to engender a sense of competition between individual units, with the clear aim of improving efficiency and performance in general. In terms of education, a school was clearly seen as being a company. The change in ideology and hence in practice is very easy to see. Instead of viewing themselves as integral parts of an educational authority, working both with each other and with the officers of that authority to provide a comprehensive service to parents and children, schools must now of necessity view themselves as independent units, working against one another in the competition for children in their schools. This change in perspective – and practice – can exhibit itself at the level of a head ringing another for advice. In the past, there would be few problems with such an action, for both were working towards the same goal. However, with the advent of direct competition between schools, and if numbers on roll are precarious, the headteacher being asked might well consider whether limiting such help and information to a potential competitor will be to the advantage of his or her own institution. Moreover, where finance is devolved down to heads and governing bodies, and they have to make the difficult decisions about dismissing staff when numbers decline, the relationship between head, governors and staff begins to change radically from one in which they perceive each other as members of a team in a co-operative endeavour, to one in which some are bosses and some are workers. When many of the most successful companies throughout the world devote considerable time, energy and resources to reducing the distinction and distance between these two groups in a company, it seems extremely curious that current legislation should be actually encouraging such divisions.

Competition, adopted as a simplistic free-market mechanism, would probably lead to the kinds of operations used for selling products in the shop, and increasingly in politics – a quick slogan, a catchy phrase, a simplistic idea designed to appeal to those without the time, or sometimes the interest, to appreciate the richness, the paradoxes, the variety of problems. If consumerism has a point in education, it is the (ethical) point that those affected should also be consulted, and this applies to parents and to children as well. It means their involvement, their consultation, and also their eduction, for it would be a retrograde step for education if those making decisions about its content, structure or organization were not aware of the complexities within it. Concerns, then, about standards and quality in education should not be addressed by the threat of extinction, but by the closer involvement of all those engaged in the process. The literature is too strong in its conclusion that leaving practices and standards to be determined only by the professionals is inadequate (Lipsky, 1980): other voices need to be heard. Closer collaboration between interested bodies is the best way forward to an improved and more responsive service. It suggests that co-operation within a team is the answer, but a team whose members are increased to bring in other parties besides the traditional ones. It does not suggest that the best way forward is to set professionals at each other's throats.

## WHAT CAN BE BORROWED?

There would seem to be a number of things that could profitably be translated from other contexts and used in education, but they are not the kind of things which can be taken down ready-made from the shelf and bolted onto the educational organization. They must be moulded, adapted, re-invented almost. In so doing, one is refusing the quick prescription from those who should know better, and one is urging sensitive adaptation by practitioners. Correct utilization, then, necessarily demands the acceptance of teacher professionalism.

A first requirement would be a good knowledge of business-theory history, not because business theory *per se* has so much to tell schools, but because many concepts are common to both. An acquaintance with the problems which business theory has wrestled with over the last 80 years or so may help teachers to take less time in arriving at suitable methods for their own organizations. Thus, the work of Michael Rose (1985) on the development of theories about industrial behaviour, or the analysis of the history of American business theory by Richard Scott (1978), using the two dimensions of open/closed and social/rational, may have mileage for educational readers – if only to alert them to which ends of these continua they are being exposed in current prescriptions for 'good educational-management practice'. Similarly, the models which have been suggested for business may find a place in educational theory, in helping the educationalist to better understand what he or she is doing. For example, things like Handy's (1985) gods of management, or Deal and Kennedy's (1982) corporate cultures, may provide a theoretical framework within which one can conceptualize the kinds of changes that have been happening to organizational and leadership styles in schools in the last ten to fifteen years or so. Certainly, people like Holt (1987) have begun to use them to good effect. In similar vein, a knowledge of Morgan's (1985) metaphors for organizational analysis may well do the same kind of job.

A second translation would be at the level of saying something about organizations and the human condition which strikes a deep chord, and makes one sensitive to the direction one must face, the perspective one must adopt, if one is to use the correct strategies in a specifically educational context. Is the following, for example, *only* about the Roman Empire?

> One reason why the Roman Empire grew so large and survived so long – a prodigious feat of management – is that there was no railway, car, airplane, radio, paper, or telephone. Above all, no telephone. And therefore you could not maintain any illusion of direct control over a general or provincial governor, you could not feel at the back of your mind that you could ring him up, or he could ring you, if a situation cropped up which was too much for him, or that you could fly over and sort things out if they started to get into a mess. You appointed him, you watched his chariot and baggage train disappear over the hill in a cloud of dust, and that was that. There was, therefore, no question of appointing a man who was not fully trained, or not quite up to the job; you knew that everything depended on his being the best man for the job before he set off. And so you took great care in selecting him; but more than that, you made sure that he knew all about Rome and Roman government and the Roman army before he went out.
>
> (Jay, 1967, pp. 63–4)

This says timeless things about the selection of staff, about getting the philosophy of the organization right before anything else can happen, about the necessity of centring around core values. It says that if you get these right, then much of the niggly, form-filling, bureaucratic, demarcational style of management becomes not only superfluous but also positively damaging. It does not say *how* one selects staff, nor which values must form the core – these will be peculiar to the organization – but it does say something vitally important, something which swings one's whole conception of organization facing in one direction rather than in another.

Similarly, the old story of the three stone-cutters talking about what they are doing expresses a deep point about what it takes to think like a manager. The stone-cutter who says (a) 'I am making a living', clearly is not thinking like one, the stone-cutter who says (b) 'I am making the best job of stone-cutting in the entire country', is someway there, and the one who says (c) 'I am building a cathedral', clearly is. Asking why their replies tell us so much about their understanding of management elicits answers which are directly translatable into any organizational context. One needs a vision of the entire project to be a manager. This, of course, is why the good class teacher does not always make the good headteacher. And sometimes, it is through distancing the problem, through asking the class teacher about the stone-cutters, that he or she comes to realize what his or her problem is. The wood is sometimes seen better when the trees are not educational.

Finally, many aspects of the human psyche are translatable into all forms of management. Look, for example, at Drucker's (1968, pp. 324–5) description of humanity's reaction to change:

> Change is not only an intellectual process but a psychological one as well. It is not true ... that human nature resists change. On the contrary, no being in heaven or earth is greedier for new things. But there are conditions for man's psychological readiness to change. The change must appear rational to him; man always presents to himself as rational even his most irrational, even erratic changes. It must appear an improvement. And it must not be so rapid nor so great as to obliterate the psychological landmarks which make a man feel at home: his understanding of his work, his relations to his fellow-workers, his concepts of skill, prestige and social standing in certain jobs and so forth. Change will meet resistance unless it clearly and visibly strengthens man's psychological security; and man being mortal, frail and limited, his security is always precarious.

This is prescriptive, but at a level which allows its artistic rather than mechanical translation, and therefore allows its fit to the idiosyncrasies of institutions and people.

In like manner, Peters and Waterman's (1982, pp. 55–6) research into America's most successful companies led them to suggest that the following factors about human nature must be taken into account when devising any system of organization:

1. We are 'suckers for praise', and whilst we aren't really as good as we like to think we are, it's demotivating to rub our noses too much in reality.
2. We're as much intuitive as rational. 'Does it feel good?' is as important as 'Does it add up?' or 'Can I prove it?'

3. Experience is an excellent teacher – it allows us to store patterns to evaluate future situations.
4. We are strongly motivated by external rewards and punishments, but we are also strongly self-motivated.
5. People believe in actions more than words, and evaluate you accordingly.
6. We need meaning in our lives, and will sacrifice a great deal to institutions that provide it, but we also need independence, to feel we are in charge of our destinies.

These kinds of insights are as applicable to the educational as the business organization, but again *how* they are translated will depend upon the organization – and thus will be best translated by those who know such organizations intimately.

What these suggest is a consciousness-raising exercise of such insights by the DES, by the LEAs, by the universities, and by the management teams of schools, and the devolving of the implementation of such insights down to the class teacher, for only those at the chalk face can know the particular applications necessary.

## CONCLUSION

The conclusion will not be the one that those seeking quick or management-led solutions will enjoy. Management theory came to education from business mainly because education had systematized so little of the subject itself. Proponents of the adoption of business strategies may feel slightly rebuffed – and suspect an irrational conservatism at the bottom of the tentative reaction to their transference – but that is how it must be. Insights from business may be extremely suggestive, but need to be couched in the terms peculiar to education. The theory must be transformed before it can be accepted, and it must be implemented by those who know the particular institutions. It means, unpalatably for many in the upper echelons of the educational hierarchy, that whilst they may prescribe general principles, these general principles must be based upon a belief in the teacher's professionalism, upon a relaxing of central control and a devolvement down to schools. Whilst much of the legislation of the past fifteen years or more in the UK appears to run counter to this argument, this does not affect its validity. If good management practice is wanted in education, then control defeats this purpose, for it strangles the very qualities it is seeking to implement. The practice of management in the schools must be entrusted to those who practise it. As one commentator said,

> It is an injustice, a grave evil, and a disturbance of right order for a large and higher organization to arrogate to itself functions which can be performed efficiently by smaller and lower bodies.
>
> (Handy, 1985, p. 185)

And that was said by Pope Pius XI, head of the Roman Catholic Church, an organization not noted for its devolutionary tendencies.

# Chapter 9

# What can we learn from the Japanese?

## INTRODUCTION

If educationalists are constantly being urged to learn from business and industry, business and industry in the UK and in the US are constantly being urged to learn from the Japanese. Such exhortations are also beginning to be heard *vis-à-vis* education. The rise of Japanese influence, first in the Pacific, and now in the world as a whole, is nothing short of phenomenal. Crippled, humiliated, totally defeated after the Second World War, it has come to be, as from 1990, the world's richest nation. There is, then, extremely good reason for examining such a prodigious rise. This chapter, therefore, will be devoted to an examination of the organization and behaviour of Japanese culture, education and business. An examination of all three is necessary, for Japanese cultural history explains why Japanese capitalist and entrepreneurial activity has taken such a distinctive turn, and how this in turn has led to the particular form that Japanese education and its organization takes. Despite Japan's economic success, the picture, it will become clear, is not an entirely positive one, nor is it one which Western societies could copy wholeheartedly. There is much to be learnt, much to be appreciated, but much to be avoided, or accepted as unworkable, in Western democracies. As Merry White (1987, p. 8) put it, we should hold Japan up as a mirror, not as a blueprint.

## HISTORICAL AND CULTURAL BACKGROUND

In common with other countries, much of Japan's individuality can be learnt from studying its past. It is isolated geographically, and culturally homogeneous, and from early in its history there has been a stress upon harmony and like-mindedness. When Prince Shotoku established the first centralized state in AD 604, *wa* (concord) was established as the most important societal and communal principle. In the seventeenth century, the Tokugawa rulers, in order to strengthen their control over the country, increased this sense of oneness by making a conscious effort to isolate Japan even further, banning, in 1614, all foreign missionaries, and going on not only to prohibit all further intercourse with foreigners, but also proclaiming that any Japanese who tried to leave the country did so under punishment of death, as did any who tried to return. Only a few Dutch and Chinese continued to trade, and this only from a small island in Nagasaki harbour. In addition to this, the Tokugawa shogunate established a rigid feudal system in which the *daimyo* (the feudal lords) were given virtual autonomy within their territories, but were controlled by a system of spies and hostages, and having to spend alternate years in the capital of Edo (Tokyo). The common people were controlled by means of a set of meticulous rules, which governed not only their manner of social intercourse, but also their work, their clothing, and even the way they ate. A person could thus only have individual identity commensurate with his social status. Along with *wa*, the moral code of *bushido*, or self-sacrifice and self-effacement, was enforced to such an extent that it became 'natural' for individuals to regard the highest virtue as serving their feudal lord. Other related virtues of *on* (obligation), *giri* (duty) and *gaman* (patience) became so much a part of the Japanese psyche that they have infiltrated all aspects and all levels of the society. Individualism, and independence from others, simply was not possible, and is regarded as abnormal today. Personal development was achieved through harmony, self-sacrifice, dependence and service, instead of, as in the West, in spite of them. The norm, then, became predominantly one of hierarchy, a fact reflected in the Japanese language and manners today. Differences in terms of address are used between older and younger, senior and junior, and even those only months apart in appointment within the same company. Brother and sister address each other in terms of whether they are older or younger. From the earliest age, the Japanese see themselves in relational, hierarchical contexts. As Ohta (1986) points out, Wittgenstein's dictum that the limits of one's language determine the limits of one's world is especially marked for the Japanese.

This being the case, when, in 1853, Commodore Matthew Perry of the United States navy sailed his 'black ships' into Tokyo harbour and forced the Japanese to accommodate to the rest of the world, they were to do this in terms of rapid economic and industrial development, but with a very different social structure and approach from that of Western individualism. Theirs would be a communal, collaborative approach, one in which individual satisfaction would be located within the group, and in which groups would have distinct hierarchies of command and obedience. Whilst this renaissance would be accomplished under the new Meiji imperial dynasty, Masatsugu (1982, p. 10) is right when he argues that this

> ... is Japan's inheritance from the Tokugawa society – the belief that the virtues of self-sacrifice and self-effacement are not necessarily incompatible with those of self-assertion and interior self-possession, and that self-respect exists in the successful devotion of oneself to the group.

This development is accomplished within a fundamentally feudal society and outlook, with rigid distinctions between people, steep and unbroachable hierarchies, and clear and explicit class differences. By giving each person in society a defined role, by transforming the militaristic samurai into the leaders of business and industry, and by importing Western ideas, and then transforming them and running them in a distinctly Japanese manner, the Meiji dynasty accomplished in less than 50 years what many countries had taken hundreds to achieve: but all with a social structure very different from that of their Western counterparts.

And education? What role would it play? This was clearly stated by Mori Arinori, the Japanese Minister of Education in 1887, when he said

> ... it is a big mistake to think that the primary aims of education should reside in instruction in the 3R's ... what kinds of persons should we be relying upon our educational system to produce? The kind of person who will be the virtuous subject our Empire requires. What will these virtuous subjects be like? They will be Imperial subjects who completely fulfil

their duties, which means that when called upon to do so they will willingly give their lives for the State. Thus the aim of education is to cultivate persons who can be of service to the State and nation.

(Horio, 1988, p. 47)

The Meiji dynasty had clearly seen how they needed to learn from the Western industrialized nations, but were careful to take only what they needed, and then in a way which gave it a distinctively Japanese flavour. It was on such a basis that a fundamental distinction was drawn between scholarship and education in Japan in the 1880s, one in which education was not intended as an individually liberating experience, nor necessarily as an intellectually enlightening one, but rather as a socializing one with a very specific purpose in mind – the cultivation of persons who would be of service to the state. As Ohta (1986, p. 28) said,

... the school system took the part of a locomotive pulling the whole of the society towards modernisation.

Indeed, Horio (1988) argues that this distinction between scholarship and education, seemingly destroyed with the introduction of the 1947 Fundamental Law of Education, has increasingly been reinstated, though this time for economic rather than military–imperialist reasons. This topic will be returned to later in the chapter.

This process of socializing for conformity was aided by Japan differing markedly from Western society, where separate institutions evolved dealing with on the one hand public and wordly matters (through secular governmental and commercial institutions), and on the other personal and spiritual matters (through organized churches). Japan never made this division. Its moral codes, and its religions, notably Confucianism, Shinto and Buddhism, were blended in such a way that the public and the private were virtually inseparable. The result in this century has been a genuine contrast between the ways in which major concerns have been dealt with in the West and in Japan. The former has tended to look to organizational structures and formal systems to solve its problems, the latter rather more to social and spiritual means. What this means in practice is that Japanese management has tended to believe that one must attend to the whole person's needs within the subculture of the organization employing them before that person will be fully motivated to make a wholehearted contribution. This is the primary reason why the major Japanese companies offer the security of lifetime employment, deal with pensions, sickness benefit and housing, and even provide holidays for their workers. A welfare state does not exist because its functions are taken over by individual companies. The individual is not seen as having two separate parts – the part that goes to work, and a separate social part – but is seen as achieving fulfilment through all parts being woven into the same existential identity. Such a view of human beings reduces the likelihood of individuals being viewed either in the narrowly economic manner of free-market economics, or in the interchangeable, mass-production manner of scientific management and bureaucracy in general, though it does pose the problem of excessive involvement (as some would see it) in the personal life of the individual. The tension between individual and institution is played out in all societies, and Japan's response is clearly very different from the West's more individualistic approach.

## THE ROLE OF THE MOTHER

This difference between East and West is particularly well brought out with regard to the role of the mother and child-rearing. As White (1987) points out, Western children are generally raised to grow towards independence and away from their parents. It would be looked on as misguided practice were the parent to nurture the child to greater dependence as they grew older. And yet this is precisely the normal view in Japan, for it is the mother (and almost exclusively the mother) who sees it as her duty to ensure that as the child grows, so it comes to need her even more, for it is only in this way, by the gentlest of persuasion, that the child comes to be socialized into the acceptable mode of interdependency. It is, then, at the breast that the interdependency of the work group is created. White puts the matter succinctly when she says

> The American mother wants to see her child develop as a fully separate person, prepared to discern and select among choices life will offer, to maintain the value placed on the concept of 'freedom'. The Japanese mother wants to cement a bond, to merge with the child, to raise him prepared for other interpersonal linkages in life.
>
> (White, 1987, p. 41)

However, there are prices to be paid. The major link within the family is generally seen as between mother and child, and not husband and wife. There is a clear division of labour for most families, with the husband leaving for work early, and arriving home late, after the almost compulsory after-work socializing drink with superiors. The wife's job is to look after and raise the children, and any deviation from such duty by the mother is seen by society at large as 'selfishness' – selfishness because she wants to do other things like having a job, or spending time with other adults. But whilst most mothers *do* see their function as that of child-raiser and are happy to be accorded such a role, the job is a difficult one. Less and less does the extended family take some of the burden from the mother, and more and more is she an isolated housewife in a block of flats with no company save her children from morning to night. Even socializing with other mothers in a similar position is constrained, for it is more than likely that their husbands work for the same company, and there is always the danger of letting slip some piece of information which may go against him.

Were a woman to decide to choose a path in life which did not include motherhood, life would be difficult. Because the male is seen as the provider by most people in Japanese society, less is expected academically of the girl, and less will be spent on helping her. Perhaps the worst thing she could do would be to go to a prestigious university, for then she would be classed as virtually unmarriageable, being clearly not the sort who would be prepared to spend a life raising children. And if she did try to get into one of the major companies, she would find it extraordinarily difficult. This can be understood if the practice of management in Japan is examined more closely.

## THE JAPANESE APPRECIATION OF MANAGEMENT

The two major influences on the Japanese psyche mentioned above – that of a historical record of (sometimes enforced) hierarchy, harmony and self-effacement, and a constant conjunction of structural, social and spiritual matters – have blended to produce a quite distinctive Japanese approach to management. For example, the notion of ambiguity, uncertainty and subtlety are generally appreciated by the Japanese as being part of a life situation, and ones which should be worked with and accommodated to, rather than forced to premature resolution. As Aquila (1983, p. 182) puts it,

> ... the Japanese approach accepts that *human interaction and behavior are so complicated that it is impossible to formulate specific rules for all occasions.* (Italics in original)

Such a concept is much more difficult for Americans and Europeans to adopt, for the Western manager is encouraged to see himself as someone of action and decisiveness, where aims and objectives are clearly specified, and rationality and analysis are used to pin down the nature of the problem in order to resolve it as soon as possible. This, however, is not always the best manner of dealing with it. Sometimes to resolve a problem at too early a stage actually makes the situation worse. Pascale and Athos (1982) give an example of this through the problems of the regional manager of an airline, who is confronted by a deputation of cabin cleaners who complain that their white foreman is assigning them all the most unpleasant jobs. They have come to the top man to get him to change the situation immediately. A more bullish manager might have gone in with guns blazing, but this manager, a Mr Kemper, was more careful, more circumspect. There were, he realized, other issues at stake here, which would be seriously damaged by resolving the uncertainty too quickly. Pascale and Athos (1982, p. 88) outline his concerns succinctly:

> The challenge for Mr. Kemper was manifold. As a senior manager in a firm priding itself on its open-door policy, he sought to reaffirm the company commitment to having all levels of management open to communication from below. Moreover, the problem had clear racial overtones, which he needed to grasp and defuse lest the issue mushroom into something larger. Furthermore, he needed to conduct himself so as not to undercut the seven levels of management between himself and the supervisor of the aggrieved cleaners. Finally, there was the union issue. Although members of the airline mechanics union, the cleaners had chosen an independent channel outside the traditional grievance machinery. The problem had to be handled in such a way as not to offend the union or set precedents that would bring an avalanche of such grievances to Mr. Kemper's desk.

What Kemper needed, he realized, was time to listen to the cabin cleaners, to talk to the other interested parties, to 'massage' the problem down to the organizational level at which the dispute occurred, so that the organizational structure would not look irrelevant, and so that it could adjust to it and learn from the problem. At the same time, he had to maintain the cleaners' faith in his and the company's sincerity. His decision, then, was to take no decision, to hear the cleaners out, and to promise them that he would investigate the matter further.

Clearly, this is a management problem which any culture could face, Japanese, English or American. What makes it the more resolvable for the Japanese is that for them a good manager is one who can resist the drive to resolve a problem until he sees what is needed to resolve it. The Western manager, on the other hand, finds himself in a culture which places more value on speed of decision-making, incisiveness and clarity, sometimes to the detriment of the problem to be solved. As one American manager put it,

> It's tough choreographing a ballet when you've been trained as a boxer.
>
> (Pascale and Athos, 1982, p. 101)

Such emphasis upon restraint, upon the appreciation of ambiguity, is illustrated by the use of language. The word *ma* has no exact equivalent in English; what it does is to instruct the reader to stop and consider the word previously read before moving on. So in the Japanese poem

> Spring (*ma*) is dawn

the reader is asked to imagine what the word 'spring' evokes within him- or herself, and only then, with such images in the mind, move on to the completion of the metaphor. In such a way is the reader urged not to charge on, but to pause, reflect, and savour, before proceeding, for only in that way will the full richness of the situation become apparent.

Such ambiguity is also seen in the manner of social interaction. It is a fairly constant complaint by the uninitiated Westerner that Japanese business talks never seem to get anywhere, for whilst the Westerner is trying to clinch a deal, the Japanese party seems to be talking in circumlocutions, always hinting and suggesting, dwelling near the centre, but never staying there. This is not rudeness, nor lack of interest, but genuine and intended, an extension of the appreciation of ambiguity. Such conversational style allows each person to know the centre of concern, but for the issue to be examined completely and thoroughly, for *wa* (harmony) to be maintained, for neither party to 'lose face' by having a blanket refusal given. There is always room for more discussion, for the world is perceived as necessarily one of shades of grey, and not the more general Western world's black and whites. A Western exchange might go very much like this:

> 'I think we can do it this way.'
> 'No, I don't think we can.'

The Japanese equivalent is much more likely to be:

> 'It isn't that we can't do it this way.'
> 'Of course. Still, we couldn't deny that it couldn't be done, could we?'
>
> (Pascale and Athos, 1982, p. 99)

It is not surprising, then, to find that there are nineteen ways of saying 'no' in Japanese, for such variety allows for all of the above – for the extension of ambiguity, for the time for reflection, and the continuation of harmony. The culture, through its history of concern for others, and for the maintenance of harmonious relations, for seeking personal fulfilment through interdependent social relationships, has tended to provide a structure which is a very sophisticated mechanism for resolving conflicts and difficulties.

This is not, of course, to say that Western organizations cannot do the same thing, only that much of Western culture works against it, emphasizing as it does the (too) logical and the (too) clear and explicit. Ouchi's (1981) work comparing Japanese and American companies shows that many of the successful American ones employ the same kinds of techniques as the successful Japanese ones. Ouchi calls these the 'Theory Z' organizations. The key concepts for successful organizations – East or West – which Ouchi describes are ones already dealt with at some length. For high productivity, he suggests, you need both subtlety and trust. Subtlety is necessary simply because human relationships are subtle. As Ouchi (1981, p. 7) says,

> A foreman who knows his workers well can pinpoint personalities, decide who works well with whom, and thus put together work teams of maximal effectiveness. These subtleties can never be captured explicitly, and any bureaucratic rule will do violence to them.

Trust is essential, for only through it can one show the support, the respect that liberates people to give of their best. Workers, by being given their head, find their personal fulfilment through and in the company. This can only be built up over an extended period of time and through a variety of mechanisms instituted by the company. The lifetime employment and the other benefits mentioned above all aid in this process. Two more which have achieved some fame in the West will be mentioned here.

The first, the *ringi* system of management, brings out a consensus form of decision-making by beginning the process at the bottom. When a problem is encountered, it is given to someone at the bottom of the hierarchy, a new member of the team. He has to then sort out a strategy, which he passes to next up the ladder for approval. Only if this approval is given does it move on to the next. The newcomer, therefore, is not only being shown a faith in his abilities, but is also being tested with more than one sort of problem, for he is being asked to understand the culture of the organization, and what it and its members can and cannot tolerate. By the time the solution is agreed upon completely, a number of things have happened. Firstly, the problem has been so picked over that most if not all possible solutions have been aired. Secondly, because all have agreed to the eventual decision, implementation takes virtually no time at all. Lastly, the individual given the problem in the first place has not only been given a real boost to his self-esteem, but has also shown his abilities to the company, and found out about how it is structured and what its values are. The *ringi* process may be lengthy, but its benefits are substantial and long-lasting.

The second mechanism is that of the quality circle, which consists of small groups of workers, usually no more than ten, who meet on a regular basis (about one hour a week) to identify, analyse and solve a company's problems. Such meetings seek to increase efficiency, improve product quality and improve communication. Their benefits are well testified, and work on the anti-bureaucratic principles that (1) staff should take personal responsibility for the success or failure of the company, and (2) those people closest to the product are more likely to produce creative solutions to difficulties. Clearly, both of these mechanisms have underlying principles which could be of major benefit to education, and this will be returned to later.

Another significant spin-off from such social arrangements is that the individual worker, because he is committed to long-term relationships, and because he is raised in a culture which views the individual as achieving individual identity through the group, is cushioned, aided and cared for by the group. If a member of a team makes a mistake, he feels the shame of that mistake; but if he has a success, the rest share in the glory as well. This explains the story recounted by Ouchi of an American company who set up a factory in Japan, and installed a suggestion box, with the promise of rewards for individuals who made helpful suggestions. For the first few weeks not one suggestion came in. The American management were puzzled, until they asked one of the workers why no suggestions were being made. The answer was simple, granted one understood Japanese psychology: the workers believed that no one person was deserving of a reward, as each worked within a team who supported and inspired them. If a suggestion came from the lips of one, it was the inspiration of many. On the basis of this, the management made a small change to the suggestion box. From now on, rewards would be given to *groups* who made suggestions rather than individuals. The suggestions came flooding in.

The lifetime employment also works in another beneficial way, for not only does it provide security and display trust in the worker, but it also provides the opportunity for the worker to fully understand and be socialized to the company's values, which in turn means that much co-operative decision-making in the Japanese company can be subtle, trusting and intuitive, simply because the members of that company are so imbued with the company's values that they all begin from the same value premises. Because they begin from the same position, they will probably all reach the same decision. It is important to stress that it is only by having this commitment to the long term that trust and subtlety are possible in relationships, and it is only by trust and subtlety that the full commitment of the worker is achieved. This is in stark contrast to a (Western) company which is less convinced by the importance of long-term values. Fixated with the idea that productivity can be gained by focusing primarily on structures and systems, it takes a much shorter-term perspective. In such a company, people will not be selected from college and gradually socialized, but rather brought in at any point in their career (a Japanese company worker would have enormous difficulty moving from company to company, for the reasons given above). Such people arrive with different value stances, and are well aware that they may be 'let go' at any time in the future. When both companies and people have such short-term commitment, there is neither the time to socialize them into the company's values, nor the need or opportunity to inspire them with any sense of trust or responsibility to it. The problems for such companies are obvious. Not only do people within the same company clash through having different philosophies, but also there is not the time to build up the trust, subtlety and intimacy which liberates workers and allows them to harmonize their personal development with that of the company's. What must be instituted instead is an organization based on explicit rules, distance, formalities and contracts – the essence of bureaucracy. It explains Aquila's (1983, p. 185) remark that the Japanese believe Americans spend 10 per cent of the time making a decision, and 90 per cent of the time implementing it, whilst the Japanese spend 90 per cent of the time making the decision and 10 per cent of the time implementing it. The Japanese are much more concerned with getting the culture, and the homogeneity within it, right; after that is achieved, implementation is straightforward. The majority of American companies, on the other hand, with such short-term socialization, may make quick decisions, but then have to spend an inordinately long time communicating why and how to the workforce, who have not been socialized to the company's values.

This agrees substantially with the findings by Axelrod (1984) which argued that it is only by 'enlarging the vision of the future ' – by making future interactions certain, predictable, soon, and significant – that one induces co-operative behaviour in self-interested individuals. This applies to the behaviour of not only individuals but companies as well. It is precisely what Ouchi (1981, p. 34) is saying when he argues that

> A Japanese company committed to lifetime employment will go to great lengths to build loyalty among its employees by ensuring fair and humane treatment ... People committed to long-term relationships with one another have strong commitments to behave responsibly and equitably towards one another.

## IMPLICATIONS FOR EDUCATION

The description of Japanese management given so far raises significant questions about schools. It becomes even more clear that a school organization founded upon, or proceeding no further than, bureaucratic organization is not getting the best from its members, nor is it facilitating their personal, social and political development. When bureaucracy predominates, the essentials of good organizations *and* good social relations – subtlety, intimacy and trust – are stifled. Moreover, the free-market, competitive model does little better, for it also fails to utilize the strengths that groups can give to individuals. As Belbin (1981) said of the best kinds of groups, they are not the ones who incorporate only well-balanced individuals, but rather individuals who balance each other well. The market, by pitting individual against individual, prevents strengths from being expressed. Finally, if one of the great strengths of Japanese companies is their understanding of the need for clearly articulated values underlying the practice of the company, and their ability to imbue members with these values over an extended period of time, what does this say about schools, where staff arrive with very different educational values, little attempt is made to establish formally a set of values for the school as a whole, and even where it is, that set of values may well disappear when the head does? Pascale and Athos' (1982) examination of the management style of the three very different, but highly successful, managers – Harold Geneen at AT&T, Ed Carlson at United Airlines, and Konosuke Matsushita at Matsushita Electric Company – demonstrated that the only company whose philosophy survived the departure of its chief executive was

Matsushita, and that was because he was there considerably longer than the other two, because the company did not rely so completely upon his particular expertise to run, and because his company, more than the other two, recognized the importance of such underlying values, and spent considerably more time hiring and inducting employees, and reinforcing these values. If the recognition of the values that an organization wishes to adopt, and their deliberate implementation, are seen as crucial to the health of the organization and the individual (and this is perhaps the central message of this book), then many schools have a long way to go.

## PROBLEMS IN BUSINESS AND EDUCATIONAL PRACTICE

The Japanese employee whom this chapter has so far described works for the *zaibatsu* – the giant business combines, like Nissan, Honda, Matsushita, and Sony. Whilst much has been written that is positive, there are some commentaries, such as Wolf (1983), which suggest that the life of the blue-collar worker in the larger corporations is not as rosy as portrayed elsewhere. The critique takes the form of saying that the kind of culture and upbringing the Japanese are subjected to leads to little more than indoctrination, such that employees learn the importance of three 'virtues' which do little for them, but go a long way to explain the high production, and the lack of strikes – these being *on* (obligation), *giri* (duty) and *gaman* (patience, putting up with it).

Moreover, even the most enthusiastic commentators point out that the sorts of relationships which have so far been described only occur to any great extent in these major companies. Lifetime employment, for example, is only enjoyed by slightly less than one-third of the workforce. The rest – the other two-thirds – have no job security whatsoever. They work for the large numbers of smaller firms which service the major corporations. These smaller firms act as suppliers for the corporations, being unable to obtain the licences necessary to import the raw materials necessary for manufacture. Finally, and as Ouchi (1986, p. 25) points out, the major firms keep for themselves the stable and very profitable operations, and contract out to the smaller firms those services most susceptible to fluctuation. The result is that in a period of recession, it is the small firms that are the hardest hit, the ones which go out of business, and their employees – the two-thirds majority – who suffer the most. Whilst there are undoubted benefits and worthwhile insights to be gained from the Japanese experience, there are clearly major drawbacks.

Moreover, Ouchi (1981) makes the important point (and a quite jarring one in the context of a very positive book) that there is no more sexist and racist company than the Japanese one. This can be explained very much in terms of the scenario so far outlined. Where one has a culture geographically isolated, and characterized by conformism and identification to the group, it should come as little surprise that the in-group feeling will also be expressed in terms of the rejection of those perceived as the out-group. This may be expressed in terms of militarism and nationalism, and the repudiation of international perspectives. Picken (1986) gives two telling examples of this. The first is that of the Japanese government during the Second World War, who tried to stamp out all use of the English language. The Americans and British, by comparison, were actively training individuals in the Japanese language to improve the quality of their intelligence reports. The second concerns that of the Ministry of Education's reaction to the increasing examples of Japanese children returning from abroad being taunted and bullied by other children (and, in some cases, teachers) for being 'different', having gained international understandings and perspectives. The Ministry's reaction was to set up programmes to re-socialize these children.

At the company level, this xenophobia is not just reserved for the non-Japanese or women. It will be expressed as the rejection of those not of the same organization. Lifetime employment means lifetime socialization, and anyone who contemplates leaving one company for another knows that, if they do decide upon this course, assuming that another company will accept them, whatever position they had reached with their former company, they will be required to begin at the very bottom of the hierarchy again. Little wonder that few employees change company.

Further, Japanese education appears to suffer from other problems which many of the larger businesses appear to have avoided. For example, bureaucracy has always been and continues to be a major problem in a centralized system. It has already been pointed out that under the Meiji dynasty education had a very specific function to play, and was manipulated to fulfil it by a Ministry of Education which maintained a strong centralist grip over it. The reforms after the Second World War, instituted under strong American influence in order to democratize the system, reversed this process for a time. This, however, was only temporary. Cultural patterns are not changed overnight, particularly when reforms are seen as instituted by a foreign, conquering power. Moreover, and curiously, it was American concerns in the late 1940s, and early 1950s over too-enthusiastic demands for democracy, which smacked suspiciously of socialism and communism, which aided the implementation of legislation which reversed the trend. Local boards of education, originally made up of elected members to institute grass-roots democracy, were replaced in 1956 by boards of members nominated by central government. The system of teacher appraisal in 1957 ensured that teachers knew that appointment and promotion depended on meeting central government demands. The screening of textbook content in 1958 ensured what has amounted to effective censorship of what is taught in schools. Nationwide achievement tests measuring children's progress, instituted in 1961, provided further teacher control, and prevented individual variation. And advice on curriculum content, originally intended as little more than suggestions to teachers, has become rigid orthodoxy. Finally, teacher in-service education has increasingly been controlled and run by central government, rather than teacher organizations. The contrast, Horio (1988) argues, is that between the dissemination and indoctrination of ministry policy, and genuine problem-raising and problem-solving. In other words, through a variety of bureaucratized procedures, the government has extended its control over the content and aims of teaching.

## THE TYRANNY OF EXAMINATIONS

Many of the problems of Japanese education are encapsulated in the 'examination hell' towards which virtually all Japanese children are driven towards the end of their secondary-school years. A number of different factors force Japanese children to join in the examination marathon. Firstly, there is the peer pressure exerted by a child's fellow pupils: and we have already seen how Japanese children are treated if they are perceived as different from their fellows. Whilst there is some letting of hair down, the overriding imperative is one of work, work and more work. And in this pursuit the parents are generally more than happy to help. After all, the goal of most

Japanese parents for their children is much the same as that for parents the world over – to ensure that their children get a good start in life, that theirs will be a secure future. What more secure a future could one have than the guaranteed lifetime employment that the major corporations promise? And how does one enter these major corporations? By doing well at school. The answer, then, for parents is to make sure that this is precisely what their children do.

They are, of course, aided in this by the pervading values of *on*, *giri* and *gaman*, as well as by the Japanese predilection for conformity and harmony, for *wa*. One must add to these values that of *kuro* (suffering or hardship), the endurance of extreme mental and physical pressures, which the Japanese believe is good for the soul. Rohlen (Shimahara, 1986) described the inculcation of this in adult bank employees when, as the climax of a two-month training session, they were made to take part in a 25-mile walk, in the height of summer, and were forbidden to rest or drink during it. It is generally believed that both adults and children nurture their spiritual strength by participating in such endurance, and coming through it. For the child, this normally takes the form of intensive study, which allows the exhortation 'Pass with Four, Fail with Five' to be taken so seriously by children from the primary age onwards. And the meaning of the phrase? One can pass exams on four hours sleep per night, but five hours is courting disaster. It is this kind of admiration of the extreme which leads Picken (1986) to ask whether this is the root cause among Japan's youth of much-publicized suicides, nervous breakdowns and ulcers. Certainly, it helps to explain why in 1985 a high-school boy was beaten to death by a teacher in punishment for taking his hair dryer with him on a school trip. As Picken (1986) says (p. 62), 'the admiration of "toughness" can shade into exaltation of crude violence'.

Such engagement is further encouraged by the general belief that achievement is not based on innate intelligence, but rather more on effort. This is a major reason why state schools avoid ability groupings in classes, and why it is widely believed that anyone is capable of reaching the most prestigious universities, if enough time and effort is put into passing the necessary exams.

And exams do occupy a predominant part of the child's life. Whilst there are private, fee-paying universities in Japan, the Imperial Universities are free, so that there is ostensibly equal competition between rich and poor alike. However, to get into one entails a remarkable degree of hard work at the secondary level. Of course, the quality of secondary school that one goes to determines one's chances, so it is generally thought best to make sure by getting into a suitably positioned primary school. And, of course, to get into one of these entails the correct kindergarten . . . The result is brought out in a conversation graphically recounted by Ouchi (1981, p. 22), which is worth quoting in its entirety:

> My old friend . . . seemed somewhat subdued that evening, and I asked him what was on his mind. 'Well', he said, 'today is the day my four year old son, who is back in Tokyo, is taking the entrance examination for a special kindergarten. I'm pretty sure that he won't get in.' 'That's ridiculous' I replied. 'I've met your children – they're very bright and you have a terrific job, so of course he'll get in.' 'No' my friend responded, 'You don't understand. In this special kindergarten, there are only thirty

openings for more than 500 applicants. Of those 500, more than half have been going to a special summer school that does nothing but drill those children for eight hours a day, six days a week, in how to take the extrance exam for that one specific kindergarten. Although I earn a good wage, it's not nearly enough to afford one of those special schools, because they charge a tuition of $1,000 per week.' Of course, such special summer and after-school training does not end there, but continues through elementary, junior high, and high school, all to maximize the chances of a high score on the ultimate university entrance examinations.

The reason for schooling and examinations has changed with different demands. After Perry's entrance into Tokyo harbour in 1853, and with the Meiji restoration, there was a concerted attempt by the Japanese to industrialize rapidly, yet at the same time to retain the essence of the islands intact. A centrally directed and controlled education system was seen as a major vehicle for effecting this, and can be seen particularly in the teaching of *shushin*, or moral education, before and after the Second World War. Before the war it was essentially devoted to the teaching of the virtues described above, and was nationalistic, anti-internationalistic and increasingly militaristic. To quote Mori Arinori, the first Japanese Minister of Education:

> Education in the Japanese state is not intended to create people accomplished in the techniques of the arts and sciences, but rather to manufacture the persons required by the State. Rather than proceeding in accord with Western principle and methods, we should carefully follow the rules developed in the schools for training army officers ... In short education must be approached in basic conformity with the spirit of *chukun aikoku* [loyalty and patriotism].
>
> (Horio, 1988, p. 100)

After the Second World War, an essentially American-based school system and curriculum was instituted which aimed for universal education, decentralization, democratization and anti-militarism. This was initially accepted, but was then increasingly questioned in government circles as Japan overcame her sense of defeat and shame, prospered economically, and began to realize her influence and power upon the world stage. Many of the policies of pre-1945 were re-examined, and those instituted under American influence criticized or adapted. Interestingly, the major protagonists in the struggle for the shape of Japanese public education appear to be the Teachers' Union on the one hand, and the Ministry of Education on the other. It is the Teachers' Union which steadfastly holds on to the values of egalitarianism and co-operation within the system and it is the Ministry, under the influence of the ruling Liberal Democratic Party (both of whom are strongly involved with the major corporations), who wish to change the system. As White (1987, p. 171) rather neatly puts it,

> ... the 'liberals' want to conserve the system, while the 'conservatives' want to change it.

The result at the present time is that the schools exhibit a (by Western standards) fairly extreme (almost militaristic) conformity in manners, discipline and study – what Edmund King (1986, p. 80) calls its rigid formalities – and the continuing post-war tradition of unstreamed, egalitarian, co-operative teaching.

However, at the end of the school day, the vast majority of children swap institutions for the *juku*, the crammer school, the private fee-paying institutions which are the main vehicle for getting the children through the 'examination hell' of the secondary school. A particularly worrying trend exists in the escalating use of them: because over 85 per cent of children over elementary-school age and over 90 per cent at high-school age attend, there has been an inflation in the level of preparation for exams. Children *must* now attend *juku* if they are to stand any chance in the race. The race begins at what many would see as a ridiculously early age. Dore (1976, p. 49) reported that some elite nurseries require *parents* to undergo an entrance exam, as two-year-olds are believed to be too young to be tested. The *juku* exist for supplementary or revision teaching after normal school hours, over the weekends, and certainly during the holidays. The result is that there is little time for the average secondary child to socialize: only the unusual do not indulge in this activity, and we have seen how Japanese society reacts to the nonconformist. One has, then, the almost schizophrenic existence of the egalitarian, non-competitive state school, and the highly competitive private *juku*. Whilst media, parents and government alike seem to deplore the effects upon the youth of Japan, it seems that little is being done to change the system. For a start, whilst parents do not like putting too much pressure on their children, they see considerable good in the child enduring *kuru* (suffering or hardship), and coming through it. The result is an object lesson in what can happen when a system becomes *too* responsive to parental demands. Duke (1986) relates the experience of being at a PTA meeting where teachers were severely criticized by parents for not putting enough pressure on children to work harder. As Duke (1986, p. 42) says,

> Classroom teachers are well aware that their reputations as teachers, and the school's standing in the community, are evaluated primarily on the examination results of their students. Under these constraints, how can the school and its teachers develop individuality, especially with forty-five students in their class?

Moreover, if parents did not encourage such effort, and were not to send their children to the *juku*, this would not prevent others from encouraging theirs and sending *theirs*, and in so doing gaining a distinct advantage in the competition for the prized university place. And after all, the aim *is* to provide the child with the right start in life. The 'examination hell' is unpleasant, then, but is seen by many simply as having to be endured.

The political arguments over the examination hell are curious and convoluted. It would seem that the majority of teachers in the Japanese Teachers' Union would like to see the examination as the major indicator of future adult success done away with, and a more protracted and continuous assessment instituted. This, of course, would involve a major reorientation in the prevailing educational philosophy, and would need to convince both parents and political leaders before it had a chance. It will be clear that parents regard examinations as a merry-go-round, which they are either unwilling to get off, or to which they cannot see an alternative. The politicians, on the other hand, so a number of commentators believe, are genuinely concerned about the effects on some, but still regard it as a useful device which must be retained in one form or another. Thus Dore (1976, p. 10) comments sceptically.

> One suspects that Japan's more conservative leaders, though they are prepared to shake their heads over the system with those who deplore it, are secretly well-satisfied. The examination hell sorts the sheep out from the goats; a man who can't take the psychological strain would be no use anyway . . . And as long as you can keep adolescents, in those crucial years when they might otherwise be learning to enjoy themselves, glued to their textbooks from seven in the morning to eleven at night, the society should manage to stave off for quite a long while yet that hedonism which, as everybody knows, destroyed the Roman empire, knocked the stuffing out of Britain, and is currently spreading v.d. through the body politic of the U.S. . . . At least one suspects that must be what they are thinking.

Horio (1988) paints a rather more sophisticated picture. What one has at the moment is an extremely selective system based upon a school system still organized around an egalitarian philosophy. The result is that all pupils strive for the examinations. Now, under the rhetoric of more individualization of the curriculum, the government has in mind a selective school structure which will winnow out only the most capable to go through the examination hell. By suggesting that the curriculum needs to be expanded, diversified and opened up to much greater choice, the government would, argues Horio, be able to introduce a selective system, for not only could streaming be introduced within schools (the brighter children taking the more academic subjects), but there could be a clearer grading of schools even than today. All of this, Horio argues, is to service an industrial machine more efficiently than at present. This, for him, is the real tragedy of Japanese education: it has shifted from being the handmaiden of Japanese imperialism and militarism, to being the handmaiden of Japanese economic and industrial ambition.

Further, and particularly interesting in the light of previous material on the bifurcation of conservative politics in the UK and the US, Horio (1988, pp. 372–9) argues that there is no necessary contradiction between the tenets of the free market and moves towards greater centralization. Increased control is necessary to ensure that the opponents of free-market thinking are increasingly squeezed out of operation and out of the public consciousness. Only by increasing textbook censorship, by leading in-service training, by increasing the monitoring of teaching, so the argument goes, will the government be in a position to be able to liberalize the curriculum, and provide a greater choice of schools. In such a manner is the circle squared.

## GEMEINSCHAFT AND GESELLSCHAFT

Whilst some might applaud a greater choice for pupils, a move away from a cultural belief which pushes those not endowed with great natural ability to strive for the unattainable, and a curriculum more suited to different abilities, the reasons for such change are seen by some as cynical, and do not alter the underlying *raison d'être* of the system. The results, suggests Ohta (1986), are there for all to see. Schooling is not intended to further the personal, social and political development of a school's inhabitants, to produce what Tonnies (1957) called *Gemeinschaft* (the community), but rather to promote Japan's economic development. Japanese youngsters, Ohta (1986) claims, show all the symptoms of the effects of *Gesellschaft* (a system based on impersonal and bureaucratic relationships), suffering from what he calls (p. 27) 'aimless frustration'. Ohta (1986, p. 28) points to precisely the problems that the Aitutaki, mentioned previously, have encountered:

> ... as the material standard of living improves by the use of household appliances, children have been deprived of even the tiniest jobs in a family ... children no longer play any important roles in family life or in lives common to all in a regional community ... What has happened here has deprived children and adolescents of the basic experiences of handling everyday difficulties in a meaningful way and making friends within a communal group. In other words, the fundamental experiences indispensable to their making matured personalities have been lost.

A picture begins to emerge which strongly suggests that the Meiji restoration in the 1860s may have modernized Japan in an industrial sense, but did so through an essentially feudal political system, and feudal values. The educational system was simply moulded to fit this overall design – an industrial hegemony enjoyed by the *zaibatsu*, working hand-in-glove with the political elite, notably through the Ministry for International Trade and Industry. The American influence at the end of the Second World War has continued to some extent through the influence of the Teachers' Union, but it seems clear that in many respects this influence has been sidelined by both parents and the political–industrial hegemony through parental pressure and the use of the *juku*. Lip-service continues to be paid to co-operation and egalitarianism in state schools, but there are increasing signs that the recipients of this system are unhappy with it (though probably unable to vocalize why, or suggest an alternative), and the *zaibatsu* continue to be supplied with their socialized recruits.

## CONCLUSIONS

If the above analysis is correct, then a number of lessons can be learned by Western educationalists and politicians considering the shaping of Western educational systems in its likeness.

The first are cautionary lessons. Perhaps the most important of these lies in the fact that education in Japan fulfils a particular function within an overall societal design. Its structure and practices cannot simply be lifted and transplanted. As Sadler (1900) said nearly a century ago, educational systems are sensitive plants, which flourish in one soil, but do not necessarily do well when moved to another. The Japanese plant has roots intertwined with cultural, social, political and industrial influences and interests, and would almost certainly not respond to simple transplantation.

Moreover, the Japanese system raises the kinds of questions posed in the first chapter – of the ultimate values a society adopts and pursues through its schools. In this respect, Westerners can learn from the juxtaposition in Japanese culture of the values of personal development through co-operative endeavour (seen in Japanese state schools *and* certain of the larger companies) and the socializing of individuals for commercial–industrial purposes. Again, the achievement and transmission of such values must be located within a particular cultural history, but it is still necessary to consider whether Japan has got the balance right. As White (1987, p. 180) points out, it would appear that the West, seeing the economic success of Japan, is seduced into thinking that the educational system is similarly desirable. But one must again ask if economic success should be the major aim of a system, particularly if there are prices to be paid. Thus, even if some Japanese children are so socialized as to not only endure the rigours of the examination hell, but even positively enjoy the experience, do we wish the same for our children? Almost certainly, with current Western values, such rigour would be intolerable. So do we wish to institute the necessary socializing influences which *would* make such rigour tolerable? Again, this points one back to the ultimate values wished for a society. Educational management cannot duck such questions. To understand educational management, we must enquire as to the purposes of education, and to do this, we must enquire as to the ultimate purposes of the society in which we live, for, in the end, the main thrust of state education will be as a handmaiden to overall societal aims.

An increasing problem, highlighted in criticism of unrestricted free-market theory, but increasingly evident in industrialized countries, including Japan, is the development in society of *Gesellschaft* – the production of relationships characterized by practical concerns, impersonality, a lack of caring, and a lack of responsibility to each other. Strategies need to be instituted within organizations which re-create *Gemeinschaft* – the essence of community feelings, a social group united by common beliefs, with reciprocal understanding and obligation. As Whiting (1983, p. 152) puts it,

> . . . we need to encourage the young to feel responsible for siblings and younger community members, to feel responsible for the welfare of the social group, to interact in nonschool settings in work that is focused on the welfare of the group.

Some writers, like Brown and Solomon (1983), have begun work in this direction, by making suggestions for the restructuring of schools. Among their suggestions they include the following:

(a) School management:
   1. Mixing the ages of students at various levels from 2½ years onwards.
   2. Involving children on a regular basis in school and home chores with the approval and co-operation of parents.
   3. Involving an entire school in a programme to recognize and reward caring, helping, responsibility and other prosocial behaviour by the children in the school, the community, and at home.

(b) Class management:
1. Giving children from about the age of 6, with adult supervision, the responsibility for caring for younger children. This could range from playing and physical care to games and acting as tutors and teachers' assistants.
2. Using co-operative learning like the Jigsaw technique (Aronson *et al.*, 1978; Slavin *et al.*, 1985), which requires that children work with each other to master a lesson, as a regular part of the curriculum.
3. Involving children in programmes of activities for helping others, such as visiting old people or people in hospital.
4. Providing the children with opportunities to see adult models exhibiting prosocial behaviour.

(c) Curriculum management:
1. Involving children in the practice of role-playing, both as helper and victim, in situations involving persons in need of help or in distress.
2. Providing training in the development of empathy.

By the use of such strategies, it becomes possible to begin to counterbalance the kinds of relationships exhibited increasingly in free-market and industrialized countries, to create a philosophy of a community and society devoted primarily to the personal, social and political growth of its members, though it hardly needs to be said that the school cannot take the full responsibility in this area.

On the positive side, the enquiry in this chapter into the management strategies of a number of Japanese companies suggests that, with suitable caveats about the cultural-boundedness of such practices, neither thoroughgoing bureaucracy, nor competitive individualism, is necessary for a company to be successful. The values of subtlety, intimacy and trust can be seen to be desirable not only from a 'humane' point of view, but also from a pragmatic, productive point of view. Further, use of a *ringi* system of decision-making, and the introduction of quality circles, could be adapted to the school situation to increase the involvement, participation and personal growth of all involved. They would clearly signal to school inhabitants that no matter what their position was within the school community, they and their opinions mattered. Such strategies promote optimism in the belief that there can be an identity of interests between humane, personal and existential interests, and institutional and productive ones, and that exclusively bureaucratic and competitive theses can be rejected.

Finally, perhaps the major point to come out of this chapter is that the most successful companies, East and West, have clearly articulated value systems which employees know, respect and practice. And those companies which have remained at the top of their respective fields for decades have done so precisely because the values have been more important than the individual chief executive. Perhaps the major question which schools might ask themselves is whether it is possible to implement the same practice to a much greater extent than at present. For only by the creation of a continuous philosophy within a school – a set of educational values which transcends particular individuals – can those within the institution fully develop the kinds of relationships based on caring, intimacy and trust which characterize both the successful institution and the successsful relationship.

# Chapter 10

# Children, management and citizenship

## INTRODUCTION

If the management of business and industry is primarily concerned with the development, production and sale of products, with the ultimate aim of keeping a company profitable, the management of schools should be more centrally concerned with the personal, social and political development of the individuals within its sphere of responsibility. Children, then, should not be seen as products but as participants in the exercise of schooling. However, school management, for both ethical and practical reasons, must address the development of both the children and the adults within the institution. Both groups have developmental needs which a school can go a long way towards satisfying. And only by schools being seen as embodying good practice through their treatment of their adult members can pupils fully understand management processes. The next two chapters, then, will be concerned with the rights and responsibilities of these two groups.

Whilst there will be similar questions to address when considering pupils and adults, there will be different questions as well. The one most particular and most central to any discussion of the managerial involvement of pupils will be concerned simply with whether they are capable of benefiting from strategies which aim to further this development, for if they do not understand what is being asked of them, then precious time and resources are wasted in attempting something which should be left for later in life. Rights and responsibilities, it might be argued, only make sense when people are able to understand and profit from them.

Indeed, it seems fair to say that at the present time most people see involvement in the management of schools as something beyond the capabilities of pupils. Such doubts begin at a psychological level with deep-seated assumptions about children's abilities, an almost knee-jerk reaction that 'oh, they can't do that yet'. This is then translated into beliefs about pupils' involvement in school management. Handy (1984) tells the story of asking teachers at a large school how many people there were in the organization, and them quoting only the teachers in the school, leaving the children out of their calculation. These doubts are finally enacted legislatively, for example through the 1986 Education Act, which effectively removed pupils from school governing bodies. When such legislative psychological and managerial beliefs are interwoven, and are then incorporated into the framework of the school, they become part of the hidden curriculum of the institution, and part of the thinking of practitioners about how their places of work should run.

This chapter will run counter to such assumptions, and argue that pupils have a need and a right to be involved in the running and management of schools from a much earlier age than is normally assumed and are capable of profiting from this. This will be argued in four main stages. Firstly, a conception of the 'child' will be advanced which suggests that most present conceptions are not sufficiently catholic to capture the huge diversity of capabilities and behaviours, or are too conservative in their estimates of children's potentials. Secondly, the kinds of rights to which children should increasingly have access will be described. Thirdly, an assessment will be made of those arguments which purport to show that children should *not* have these rights. Central to this assessment will be an expanded and optimistic description of the concept of 'childhood' Finally, by looking in detail at what is believed to be the strongest of these arguments, the limited-rationality argument, and seeing why, in many respects, it fails, a view of pupils' involvement in school-management decisions will be arrived at which suggests the early and increasingly democratic involvement of the child, an expanded concept of political literacy and citizenship, and genuine benefits for both children and society.

## THE NOTION OF 'THE CHILD'

The very idea of a child's right to participate in school-management decisions can be a ridiculous notion, for how, it might be asked, can two-year-olds be expected to vote sensibly or make decisions crucial to their welfare? How can they be expected to participate in decision-making which involves the assemblage and balancing of a host of different but interacting factors, and the sensitive handling of a variety of different people's desires and motivations? The answer simply is that they can't. The very notion of children's rights can be a ludicrous idea. And it is usually with this kind of example that the whole idea is summarily dismissed.

Two things, however, should be noted about the above. Firstly, the person inclined to dismiss the notion of children's involvement should first ask the question 'What is a child?' This surely is crucial, for within the simple term 'child' resides a huge variety of definitions. As Franklin (1986, p. 7) points out, the present definition of childhood actually covers a wide age range from early infancy to late adolescence, and encompasses within it an enormous range of abilities, needs and potentials. If the 'child' is seventeen rather than two, then the notion of voting, debating, negotiating or taking important decisions makes much more sense.

Secondly, implicit in the argument against children's involvement is the acceptance that even if children *are* capable of exercising such rights, then they should not be allowed to do so. There may be a hidden agenda which disputes children's rights, which begins from a business–industrial premise, and which quietly asserts that children are in schools to be trained for their place in the workforce, and if their personal, social and political education conflicts with this, then it is this development that should suffer. This is an agenda that we need to be keenly aware of in the real world, but which, ethically at least, is not possible to sustain if we are determined that schools are to be utilized for educational purposes which value people for themselves and develop them for their personal betterment, rather than some industrial–managerial complex.

There are, it might be argued, strong similarities between arguments against children and against other groups like blacks or women having rights and involvement in decision-making processes within society as a whole. The hidden agenda – of their use as cheap sources of labour in an economic scheme of things – might well be the same as for children, and so might the more overt reasons given for their non-participation. Thus, if a section of the population is to be prevented from enjoying the same rights as the dominant group, then the first thing to do is to impugn their capabilities. If they are black, say that their IQ is significantly lower than that of whites – that they need to be treated in much the same way as children. Or if the disadvantaged group is one of women, argue that they are constitutionally, biologically or temperamentally unsuited to taking on the reins of responsibility that men normally have held in the past. If they are children, convey in the description of 'child' the idea of an emotionally immature, inexperienced, gauche, cognitively undeveloped person. Assert their incapacity and carry the argument. It is, therefore, very important to scotch this idea of there being one kind of 'child'. The variation is enormous, and one which a simple 'incapacity' argument cannot fairly counter without looking at individual cases much more closely.

## CHILDREN'S ABILITIES

Even granting this, one has to be enormously careful concerning assumptions about children's capabilities. These tend to be heavily ingrained, and yet there has been a steady stream of developmental psychological material over the last fifteen years or so which suggests that 'children' are much more capable of complex logical and moral thinking than had been believed by Piaget (Piaget and Inhelder, 1956; Piaget, 1977), who still exerts an enormous hold over current thought in this area. Wood (1988), for instance, in reviewing the research, is much more convinced by the thought of Vygotsky, and the possibility of increasing children's performance in a variety of areas by active teacher intervention, as opposed to the rather passive 'wait until the child is ready' philosophy suggested by Piagetian notions. Evidence comes now from a large variety of sources. Dunn's (1988) careful taping and examination of young children's understandings of social interactions shows a sophisticated understanding by preschoolers of such relationships. Similarly, Harris's (1989) extremely detailed examination of research into the development of young children's understanding of their own and others' emotions paints a similar and, for many, surprising picture of the early development of supposedly mature processes. Other research continues in the same vein. Johnson (1982), for example, showed that children of as little as eighteen months of age understood distress in another, and tried to do something about it. Borke (1971) demonstrated quite clearly that children of three and four years are quite capable of understanding another person's emotions and the kind of face they would have with such feelings. Both Hughes (1975) and Donaldson (1978) have also shown that children of much the same age can take the cognitive perspective of another and imagine how another person would see things from a different angle from themselves. Jahoda (1972) has produced research to show that young children of six to eight years are very aware of what alcoholic drinks look and taste like, of what sorts of behaviour people exhibit when they drink in quantity. They clearly understand the concept 'alcohol' – strongly suggesting that education in this area could start much earlier than is normally assumed. Furthermore, Davies (1984) produces evidence to suggest that it is not so much 'children' who are incapable, in some biologically predetermined sense, but rather that it is adults who impose their definitions and assumptions of 'childhood' upon children, who then conform to these adult expectations, and consequently undersell their abilities. In similar vein, Mueller (1972) found that three-, four- and five-year-olds were more verbally explicit when communicating with a person who could not see, compared with one who could: whilst Shatz and Gelman (1973) found a difference in the way in which four-year-olds speak to two-year-olds and to adults that was appropriate to the differential characteristics of the listeners.

It is therefore rather worrying to read a philosopher like Hobson (1984, p. 70), when considering methods of teaching, rather glibly stating

> In the early years it will be mainly a matter of instructing, with little in the way of intellectual backing or full rational explanation of what is taught . . .

The assumption here is that children cannot understand such matters; and yet there is not a single mention of any of the recent findings in developmental psychology. This kind of armchair philosophy enshrines existing dogma, and makes it that much more difficult to force a reappraisal.

Furthermore, since the seminal work of Ariès (1962), there has been a steady stream of historical studies suggesting that 'childhood' as such is not so much a biological event as a social construction, that 'childhood' as we know it is really an invention of little more than 300 years ago, caused, depending upon one's point of view, by the emergence of an education system (Ariès, 1962, pp. 306–7), changes from an extended to a nuclear conception of family structure (Shorter, 1976), the rise of capitalism (Hoyles, 1979), or the increasing maturity of parents (Demause, 1974). This emergence of childhood, it has been claimed, can be seen in such things as children being given special clothes distinct from adults; their having their own toys and games for the first time; a growing tendency to express children in art as children and not as miniature adults (Ariès, 1962); and a more friendly association of child with parent, characterized by a decline in the infant death rate (Demause, 1974).

To be fair, the evidence for the thesis is not conclusive. Pollock (1983) has taken considerable pains to point out the inaccuracies, exaggerations and poor source material of many commentaries, suggesting that the historical thesis is at best not as strong as its proponents would claim. But even allowing for this, such a theory, like the findings in development psychological theory, does make one sit up and re-think one's comfortable assumptions about what a 'child' is. The answer to the question 'what is a child?' must of necessity remain incomplete, but the areas of incompleteness do point to the idea that 'children' are considerably more capable than present adult society believes. Within certain limits (to be discussed later), it would seem that an optimistic, experimental approach to their capabilities is the most appropriate.

So an increased appreciation of children's abilities in many areas of thinking will have important implications for many areas of education. Firstly, the summary dismissal of children's involvement in decision-making in schools must be an unjustified one. There must be a pragmatic 'let's see' approach, and even initial failure by the children should not be taken as evidence of inability. As any practising teacher knows, inability to do something may come as much from previous adult expectations as from any developmental disability. When children have spent their careers in institutions which, in terms of both structure and dynamics, have excluded them from decision-making processes, and these institutions have clearly indicated the adult population's belief in the pupils' inability, is it any wonder that it may take time for children to believe that they can do these things?

Secondly, consideration of such research will suggest attitudes to values education for children. For example, if children have certain rights with regard to their development as autonomous beings, then education conducted in a didactic or indoctrinatory manner would breach these rights. Hand in hand with this would go the argument that even when children had not reached a level of maturity which allowed them to exercise these rights, space should be left for their development. For example, because many of the complexities of the ethics of nuclear power will be beyond the primary-school child, this indicates that these issues must be delayed in treatment, rather than a simplistic answer given. As Rawls (1971, p. 197), has argued, even were there a process for brainwashing people so that the outcome was that they would subsequently welcome their 'conversion', this would still not be morally justifiable. In like manner, just because children, on 'maturity', may embrace with enthusiasm the doctrines and dogmas of the faith in which they have been schooled early in life, this does not justify the approach.

Instead, an approach to education would be suggested which is tolerant and responsive to differences of opinion, and therefore allows the children to develop their own opinions within the framework of the school or the home. Such an attitude to education will be found to harmonize in interesting ways with the kind of subjectivist attitude already advocated, one which not only has implications for the holding and practising of values, and for epistemology in general, but also is aware of its tentativeness and changeable nature, is tolerant of criticism, is open-minded, and is aware of its fallibility.

## CHILDREN'S RIGHTS AND ARGUMENTS AGAINST

Do children, then, have any rights to participation in the management of schools? In this respect, there seem to be three distinct rights in particular which adults in our society enjoy, which are denied or severely limited when applied to children. These rights are:

1. the right to decision about their own actions;
2. the right to expression of opinions;
3. the right to involvement in institutional decisions.

Ranged against these rights for children, there appear to be four different arguments.

### (a) The power argument
This argues that adults are stronger than children, and until children acquire the physical strength and mental prowess to compete with adults, they must pay due deference. Little time will be spent on this argument, other than to say that whilst it undoubtedly is the case that some people do act in accordance with this argument, I can think of no *ethical* argument to support their doing so. Indeed, the use of such power clearly breaches a fundamental principle, that of an equality of respect for other human beings, regardless of their power or size.

## (b) The non-contributory argument

This suggests that because children have no financial stake in the running of schools, they should be debarred from decisions in their running. However, it might well be argued that it is precisely because they are financially dependent that they are most likely to be affected by decisions, and therefore must have a say. After all, it is precisely because unemployed adults, or the very poor, are financially dependent that they need a stake in the running of society, otherwise they might find themselves in an incomparably worse situation.

This is not to deny that adults should have a large say – after all, parents and teachers are the taxpayers, and so it *is* their money which builds the schools. But arguments that adults have a better knowledge of value for money are, strictly speaking, nothing to do with the non-contributory argument at all – they are claims relating to children's limited rationality, and we shall come to this now.

## (c) The limited-rationality argument

Simply stated, this argues that because of children's immature, unrefined reasoning processes, and their limited experience, their rights to participation should be drastically curtailed. Now a number of problems immediately present themselves with this argument. Firstly, as noted at the beginning of this chapter, the developmental evidence suggests that children are much more capable in their general abilities than is normally credited, and almost certainly could handle decisions better than normally imagined. At the very least, the limited-rationality argument must be tailored to such evidence. Secondly, there are enormous difficulties in simply determining when a child or an adult *is* capable of such decisions. Is, for example, Piaget's (Piaget and Inhelder, 1956) description of an abstract stage of reasoning in the human being the watershed for differentiating between child and adult? If so, then 12 to 14 years would seem to be the age at which the changeover is made – an age that most adults in our society would think far too young. And notice that this is using research which is now increasingly seen as too conservative in its estimate.

Even if criteria for 'mature' thinking could be established, it might still be argued that it is the child's experience in management that is lacking. Here we are in a Catch-22 situation. Children may not be granted the right to gain experience, because their experience is lacking! It is sometimes of a truism to say that things are only fully understood when practised. If many 'children' seem incapable of exercising rights, it may well be that this is not due to some biological immaturity, but more to a combination of lack of experience and practice in such skills, and, more importantly, lack of belief in their ability to do so, precisely because the society in which they have grown up has fed them with the idea that they *are* incapable. This is *not* to suggest that the world is peopled with little supermen and superwomen, but rather to suggest that unless people adopt high expectations of 'children's' capabilities, and give them the opportunity (and the belief) to try such skills out, how shall we ever know?

A further difficulty with this argument lies in the fact that adults may well have the required reasoning processes, but have lived such sheltered lives that they do not possess the range of experiences which particular 'children' have. There must be many cases, then, where adults (in the chronological sense of the word) do not meet any proposed criteria of reasoning and experience, whilst some children do. Wringe

(1981, p. 123) describes this problem as the distinction between 'normative' and 'institutional' definitions of maturity. He suggests rightly that the normative definition is logically prior to the institutional: that determining who should be classed as an adult must precede the legal definition of adulthood. The complaint is that there must be many more cases at present than most people would credit where the institutional violates the normative.

## (d) The apathy argument

This argument was touched on in Chapter 3 when, in describing the alienating and apathy-creating effects of bureaucracy, it was pointed out that, in the sphere of politics, these have not been regarded as wholly negative outcomes. Writers like Schumpeter (1943) have seen considerable merit in having a system of representation which involved as little participation by the electorate as possible. This was because the electorate were viewed as unskilled and very likely to make irrational and destabilizing decisions if given greater participation. Schumpeter (1943, p. 283) argues that 'the electoral mass is incapable of action other than a stampede', because the only thing that the ordinary man can understand is that of which he has everyday experience. When he has to deal with political affairs 'the sense of reality is . . . completely lost' and so, whenever he deals with such issues, he exhibits a 'lower level of mental performance' (Schumpeter, 1943, p. 270). Democracy, then, is seen as being rather like free-market economics; voters, like consumers, choose between policies/products offered by different parties/companies, but they do not take part in the productive process.

The argument, then, would be applied even more strongly to pupils, for, it would be argued, if adults are likely to make irrational and destabilizing choices, how much more so are children?

Against this, a number of things can be said.

Firstly, Schumpeter's argument could be used against himself for the increased participation of children in school management. If the argument boils down to lack of understanding because of the distance of processes from the ordinary person's experience, then it is quite clearly incorrect for the child and school management, precisely because the school and its organization is very much part of their normal experience. The question then becomes not whether participation at such a level is allowable (for clearly it conforms to the criterion of being within their everyday experience and understanding), but whether it would have an educative effect for participation in the wider, societal sphere.

This question can be substantially answered by referring to the work of Almond and Verba (1965) and Pateman (1970). Almond and Verba's cross-cultural study, covering the US, Great Britain, Italy and Mexico, strongly indicated that there existed a positive relationship between political participation and political efficacy: the more that structures and institutions exist within society, both at local and national level, which enable people to engage in influencing decisions, the more that they feel they can, and the more that they try to do so. Their work indicated, as did Pateman's survey, that individuals do benefit from local participation and make greater and more informed choices at the national level as a result of it. As Pateman (1970, p. 110) says,

The ordinary man might still be more interested in things nearer home, but the existence of a participatory society would mean that he was better able to assess the performance of representatives at the national level, better equipped to take decisions of national scope when the opportunity arose to do so, and better able to weigh up the impact of decisions taken by national representatives on his own life and immediate surroundings.

Crucially, and as Dickson (1975, pp. 9–10) says, 'commitment is a consequence – and not a pre-condition – of involvement'. This echoes a whole tradition of participative democracy, from writers like Rousseau, Mill and G. D. H. Cole to the present time, which suggests that the crucial role of institutions like schools lies in their educative power – democratic psychological characteristics are a *result* of the influence of institutions within which people are socialized, and *not* the preliminary qualification. Again, the research of people like Almond and Verba supports this assertion – the average individual is not, as Schumpeter and others would assert, basically fascist and totalitarian in outlook, and therefore not to be trusted with participation, but is the product of the society and institutions within which he or she lives. If such individuals have 'totalitarian' personalities, this is a criticism of existing society, and not of them. We become totalitarian in outlook by being constrained to act and think in this way; we learn to be better citizens by practising being such. And if one accepts the evidence of children's increasing rationality, then the evidence suggests that schools should play a vital role in this area. The argument from apathy, I suggest, can be discounted as being little more than a self-fulfilling prophecy. The focus of attention must return to the concept of limited rationality.

Applying the limited-rationality argument, then, to the right of children to involvement in the institutional decisions of schools, one can begin by dividing the notion of 'institutional decisions' into two categories:

1. decisions to do with the curriculum taught – with its composition, value orientation and selection;
2. decisions to do with the organization of the institution – with its efficient running and management.

## CHILDREN AND CURRICULAR DECISIONS

What, then, is one to make of the first category – the proposed right to institutional decisions with regard to the curricula? In this context, a good point is made by Moore and Lawton (1978, p. 262), when they argue that

> ... teachers are, to some extent, *authorities* on what they teach ... they must be authorities relative to those they are trying to educate ... Pupils are not authorities in this sphere, since if they were they would not be pupils. There is thus a conceptual connection between *educating* someone and being *an authority.*

This can clearly be the case without contradicting the stand of subjectivism which this book has taken, if it is accepted that there are different levels of subjectivity.

The teacher does not have to be all-knowing or infallible to be an authority for the child. Broadly speaking, what Moore and Lawton are bringing out is the distinction between the aims and objectives of an educational enterprise. The objectives, the lesson structures, the short-term teaching strategies, are, as we have argued, very much within the capacity of the average child to criticize. Who better to judge the quality of the food than those who are eating it? Having said this, one must add the large caveat that judgement also depends upon the food that one is used to eating, and what one likes to eat. Consumerism is a good argument to an extent, but one needs to be aware of their gastronomic experience and preferences before accepting the judgements of consumers.

Whilst a degree of participation is acceptable in terms of objectives, the aims, on the other hand, are rather more problematic. They are the long-term goals, the ultimate ideals pursued by the teacher. This, if properly done, is an immensely sophisticated enterprise, combining as it does reflection upon different philosophical ideals, the application of psychological findings, a grasp of the range of relevant content areas, the use of practicable and effective implementation strategies, and an ability to apply relevant and workable evaluation techniques. There must be a gulf of understanding and expertise – and authority – between teacher and pupil here, but a number of things can be said which indicate that the child should still not be left out of the consultation process.

For a start, a gradual education towards such an understanding can be seen as not only something which would enrich a child's enjoyment and appreciation of the area involved, but also part of the process of increasing their understanding and hence participation in the running of the school. The ability to communicate such concepts and issues should not be more beyond the capabilities of a teacher than the teaching of any subject, for both involve an appreciation of their deep structures, and an ability to understand and communicate these should be the essence of good teaching.

Moreover, there will come, very early in the child's education, situations which put teachers on the spot, where they can either acknowledge that there is more than one opinion upon the matter at hand, that they are not all-knowing authorities, or they can duck the issue and leave the educational aim of developing the child into a rational, questing, autonomous individual to some future teacher. What, for example, does the teacher answer when the child asks:

- Does God exist?
- Does grandma go to heaven when she dies?
- Is it wrong to eat meat?
- Is it wrong to fight wars?
- Do we go to hell if we are bad?

These are questions which can be and are asked by the youngest of schoolchildren. Much more is at stake than deciding between giving a quick 'yes' or 'no', which disposes of the question, or spending time on a more detailed answer. More important is the teacher's art and the child's autonomy – can he or she deal with this question in a manner which does not leave the child feeling marooned and adrift in a sea of uncertainties, but rather in a way which begins to open up for the child the huge areas of human knowledge – some would say all knowledge – where no answer can be final and definitive, which introduces to the child the infinite wonder and variety of human enquiry and existence? In all curricular areas where the subject under discussion is capable of different interpretations – literature, history, the social sciencies, and the sciences themselves (Chalmers, 1982) – this element of individual interpretation can and should be introduced at the start, and not as some top-dressing once the 'facts' are known.

The point is that if one of the aims of an educational establishment is to develop the child's sense of autonomy, then this must be recognized in matters curricular, as well as matters organizational. This is not just an epistemological point, but is a moral point as well. It is a child's right to be made aware of the differences of opinion, to know that an 'authority's' judgement is not the only one, and the acknowledgement of this right must inform the teaching of all subjects. This is not to undermine the authority of teachers, if by this is meant their greater degree of expertise in matters curricular when compared with the pupils. Nor is this to undermine the over-arching authority of logic and rationality which must apply for both pupil and teacher. It is to undermine, however, the authority of those teachers who *would* claim to be infallible and all-knowing.

An acknowledgement of children's rights and their developing responsibilities suggests that respect for their developing autonomy and rationality, and an understanding of the tentativeness and changeability of all curricular knowledge, come together in a mutually reinforcing way. As children develop in understanding, so they can come to see that teachers, like themselves, are only seekers after the truth. The teacher may be further along the journey, and can thus point to some of the paths the child may take, and some of the pitfalls to avoid. But the teacher, like the child, is still travelling. This necessitates that as the child progresses, the teacher increasingly acknowledges the child's developing grasp of the nature of learning. The paradox of teaching seems to be that a major criterion of its success must lie in the extent to which the pupil can progressively do without it.

## CHILDREN AND ORGANIZATIONAL DECISIONS

Regarding the second category, it is surely a deficiency in the running of the school if those taught are not consulted about the manner of their treatment, and about suggestions for improvement. Firstly, the reactions and suggestions of pupils constitute an invaluable source of assessment material. As Barry and Tye (1975, p. 98) remark,

> If there is one lesson more than another which teachers (including heads) need to learn, it is to talk less and listen more . . .

However, and more importantly, not to consult children would specifically be a failure to educate them towards democratic involvement within the community as a whole. Further than this, and as Jeffs (1988, p. 44) points out,

> . . . a clear relationship can be perceived between the long term health and survival of a democratic system and the ability of schools to prepare young people for their role as citizens.

We are talking not just about the rights of pupils, important as they are, but about the kind of society we wish to live in.

Quite clearly, we are beginning to talk of an inseparable link between the management and organization of schools, and the politics of school and society, for how schools are organized and managed, the role that is given to pupils within such institutions, will crucially affect their political literacy and and concept of citizenship in later life. There is therefore a great need to expand teachers' concept of political education in schools to one which recognizes that its existence enhances the educational function of schools. They must, moreover, come to acknowledge its function as more than a timetabled activity for certain, usually older, groups of students; it is something which must permeate the hidden curriculum of the school, and provide a political literacy which produces, through participation, an understanding of genuine citizenship.

There are clear barriers to this. Firstly, teachers must cease to view political or citizenship education as a member of that dangerous, slumbering species 'controversial issues', all of which are best left unwoken. They must, as Pollard (1988, p. 63) argues, come to the understanding that

> Controversial issues . . . have a place in the school curriculum not only because of the substantive importance of the issues which may be raised . . . but also because they provide an introduction to peaceful processes by which such issues can be fully aired and conflicts resolved. This is a very important educational experience for children and thus, in many ways, a condition for the future health of our democracy.

Pollard thus takes the argument one stage further. We are not talking about the introduction of political education as essential for future citizenship and democratic involvement, but of the introduction, as early as possible, of *all* controversial issues into the curriculum, precisely because they can be discussed in the one forum which encapsulates the best of the democratic process; active participation, conflict expressed within a framework which grants order and respect for one's opponents to express their point of view, the use of reasoned discussion. Can one think of a better way of introducing the process?

A second barrier is that of pupils themselves. The Newsom Report (1963, p. 16) argued that

> A man who is ignorant of the society in which he lives, who knows nothing of its place in the world and who has not thought about his place in it, is not a free man even though he has a vote. He is easy game for 'hidden persuaders'.

Yet Robert Stradling's survey (1977) showed that 80 to 90 per cent of school leavers were desperately lacking in the knowledge, skills or attitudes which would enable them to be effective citizens, whilst the DES (1983) reported that over 70 per cent of young people declared themselves to have little or no interest in politics. Here is ripe evidence for a Schumpeter-type analysis, and yet, as we have seen, such conclusions would be incorrect and unjust. When schools make so little attempt to democratize themselves, it is hardly surprising that pupils should show such little interest. And, as importantly, it prevents them from acquiring the kind of skills needed to participate effectively in later life.

A third barrier is one of adult resistance yet again, boiling down to a lack of belief in pupils' abilities. We are in a Catch-22 situation once more: children are not capable because they have not been given the opportunity, and they will not be given the opportunity because it is believed that they are not capable. In this respect, four pieces of research, all from different countries, are especially noteworthy.

The first, by Cohen (1981, p. 261), begins from the premise that

> ... only a tiny minority of the population have received enough basic training in politics to be conscious of their potential political role and to know how best to influence political decision-making. The channels of political communication may be blocked as much by ignorance as by apathy.

He goes on to describe an experiement in a Dutch primary school in participatory democracy which suggests (though it is insufficiently documented to prove) that political education in the early years is not a fanciful notion. Each class at this school elects two representatives who will represent the class in a monthly school 'Parliament' on issues which matter to them – questions like keeping animals at school, the various uses of the playground, or start and finish times of school. Minutes are taken and discussed by each class the next day. Some crucial details are left out of the account – such as the extent to which children's decisions are actually implemented – but the article reports that important political lessons are being learnt, such as that a class tends to elect no longer the most popular person, but the person most likely adequately to express their point of view. Further, it has been found that the children were much more likely to obey rules they had been instrumental in forming.

The second, by Stevens (1979) in the UK, uses the technique of recording conversations between children of primary age to show that, despite lack of help or training in this area, and a genuine problem with articulating thoughts, basic political concepts are being used in a quite sophisticated way. One can only guess at what such children would be capable of if the same time and patience were given to this areas as to say, the mechanics of reading or the development of computational ability. Again, one is struck by Vygotsky's concept of the 'zone of proximal development' (Wood, 1988, p. 124) – the gap between what children can do, and what they are capable of doing with adult help. This seems to me very clearly an area where such adult assistance would have immense benefits for individuals and society alike.

The third is the later work of Lawrence Kohlberg and his associates with secondary-school pupils in the US (Power *et al.*, 1989). For much of the 1960s and 1970s, Kohlberg's work was concerned with the effect of moral-dilemma discussions on children's moral and justice reasoning, but he became increasingly convinced of the necessity for such development to take place through the school's structuring as well as through instructional programmes in the classroom. It was for this reason that a number of experimental high schools were created: Cluster School in

Cambridge, Massachusetts; Scarsdale Alternative High School, New York; and School-within-a-School, in Brookline, Massachusetts. All are small in size, from 60 to 100 pupils, so that direct participatory democracy is possible. All are concerned with opening up to students the nature and necessity of school rules, for Kohlberg, like Durkheim before him, was convinced that schools cannot dispense with authority, for people must live together. It is the central purpose of these schools for the students and teachers to devise structures and rules by which they can live together as a community. They must learn, then, that citizenship involves responsibilities as well as rights. The research published so far indicates that students generally have higher reasoning on standard moral dilemmas than on practical issues, but that their scores improve with the students' continuing involvement in the 'just-community approach'. Further, and as one might expect, the process described has been a difficult, at times unpleasant, but educative experience for all involved. But then, when people have little or no experience of having to structure their own lives in schools, one should not expect an easy road.

The cluster schools, like the two examples described before, still suffer from being isolated experiments in a society which is not really sure if it wants to pick these ideas up and run with them. More chance of success comes with schools engaged in participatory democracy which have political and society's backing. The final example, then, is a description by Halsey (1983) of the Yugoslav education system, which has moved some considerable way towards the principle of school self-management, principally because the society as a whole is committed to this ideal. The smallest self-managing educational unit, what Halsey calls a BOAL (basic organization of associated labour), is an elementary or secondary school, which has a governing council of representatives from the school staff, local citizens and parents for elementary schools, and local work organizations and students for secondary schools. This clearly does not directly involve children as young as those in, for instance, the Dutch primary experiment described above, but it does have a number of things in its favour. For a start, it is not an isolated phenomenon, the creation or brainchild of an enterprising head and/or staff, existing in a society which looks on with interest, but sees no real connection between it and the concerns outside of the school. As stated above, the Yugoslav experience is undergirded by a societal belief in the value of self-management, and therefore such structures are bedded into the workings of society. Self-management, being an ideal sought by the community, is therefore that more likely to be encouraged and to succeed in schools. As Watson (1985, p. 22) points out,

> ... the expectation is that all students will end up working in self-managed enterprises, and that therefore they should have experienced and learned about the concept of self-management.

Whilst the participation of students only begins at the secondary level, all students see this participation from the earliest of ages, and begin to experience it once they reach senior school. There seems no reason why its prosecution at an earlier age should not bear excellent fruit, precisely because it is deemed important by society as well as by the school.

One final point is worth making about the Yugoslav experience: both Halsey

(1983) and Pateman (1970) note that the larger the organization, the more difficult direct participation becomes, the more representative democracy is needed, and the more is it the experience that this subverts the original enterprise. The answer is clear, and one echoed by the Kohlbergian experience, but also at other points throughout this book: schools, if they really desire to define personal, social and political development as their major task, need to find ways of reducing their size, or of breaking the institution down into smaller and more personal communities, so that direct participation becomes a genuine possibility.

## CONCLUSION

The final barrier, then, becomes very clear from all of the above; it is a lack of societal and political will. It seems to be an excellent example of where politicians can and should lead public opinion rather than merely follow it. So why do they appear to lack the political will? It can stem from a variety of sources – from ignorance of children's abilities (how many politicians know of Piaget's work, never mind the research after it?); from fear of raising the issue (it will probably lose rather than gain votes at first); from time pressure (there are other, more immediate concerns on the political agenda); or from a dislike of genuine participatory democracy (it is, after all, that much harder to control the political and economic process when people really do have a say).

However, to ignore this need – this right – represents much more than just inertia by politicians, parents, teachers and administrators. For, as Stevens (1979, p. 271) says,

> ... to ignore, educationally, a developing capacity for rationality in any area of knowledge constitutes an ideological stance per se.

Ignoring children's right and needs in this area – denying them a say in the management of schools – says an awful lot about the schools and the society in which they exist.

# Chapter 11

# Teachers and the ethics of participation

## INTRODUCTION

If the previous chapter discussed a subject still alien to many people, this chapter deals with one with which many people will feel more comfortable. Yet teachers, I believe, participate in management decisions far less than they should. Part of this is due to the way in which the concept of participation is normally viewed: both the business and educational literature tend to view participation as the gift of management, to be invited or withheld when it suits management's aims. This view of participation, it is argued, stems from limited managerial concerns in business and industry for improving relationships in the workplace, and/or concern for increased production. This chapter suggests that in education a further, ethical, dimension needs to be added, one which argues for participation as both the right and duty of teachers. Such a position is based upon the kind of position developed so far regarding a school management's ultimate purposes – that it must develop each person, whether child or adult, that it must be based upon an examination of the nature of the educational process, and that it must recognize the role that the school plays as an agent in the development of a society's citizens. If these arguments are accepted, they will have important consequences, not only for the role of both teachers and pupils in the management of schools, but, just as importantly, for their personal, social and political development.

## THE DECLINE OF TEACHERS' INFLUENCE

Throughout the Western world the teaching profession is very much on the defensive at the moment. This is particularly so in the UK. Over the last twenty years it has seen its power and influence diminishing, the real authority for decisions being shifted from the educators either to the governing body of the school (on which they have some, but fairly minimal, representation) or to the DES (which has become increasingly deaf to teachers' opinions or complaints). Decision-making is moving, it seems, inexorably away from the staffroom. There is a clear paradox in policy here, for one thrust of such policy decentralizes power, whilst another centralizes it. This, as pointed out in Chapter 7, is a reflection of the very real tension within British politics at the present time – the devolutionary beliefs of free-market thought, and the centralist tendencies of more traditionalist elements. Free-market thought, it has been argued, can be seen clearly in, for example, the policy of open enrolment, which attempts to put the power to select the school into the hands of the parents, as well as in moves towards the local management of schools, which are intended to increase the power of the governing bodies and the parents.

Centralist tendencies, on the other hand, can be seen in the creation of a national curriculum which has very largely taken away from teachers a say in the choice or amount of subjects to be taught in school, the concepts to be examined within these subjects, and those areas to be examined and assessed, and moved such decisions to Westminster. Further, despite the fact that it is claimed that teachers will be left to accomplish these tasks in the ways they think fit, it seems much more likely that teachers will be forced into compromising their pedagogy in order to accomplish the tasks at hand. It is clear, then, that there are forces moving decision-making upward and downward (or outward?), but away from teachers themselves. What has happened is that the teaching profession as a whole has hardly been consulted on probably the most sweeping educational changes of this century.

There would appear to be at least three reasons for this lack of consultation and participation by the teaching profession. The first, noted earlier in the book, is the belief, starting in the late 1960s and continuing to the present day, that education in the UK is in a bad way, and needs shaking up radically. Populist tirades like the Black Papers created the belief that education was a stumbling block rather than a catalyst on the road to national prosperity. Change within education was regarded as something too important to be left to the educators: if bad practice was the practice of the teaching body, then it would need an external force to change it. And clearly you do not consult with someone, or ask them to participate in putting their house in order, when you do not trust them.

The second and connected reason comes from part of the analysis of the problems of the welfare state performed by monetarist thinkers like Milton Friedman and Friedrich Hayek. As we have seen, they argue that part of the problem with the ideology of social democracy is that by expanding the role of government past the 'referee' status of free-market thinking, the welfare state takes on board a large number of interest groups who, through the protective qualities of nationalization and welfarism, come to control what is to be provided by the various institutions. The classic examples given are the health service and education. Those professionals who work within these sectors, it is argued, so control the structure and output that the consumer has very little say in how these services should be run. And crucially, they argue, it is for the customer/consumer to decide what is to be provided, for it is only through this mechanism that the institution can respond to what those using it really want. Without this pull, institutions will become (and have become) increasingly self-interested, unresponsive to the needs of those who use the service, and hence increasingly inefficient in producing what is really required. Clearly, if you subscribe to this scenario, then you are hardly likely to listen to the producers – the teachers – for they are the central reason for the problem in the first place. Indeed, one could go further than that, and be reasonably confident that arguments for participation are little more than the bleatings of the self-interested, and will only tell you precisely what you must *not* do.

The third argument is rather different from the other two, but makes the position even more perilous. It is that some teachers, especially but not only at the primary end of schooling, have shown a marked reluctance to seek this participation. Instead of giving the time and commitment at school necessary for the process, there have been, it would seem, many who have been happy to avoid this right, and have perceived it as little more than a burden. As this book has been arguing, participation and democracy in schools must be seen by staff as a duty rather than as just a right, for it is only by its practice that children can see what it could really mean in the larger world. Where staff abnegate their responsibility in this area, they present a role model to children which is destructive to the maturing of political attitudes, to the development of a true citizenship. This third argument suggests, then, that lack of participation stems not only from those at the top of the hierarchy of educational management, but also from the practices of those at the bottom. If there then exists a situation where those at the top do not wish to allow participation to those at the bottom who do not want it, very little is likely to happen. The results have been all too clear in recent years.

And yet, if there is an in-phrase in the educational management literature at the present time it is that of 'participative management'. Such phraseology, however, can be rather woolly, for there are considerable variations as to the meaning and applicability of the term. Firstly, it needs to be specified whether this participation is, as noted at the end of Chapter 3, *pseudo*-participation (where no real decision-making is allowed), *partial* participation (where equality of decision-making is not allowed, but influence is), or *full* participation (where there is equality of decision-making). This book has so far argued for a genuine form of participation, which confers upon participants a real opportunity to affect outcomes. This means going beyond pseudo-participation, and yet, as we shall see, much of the literature is actually advocating pseudo-participation, with less of the partial type, and very little full participation.

Secondly, Schein (1988) suggests that one should also consider that there are at least three different areas within which different types of participation might be considered. These are (1) the policies of the organization – its basic mission, its structure; (2) the design of the physical and social environment of the workplace itself; and (3) the implementation of the work. The interaction of these two dimensions is illustrated in Figure 11.1.

It will be clear that any combination of the two dimensions is possible, from full participation in the area of implementation, to pseudo-participation in the area of policy. Schein argues, I think correctly, that any form of participation is increasingly discouraged the more one moves from area (3) to area (1). However, it is interesting to note that this is not a particular problem for Schein. In describing a grid showing these job dimensions and the degrees of participation, Schein (1988, p. 135) says

> The purpose of this grid is to aid the leader or manager . . . in deciding how much involvement on the part of subordinates is appropriate to that decision area.

Participation is therefore seen, unproblematically, as a gift of management, rather than, as this chapter argues, a right and a duty of staff. Schein's is a view which will be constantly encountered. One thing from Schein's analysis which is particularly appropriate here, though, is the comment

> . . . in the final analysis, the degree to which organizational policies are handled participatively depends largely on the economic and political system within which the organization exists and what its basic mission is defined to be.
>
> (Schein, 1988, p. 135)

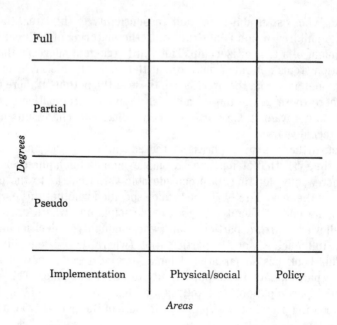

**Figure 11.1** A participation grid. After Pateman (1970) and Schein (1988).

The earlier chapters of this book have testifed to this particular insight. And yet, the days of the paternal headship are deemed, by some at least, to be now coming to an end, and a much more structured, professional approach is demanded. This entails the adoption of new management techniques, and, in this respect, educational management literature has generally followed the literature from business and industry. With the discriminations and caveats listed above in mind, it is clearly important to begin with an examination of this literature.

## THE PARTICIPATION LITERATURE

Dill (1964) argued that there are in fact five different reasons for employing participation in decision-making. These reasons are:

1. to ensure that decisions do get made, and that there is somebody with whom to talk over and evaluate the results;
2. to involve and motivate more people through making them feel that the decision was partly of their own creation;
3. to improve the quality of decisions by involving more of those who know something about the task at hand;
4. to train people in the handling and motivation of others;
5. to make decisions efficiently and without wasting time or manpower.

Dill quite rightly points out that these different reasons argue for different degrees of participation, and for participation by different people. Thus (1) and (5) might argue for very limited participation, whilst (2) might argue for participation by those involved in the decision, (3) for participation only by those who are experts, and (4) for participation only for those who are being trained for advancement.

Two things seems to be clear from this. The first is that all these forms of participation are again seen as the gift of management. This applies to education as much as to business and industry. Hoyle (1986, p. 99), for instance, talks of

> a balance between two forms of power, the legal authority of the head, and the professional authority of teachers

and sees the issue as translating into

> the structure for participation which heads establish as a function of their leadership style and teachers' responses to these structures.

Paisey (1983, p. 100) is even more clear:

> Original authority lies with the person appointed as head of school. One of the most important manifestations and applications of this authority is to decide on the levels of participation which the school as an organisation shall have.

Statutory power is therefore seen as the basis for participation. Participation is, then, the gift of management.

The second point to be noted is that Dill's five reasons appear to boil down to just two:

(1) that with participation you get better results;
(2) that with participation you achieve better relationships in the working environment.

The questions still remain as to what degree of participation is being used – pseudo-, partial or full – and in what areas – implementation, physical structure and policy. The fact that this is the gift of management suggests a leaning towards the 'pseudo' degree, and the implementation area, though the 'partial' degree and limited influence in the physical and policy areas would not seem to be excluded, if the balance of power remained with management, and the results justified this transference of influence over decisions.

## MANAGERIAL CONCERNS

The work described above clearly agrees with the concerns of managers described on the axes of the 'managerial grid' devised by Blake and Mouton (1985) (Figure 11.2). Here they argue that managers will show a tendency to emphasize one or other of these axes – either results or relationships – in their dealings. The emphasis on results is clear enough, for whilst profit maximization does not have to be a company's *raison d'être*, loss minimization must be the bottom line, for no matter how altruistic a company is, it will go out of business if it does not at least break even. However, the second emphasis – the wish to achieve better relationships within the working environment – needs rather more investigation. It might be a simple humanitarian concern for other human beings, and there are companies which place

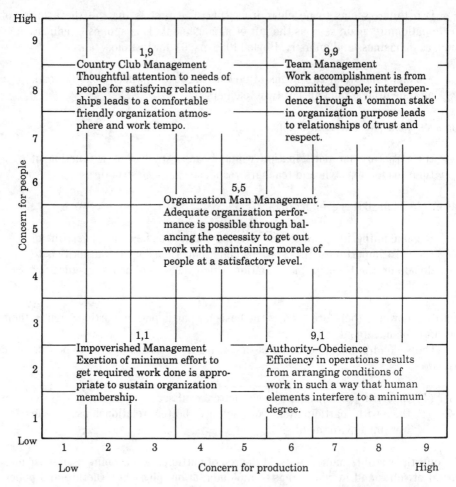

**Figure 11.2** A managerial grid. Source: Blake, Robert R. and Mouton, Jane Srygley, *The Managerial Grid III: The Key to Leadership Excellence*. Houston, Gulf Publishing Company, copyright © 1985, p. 12.

the welfare of their customers or workers high on their list of priorities for purely ethical reasons. It seems fair to say, however, that the relevant literature would not, on the whole, support such an interpretation. Much more common is the assumption that when better relationships are achieved, and people are happier, better results occur as well. Certainly, major organization theorists like Mayo, McGregor, Likert and Tannenbaum all begin from this premise. If this is the case, then it seems fair to say that the argument for participative management usually boils down to little more than an effective way of achieving better production. However, while there seems to be a fairly strong consensus of opinion that increasing participation does normally produce (1) better results and (2) better relationships, and therefore is worth pursuing, neither of the arguments is completely watertight.

## PARTICIPATION AND RESULTS

There is much argument and evidence to suggest that increasing participation does produce better results. At the common-sense level, any organization which can harness the enterprise, initiative and interest of its workers, and use their individual and local knowledge, is going to do better than one which does not use such energies. Writers like Fischer and Siriaani (1984) have gathered a great deal of evidence in favour of the idea that participation is necessary for the achievement of long-term efficiency, for precisely these reasons. At the international level as well, as we saw in Chapter 9, the Japanese use of participatory techniques such as the *ringi* form of consultation, and also of quality circles, is argued to be one of the major reasons why they are so enormously successful economically.

However, whilst the evidence for participation improving results is strong, there is some contrary evidence which needs to be noted. The research by Vroom (1984), for instance, showed that US business managers do not believe it to be an automatic benefit, and that in practice these managers varied their use of participative techniques with the particular factors in the situation. Vroom noted that the major factor behind such decisions was that of the *time* available: if these managers believed that action was needed almost immediately, and that the action was vital to the health of the organization, then they were less likely to consult. Indeed, the amount of time spent upon a particular problem was a good indicator of where these managers placed their immediate priorities. Where the task was more important, less time was spent; where staff development was a priority, more time was spent. The same task, then, might demand different strategies, depending upon the social relationships occurring in that place at that time.

So another major factor for these managers was the condition of the social relations within the group with which they were dealing. One gains some idea of the effect of group relationships on the effectiveness of participation by examining the results of exercises in group dynamics used on management courses. These may involve people being cast away on desert islands, on lunar landscapes, or in arctic conditions, and having to negotiate with other group members those articles they perceive as vital for survival. Clearly, one could use pseudo-, partial or full participation in such exercises. The results tend to show that the groups which are encouraged to use either partial or full participation tend to get the better scores in the end. However, the situation is not quite as simple as this statement makes it seem. Indeed, perhaps the most interesting situation is one of full participation where an unstructured group of people are placed in a room, given equal influence in making decisions, and told to arrive at a prioritized list. A number of things may happen, among which are the following:

- They may all get on, discuss rationally, and arrive quickly at a sensible list which gets higher marks than their individually completed sheets (unlikely).
- They may spend a lot of time discussing and eventually arrive at a consensus decision which is better than any individual decision (possible but unlikely).
- They may spend a lot of time resolving whose opinion is going to count (and not necessarily for rational reasons) before, after a long time, arriving at a number of decisions, held by different factions within the group who refuse to compromise (possible).

- They may spend a lot of time discussing and eventually arrive at a consensus decision which is better than the *average* of individual decisions, but not as good as some individual decisions on their own (possible, maybe probable).

Several things come out of such exercises. One is that democratically organized groups which encourage full and equal participation are not always the most efficient: those groups with an element of hierarchy and direction, which grant the authority to a leader to focus on specific issues, may well, in the short run, save time and avoid interpersonal confrontations. Having said this, it could plausibly be argued that as genuine participation is probably a new learning situation for many, some difficulties or even failures are to be expected, should be learned from, and worked through. Certainly, this has been the experience of Lawrence Kohlberg and his associates in the cluster schools, mentioned at the end of the last chapter.

Indeed, if elements of conflict are present where the object of the exercise is no more threatening than role-playing survival on the moon's surface, how much more so will this be when situations are real-life ones, and affect status, self-perception and self-esteem, promotion, personal values, and payment of the mortgage? If people can become entrenched over whether to give priority to a radio transmitter or to lunar flares, how much more so are they likely to when issues really *matter?* Thus, one of the major, if not *the* major, reasons for the William Tyndale debacle (Auld, 1980) was the unresolved differences of opinion within the staff over the introduction of radical curricular and methodological innovations, which were exacerbated by the democratically participative style espoused by the head, Terry Ellis. The study of Swidler (1979) of two free schools in Berkeley, California, highlighted the same kinds of problems when participative democracy is introduced. This is not to argue against genuine forms of participation, but rather to indicate that the education of people, adults or children in this process may not be a trouble-free one, and may cause some people to abandon the project. A first conclusion, then, might be that increasing participation may give better results, but these may only occur in the medium to long term. If partial or full participation is really desired, then arguments as to its effectiveness will give some support for its use, but probably not enough.

## PARTICIPATION AND RELATIONSHIPS

Perhaps the first question to ask here is how, specifically, relationships would be improved by greater participation. It could be argued that an answer might boil down to the four following reasons:

- people feel better if they are able to participate in decisions which affect them;
- people will therefore feel better about working for the organization, and this will result in better work;
- participation allows for the sharing of common goals, and the playing down of differences;
- 'management' and 'workers' have many things in common which can be highlighted by participative procedures.

And yet, whilst accepting the apparent common sense of much of this, much of the above suggests that participation is a learning process for those involved, and does not necessarily lead to the desired results overnight. People have expectations of themselves and their organizations caused by their previous socialization within them. Abilities to participate are not natural but learned, and if previous learning opportunities have been limited, one can at first expect problems. Because of the sheer unpredictability of human beings, and because managers are only human too, if not handled extremely sensitively, increased participation might have precisely the opposite effect on relationships from that intended.

Such cautions about the introduction of participation are supported by the work of people like Alutto and Belasco (1972), which indicated that desire by teachers for participation varied depending on age, sex, socio-economic position and marital status. Conway's (1980) findings that teachers' desire for participation depended upon the area of activity described also support the contention that the initial success of participation is conditioned by previous experience. Finally, the findings of Nias (1980), which demonstrated that many teachers are very happy to decline the opportunity for participation on the grounds that they have their area of autonomous responsibility within the classroom, and are happy to leave other decision-making to the 'humane' but 'positive' head, again suggest that there is some way to go in convincing teachers that participation is not only a right but a duty. Writers such as Campbell (1985) have not been slow to point out that this kind of 'restricted professional' attitude will not harmonize well with the demands for extra staff participation through increased emphasis on subject specialism and expertise in primary schools. This usually leads, initially at least, to more problems *between* staff, simply because they are having to collaborate in ways not seen when purely class teaching. This is perhaps the underlying reason for the reluctance of Nias's teachers to come out of the classroom, and one that substantially agrees with Conway's research: it demands considerably greater interpersonal skills with other adults, and is therefore far more stressful.

## THE NEED FOR AN ETHICAL AXIS IN MANAGEMENT CONCERNS

If anything can be concluded so far, it is that neither a concern for results, nor a concern for relationships, necessarily suggests that participation is the right way to achieve them. Participation as a management technique is in many situations neither necessary nor sufficient. There has to be a stronger justification for it than the two axes of Blake and Mouton's grid. There has to be a third axis. This, I suggest, is the ethical axis.

This ethical axis is clearly missing from the work of Vroom (1984), even though the title of his paper is 'A *normative* model of managerial decision making' (my italics). He moves from the description of a decision-making model to the report of how managers actually reach their decisions, and suggests that the latter is support for the former:

> A model designed to regulate, in some rational way, choices among the
> decision processes ... should be based on sound empirical evidence
> concerning the likely consequences of the styles. The more complete the

171

empirical base of knowledge, the greater the certainty with which we can develop the model and the greater will be its usefulness.

(Vroom, 1984, p. 258)

However, this clearly will not do, for no amount of empirical evidence can provide justification for a normative belief. What is needed instead is an underlying ethical argument for the model, and this Vroom fails to provide. Just because managers *do* do certain kinds of things, this is no justification for what they *ought* to do.

## ETHICAL ARGUMENTS FOR PARTICIPATION

If the major argument for participation has so far been for its use in a campaign for efficiency, then clearly it is time to question whether that is its only use. As pointed out in other chapters, efficiency may be a principal goal of business and industry, but it is highly questionable whether it should be quite as central for education. The idea of efficiency has to be argued for, just as other aims and purposes of a school have to be. One does not need, then, to find oneself caught on the hook of proving that participation is necessarily efficient. The evidence suggests that, in the long term at least, it is. But even if it were not, this would still not disqualify its pursuance. This all depends upon the goals of the institution within which it is to be utilized. In some business enterprises, it might be discontinued if it failed the test of efficiency. But are the goals of education those of efficiency as well? If education is more the subject of ethical concerns, then the grounds upon which it is tested change dramatically. A better way of adjudging it, then, is to examine it in the light of the nature of the educational process, though its implications and transference are, I think, rather more wide-reaching.

One might begin by asking the questions (1) does a teacher have a *right* to participation?, and (2) on what grounds might one base such rights? A number of reasons might be given, among which might be:

1. *Teachers possess expert knowledge.* This argument, I think, is untenable, simply because if someone is paid for his or her advice, this does not mean that it has to be used. Just as I buy a bar of soap, but can throw it away if I want to, so I may buy someone's advice but then ignore it.
2. *Teachers are autonomous in their work.* This again seems insufficient, as it appears to smuggle in the conclusion of participation. Autonomy would include participation in its meaning, for how can one be autonomous if one is not able to at least partially participate in decisions which affect one? Clearly, statements about teachers' autonomy have as much need of justification as those of participation.
3. *Teaching is a calling, a caring profession.* Again this is inadequate, because all it describes is why people do the job: it says something about their liking for it, but nothing about their rights to participation.

All three of these arguments implicitly support the belief that it is the right of those owning the means of production to participate in decision-making, and the right of such people to allow or disallow participation by those who do not own the means of production. Were I to own the bar of soap. I would have the right to dispose of it. If, curiously, I and several others owned it, I would have the right to participate in the decision as to its use. And so, the argument goes, as teachers are employees, and do not, in any sense or form, own the means of production (not buildings, materials, nor children), they have no right to participation, though their employers (LEA, DES, governing bodies, or their representatives, the headteachers) may give them that opportunity if they see it as increasing their effectiveness on one or both of the axes of the Blake and Mouton grid. It is this kind of thinking, I suggest, that has so reduced the status of the teacher, and produced such generally low morale in the teaching profession.

Must the argument, then, stop there? Has the position been reached where it must be concluded that teachers have no rights to participation, only the opportunity if their employers feel it is in their (the employers') interests?

## Participation because of the educational process

If we return to the process of education again, it will be clear to anyone who has done any teaching that education is not a transmissive one-way process. Teachers do not (or should not!) fill up pupils' minds with bits of information and remain unaffected themselves. Education is a two-way process in which both sides open themselves up to the possibility of change. A teacher gives of him- or herself in the process, and if one of the purposes of education is to change the student, then undoubtedly one of the consequences is that the teacher is changed as well. If education, the meeting of minds, is to take place, this is inevitable. Education is not about give (the teacher) and take (the student), but about give and take by both parties.

Two things must be said here. The first is that it is sad that for many, such a description of education will seem strange, romantic, and irrelevant to today's situation. Schools and teaching may well have come so far down the road as parts of a delivery system that some people have lost the sense of education as personal and social growth, of space, of patience, and of one-to-one relationships. Concepts like these are a long way from current obsessions with the acquisition of certificates, degrees, or other qualifications for the job market, and the furtherance of economic prosperity.

This leads to the second point, bound up as both are with the true notion of the educational process. This misunderstanding or abuse of the process of education is *the* major problem with the notion of aims and objectives in planning in education (and indeed planning in virtually any enterprise). It simply will not do to be told that the function of a teacher or a manager is to decide upon aims and the objectives for these aims, and then to pursue them. Certainly, when Drucker (1968) formulated the idea, he did it with the very best of intentions – it was to be the way to make business both more efficient and more caring. By allowing individuals to define their own goals, and plan how to reach them, they would be both more motivated and more self-fulfilled. In so doing, both the individual and the company benefits, for people who are motivated and self-fulfilled work harder and produce better results.

However, as noted in Chapter 2, this has encouraged in education an individualistic rather than a dualistic view of relationships, for it suggests that teaching is a process of transmission rather than, as it should be, one in which teachers come to the classroom with aims and objectives, but are able to adjust and modify these, depending upon the interactions which occur during the lesson. Where they are unable to do this, through personal or theoretical rigidity, they alienate those whom they teach, for they clearly communicate that the pupils' interests and opinions are of no value in the school.

Now, if education is a two-way process, and inevitably involves the giving of oneself, then this would suggest a strong ethical argument for participation in decision-making for those involved at the chalk face. If one is part of an enterprise which necessarily involves the surrendering of a part of one's autonomy, individuality and self, the right to partial or full participation must be there, for it would seem to be a fundamental right of people to participate in decisions which affect their personal integrity and welfare. Teachers are co-owners in the means of production, for part of the production process is themselves. Genuine participation, then, is called for at all of levels of the organization – implementation, design of the environment, and formulation of policy.

If this is the case, then the argument would seem to apply to many cases in industry. The word 'employee' does not do justice to many relationships in industry, just as it does not do justice to the role of the teacher in education. Certainly people sell their labour, but in many cases they do much more than that: they give of themselves, their aspirations, their emotions, their very personality. Indeed, this is precisely what William H. Whyte recognized with his book *The Organisation Man* (1960), in which he saw how the business organization was demanding more and more of the individual, not only in terms of time and effort, but also in terms of personality commitment. To suggest that such an arrangement is one of merely selling labour is grossly to misdescribe what is going on. Where it is more than this (and this must be the norm rather than the exception), then it would appear that the onus is on the employer to prove that participation by those employed is not justified, rather than for employees to prove that it is.

## Participation because teachers are people

This leads the discussion into the second major argument for participation by teachers in the management of schools. It seems on the surface so commonsensical that education must have proceeded a long way down business and bureaucratic roads for people to have lost sight of it. It is *not* that teachers are the people centrally involved in the education of pupils, and therefore should have a large say in the process. This was the first ethical argument for participation. Rather it is that pupils and teachers are human beings, and deserve to be treated as such. On this view, ' the good life' no longer necessarily consists in the pursuit of an increased GNP, with people being developed to facilitate that goal. Rather, the relationship is reversed, and in this new good life, GNP serves as a means to the end of the development of people, both children and adults.

This person-centred nature of education was firmly proclaimed when in 1967 the Plowden Commitee, with official backing, declared that 'the child is at the centre of the school' (Plowden Report, 1967). This had implications for teachers as well as children, for it suggested that functionalist and transmissive elements in education needed to be counterbalanced by a concern for people's personal, social and political development. Such concerns appear to have almost totally disappeared from official rhetoric in the last twenty years or so. If in 1967 Plowden could argue for the child being the school's central concern, in stark contrast, the DES could declare in 1981 that 'the curriculum is at the heart of the school'. In the process, a concern for the individual, and the dualistic nature of education, have tended to be lost. One of the consequences of this is an inability to perceive the validity of the ethical argument for teachers' participation. Where education is viewed as instrumental in purpose, so people within it are viewed as instruments. Where it is viewed as a functional activity, so people within it are viewed as functionaries. They are viewed as means to ends, because education is viewed as a means to an end. Where, on the other hand, education is viewed as an end in itself – a process of exploration and discovery, in some cases by one person working alone, in others by two people's chemistry, and in yet others by the entire school community – then those centrally involved in this process can also be viewed as ends in themselves, and as worthy of esteem and consideration as important human beings.

When one reaches the belief that teachers are first and foremost human beings, with whose development the school should be as concerned as it is with that of the pupils, then the whole managerial perspective changes. The central criterion for 'good management' becomes a concern for the morale, self-esteem, commitment, enjoyment, and personal, social and political fulfilment of those engaged in the process. The major arbiters of this process are then no longer people in economic think-tanks, but the people involved in the process. It means that teachers are viewed as important because they are part of the purpose of education, the development of people. Participation becomes a right and a duty rather than a gift, a tool or an expedient.

## Participation because of the needs of citizenship

This last reason for participation leads naturally into the final argument. Not only are teachers centrally involved in the process of education, and not only should they be given the opportunity for personal development as much as the pupils, but this personal development must be seen within the context of a community and a society. The pupils of a school need to have the education and the experience to enable them to understand the workings of their community, and the society within which they will take a part, and the rights and responsibilities which result from those involvements. How much more so should the adult members of the school, having greater experience and understanding, be given the same kinds of opportunity? This is not only for their own benefit, however, but for the benefit of the pupils as well, for if they are not involved, if they do not have, and do not take up, the rights and responsibilities of the running of the institution, what lessons, what hidden curricula, are being delivered to the younger members of the school? If one professes a serious commitment to the ideal of citizenship, then continued and increasing participation by its members is a necessary conclusion.

It will be clear as well that if one believes that citizenship education is a vital function of the school, then teachers' participation is not just their right, but also their duty and responsibility. If the pupils of the school need to see it in practice, then no matter how tedious, irksome, or even threatening participation in the running of the school becomes, teachers have an educational obligation to their pupils to be involved. Participation may not be a gift of management, but it is also not a gift to teachers, which they can use or not, depending how they feel. It is part of the definition of the job. Restricted professionals are not professionals at all: they are simply abnegating their responsibilities.

## WHAT DEGREE OF PARTICIPATION? IN WHICH AREAS?

If the general argument is accepted that increased participation is a genuine right and responsibility of the teaching profession, the hard questions still need to be asked: what degree of participation, and in which areas? In terms of degree, it will be clear that whilst pseudo-participation may initially motivate some individuals, it may well also have counterproductive effects, in that when these same individuals see that their contributions can and will be ignored if not conforming to managerial plans, they may well become cynical about the entire process, and withdraw from it, or attempt to undermine it. Furthermore, pseudo-participation does not educate people into seeing that organizational decisions have both beneficial and harmful consequences. Participation involves responsibilities as well as rights, and the only way to see this is to see its effects. Pseudo-participation, then, is probably not appropriate for any of the areas detailed.

Partial participation – limited influence, but influence which is conditioned by the greater influence of others – makes good educative sense for pupils whose initial decisions may be limited by experience, and which need to be amended by wiser councils. It would also make sense for those adults without experience or expertise. The question then becomes one of the areas of participation. In terms of implementation, it makes little sense to involve only partially those who are actually implementing the curriculum. It may, however, make good sense to do no more than this in the design of the physical and social environment, for there will be other considerations – financial, architectural, structural – which will be beyond the normal range of a teacher's experience. The same would seem to apply to policy decisions, where a host of factors, beyond the purview of the school, must be addressed. The caveat, however, must be made, that if the school is an educative environment, then part of the education of its adult inhabitants must be as that of its pupils – to help them to understand the complexities of issues beyond their present experience, to enable them to participate more fully. One can then imagine a situation where partial participation moves to full participation as individuals demonstrate their ability to contribute at this level.

Full participation – equal influence on decisions with all other interested bodies – is, I think, an ideal for any school, and for any community aiming for genuine participation. It will be limited in a variety of different ways: in terms of children's developmental capabilities, by a lack of sufficient experience and expertise, and, pragmatically, by the time available, by the commitment of individuals, and by legal statutes as to where responsibility ultimately lies. But it should not be regarded as static: if the school is to educate for citizenship, it should be actively seeking for more and more ways in which both adults and children are educated and empowered to have a voice of equal influence. Clearly, each school will be different, as they contain different individuals with different capacities. But the goals remain the same: it is the time scale of their realization which will differ.

## CONCLUSION

Teacher participation in management decisions is not likely to increase, given current ideological impulses behind legislation and training. For the time being at least, teachers will probably continue to be seen as lower-grade functionaries in a greater economic scheme of things. However, this chapter has suggested that over-concentration on such concerns has drastically curtailed discussion of other educational goals, and concern over economic well-being must be balanced against other more educational considerations. If the major goal of education is the development of all engaged in the process, then it might well be that a lesser pursuit of economic growth is still consonant with a 'good life', and there will then be room for an acknowledgement of the need and right of those engaged in the process of education to much greater participation in its management. If *this* is accepted, participation will no longer be seen to be in the gift of managers. Rather it will be seen not only as a natural right of teachers engaged in the process of education, but also as their duty to those who are in their care. The real democratization of education could then begin.

# Chapter 12

# The ethics of leadership

For many, leadership in the school will be conceptualized in terms of how the head or principal of the school treats the other members of the organization in the process of implementing policies. As long the head shows consideration for them, and an appreciation of their problems, does not attempt to impose too much of a burden, and is even-handed in dealings with them, he or she may be seen to have considered the issues raised by the ethics of leadership, and have gone some way to their fulfilment. Thus, for many, the following argument would not be very controversial:

1. The head is the leader of the school.
2. The leader's job is to implement policy in the school.
3. The leader does this through the members of staff.
4. Therefore, the head's job is persuading others to implement policy.

Indeed, it might seem like little more than common sense. However, such an understanding is built upon a number of entwined factors, some theoretical, some practical. For a start, it rests upon a fairly widespread belief in a leadership literature which spans rather more than the field of education. Fiedler, for instance, argues that 'leadership ... refers to that part of organizational management that deals with the direction of subordinates' (1987, p. 3), while for Tucker (1981, pp. 18–19), the role of a leader is to 'define the situation authoritatively ... prescribe a course of group action ... [and engage in a] mobilizing function'. In much of the literature, therefore, the concept of leadership is viewed relatively unproblematically.

More practically, it is also the sort of assumption about leadership voiced at the present time by most politicians. Schools, it has been agreed by different parties, are there to do a job for 'the country'. The staff of schools are employed to carry out such directives as are determined to be 'beneficial', and as heads are employed to lead each individual school, then clearly their job is to make sure that the staff do what is deemed good and necessary.

Perhaps crucially, though, this view takes on an air of virtual unchallengeability because of the way it has been translated into practice. And practice, and the socialization which stems from it in the school, then feed back to mould the thought and further action of practitioners. This is nowhere better illustrated than in the five kinds of restraints which heads find when they come to think about the managerial possibilities of their job. We need to consider these in some detail.

The first restraint is a legal one in that heads or principals have the principle of *in loco parentis*, common law and the major Education Acts to support their position and direct their action. Moreover, though the head's authority is mediated through the LEA and/or the board of governors, he or she is responsible for the internal activities of the school. Legal authority, then, implies legal responsibility: it will be an unusual (and imprudent) head who devolves such authority too far. Moreover, as Harling (1984) pointed out, any supposed autonomy of the class teacher has no legal basis. Teachers are assistants to the head, and nothing more. If a measure of autonomy is granted to teachers, it is in recognition of the fact that discretion is needed in applying rules to particular classes and individuals. Such discretion can be (and increasingly has been) withdrawn as doubt is cast upon the 'professionalism' and trustworthiness of teachers. In such a climate, it is hardly remarkable to find that the roles of the head and staff are seen so functionally, so unproblematically.

The second restraint, connected to the first, is historical. Allied to an increased trend to bureaucratization, and hence control, of schools, has been the development of a conception of headship which has stemmed largely from nineteenth-century ideas of public-school paternal embodiments like Arnold of Rugby. As Protherough (1984) has documented, they were seen, and came to picture themselves, as virtually all things to all men: as school entrepreneur, 'selling' the school to parents, as designer of and experts on curricula, as chief disciplinarian, as hirer and firer of staff, as the spiritual leader of the school community. Bernbaum (1976) describes how this conceptualization was exported from the public schools to the elementary and primary, the grammar and then the comprehensive schools. To paraphrase Louis XIV, it would not be too far from the mark to suggest that, for a head, *'L'école, c'est moi'* embodied much of this historical inheritance. And where history has set a particular background, it can constrain the imagination, and prevent awareness of other possible forms of leadership.

The third restraint, allied to both of the above, is pragmatic. Where heads or principals have been educated and have seen their careers develop within schools which have exhibited this paternalistic style of leadership, they may find it difficult to conceptualize different practices or forms of headship when they rise to this position themselves. They may read of other kinds, but when the legislation within which they work, their own experience, the experience of their peers and of colleagues around them, their own staff, and the parents of the children, all seem to favour such a form of leadership, it should not be too surprising if this tradition is continued. After all, for a practitioner, this is not a theoretical issue, but one of practice, which involves personal prestige, self-concept, and a salary to pay the mortgage. In such a situation, if there are few other kinds of role models to follow in practice, experience and common sense may seem to go well together.

The fourth, the theoretical, has already been dealt with at length in this book. Much of the literature, derived as it is from business and industry, suggests that a functional and managerial style of leadership is the appropriate form of leadership for education. Within such a diverse body of literature, one might see a movement of theory from the leader as the efficiency expert (Taylor, 1911) to the head as the social engineer (Mayo, 1946) and as a clinician (Schutz, 1958), to leader as hero (Deal and Kennedy, 1988). All, however, draw their inspiration from somewhere other than education, and all essentially fail to address the question of what role a leader should have if an institution like a school is to fulfil its *educational* purpose. Where much of the theory blurs the distinction between education and other organizations, it also muddies the water for any head attempting to pursue an educational form of leadership.

The fifth and final restraint is the conceptual. If the fourth restraint is concerned with problems of transferability, this vice is concerned with the ways in which the very notion of leadership has been conceptualized, and placed within paradigms which further frustrate attempts to relate the concept to educational issues. A nice summary of the possible conceptual models of leadership on offer has been given by Paisey (1984). He suggests that there are four distinct models on offer in the literature. It is instructive and informative to examine these in a little detail.

*The congenital or trait model* suggests that leaders are born rather than fashioned by the environment, and that they possess qualities which are universal to leaders. Intelligence, humour, tolerance, decisiveness, physical dominance and attractiveness have all been suggested at one time or another as qualities with which leaders are naturally endowed. The evidence, however, is at best equivocal. Stogdill (1970) investigated 124 papers in an attempt to determine the validity of this model, and came to the conclusion (p. 126) that

> ... leadership is a relation that exists between persons in a social situations, and that persons who are leaders in one situation may not necessarily be leaders in other situations.

His conclusion (p. 123) that 'the qualities, characteristics and skills required in a leader are determined to a large extent by the demands of the situation in which he is to function as a leader' were contributory factors in the development of the second model which Paisey describes, *the situational model*. This stressed the relative and ubiquitous nature of leadership, suggesting that leadership was less about natural qualities as about the right person being in the right place at the right time. What will make person A a leader in one situation will leave person B on the sidelines. And yet given a different set of circumstances, it will be B who will come to the fore. Clearly, this is the other side of the congenital model, and suffers from the same kinds of criticisms. Leadership theories which focus only upon either traits or situations leave themselves open to the criticism of having neglected the other side of the equation.

Both of these two models are very different from Paisey's next model, *the management model*. This model makes many of the assumptions of bureaucratically oriented writers, in that, firstly, it identifies leadership with the formal position of the individual in the organization, and secondly, it assumes that there are objective values which this individual is there to transmit. In educational terms, this would mean that as a particular person is appointed head or principal of a school, that person must therefore be the leader of the school, and be the person who transmits these values. Of course, by so doing such a model fails to see that people can be leaders without necessarily being formally appointed to a title commensurate in a bureaucratic organization with such a role. It ignores the role that an influential or imaginative individual not recognized by the formal structure may play in the design and implementation of a policy, and in the persuasion of other people to adopt it. Moreover, it fails to see that values may be contested within an organization, and values not necessarily in accord with those passed down the hierarchy may be adopted and practised by those within the organization. Values, then, cannot be simply held as objectively correct, but are adopted for particular purposes by particular people or groups, and are therefore contestable. The management model of leadership, then, might well constrain an understanding of or prevent the expression or development of a form of organization which wished to devolve responsibility and power (and ultimately leadership) to others in the organization, or which was attempting to appreciate that values are subjective and contestable.

Paisey's final model, *the followership model*, moves some way along this path of subjectivity, by suggesting that a necessary counterpoint to the work on the qualities and situations of leadership is attention to why people are prepared to act as followers – why individuals are prepared to listen to and act upon the suggestions of others. Such a model is a useful vehicle for investigating the subjectivities of individuals and the micropolitics of the school, as it demands that significance be attached to all the individuals in the organization and the interactions between them. Rather than painting a picture of a complex and interesting leader leading essentially homogeneous sheep, it suggests that attention must be given to the richness and complexity of the values of both leaders and followers. In so doing, it opens up the possibility of a discussion of dialectic within the organization, and shifts the perspective from the individual to the interactional and social.

There is, then, within these models, a genuine movement towards an appreciation of the nature of leadership. From leadership attribution to people's innate qualities, to an appreciation of context, to its attachment to positions in a hierarchy, to its appreciation as a subjective and interactional phenomenon, all four models have something to offer. However, it would seem that, within education, a fifth model is needed, one which links leadership with the ethics of the educational endeavour. This fifth model, *a transformative or moral model*, would argue that the concept of leadership should be linked to a concept of the ultimate purposes of the school. These, it has already been argued, should be understood in terms of the possible liberating and enabling effects of school organization upon individuals and groups within the school community. School leaders, according to this model, cannot limit their vision of themselves to that of '. . . middle management appointments', nor of their role as that of '. . . institutional maintenance in which the primary function is merely to maintain the status quo . . .', an attitude of simply 'keeping the ship afloat . . .' (Gunn *et al.*, 1988, p. 3). Rather, they need to possess a vision of a good and just community, for out of such a conception comes a practice which adumbrates that of a good and just society. They must enable others to reach their full potential, not only personally and intellectually, but also socially and politically. Ultimately, this will mean empowering others to take over the reins of leadership when these others are most suited to the task.

Such a conception is clearly at odds with the management model, in that it suggests that bureaucratic appointments do not necessarily give the degree of purpose nor necessarily indicate the right person for the right task. However, it can incorporate part of the congenital or trait model in that the qualities an individual possesses may suit them to lead at a particular time; it can incorporate part of the situational model, in that different individuals will be suited for leadership in different positions; and it can incorporate part of the followership model, in that followers could ultimately become leaders and vice versa. However, this model gives the concept of leadership an extra dimension in that it conceptualizes leadership as being concerned with more than one person leading others. The role of leadership is also concerned with one person enabling others to lead in order to harness all the elements of a fair and just society. In this respect, rather than being dominant, charismatic figures, heads or principals become facilitators, who are

> ... responsible to a process rather than specific outcomes, to the integrity of the community rather than to the needs of particular individuals.
>
> (Barber, 1984, p. 280)

It will be clear, then, that before one can discuss who is a leader in education, or what their function as leader should be, one needs to ask what the purpose of an education institution should be, and what sort of culture it is trying to create. Indeed, the concepts of leadership and culture are closely bound together because the notion of culture helps one to conjure with ultimate visions of education, and of the roles which people must play within them in order for such a culture to be created. However, one needs to be just as cautious with the concept of culture as with that of leadership, for much of the literature on cultures stems from the business world, and may not be applicable to schools. We have already seen in Chapter 1 how Charles Handy's four gods of management have a transferability to the educational domain, but how they need to be refined by noting their interactions with particular educational ideologies. In a similar way, the work of Deal and Kennedy (1988) has been immensely influential in centralizing the concept of culture, and they perform a valuable service of suggesting that one of the major mistakes in the business literature has been to assume that businesses are successful because of rules, whereas they suggest that such organizations are successful because of the people within them, and the co-ordination and meaning which a culture gives to their activities. As they say,

> ... we need to relearn old lessons about how culture ties people together and gives meaning and purpose to their day-to-day lives.
>
> (Deal and Kennedy, 1988, p. 5)

So far, so good. If education is concerned primarily with values and people, then much of what Deal and Kennedy have so far asserted can be agreed with. If their writing, and that of educationalists, is primarily concerned with the kinds of values and culture which an organization must create, then there may be much mileage in examining the transferabilities, for they may provide clues as to the construction of such cultures, and the place of leadership within it. We must examine their work in a little more detail.

Their work stems from their examination of hundreds of corporations and their business environments, an examination which led them to the conclusion that whilst traditional management skills like financial planning and cost control are important to a company's success, the really vital element of a company is the culture it creates, the set of values it holds up before its employees and customers. They eventually came to the conclusion that companies fall into four general types of culture. These, and possible implications for schools, can be seen in Figure 12.1. It will be clear from a perusal of these descriptions that there are genuine parallels and transferabilities to schools in Deal and Kennedy's cultures. However, there is still a need for caution,

| Culture | Main feature | Type of person employed | Drawbacks | Educational implications |
|---|---|---|---|---|
| Tough-guy macho culture | High risk, immediate feedback. Life is seen in terms of win or lose | Individualists, sports and show business, succeeding through own talent. Past success counts for nothing | Not for co-operators, or for team workers, or for those who take a long-term perspective | Could be an individualist charismatic teacher, tolerated by colleagues because of teaching ability. In a competitive environment, such teachers may be useful selling points for schools |
| Work hard, play hard culture | Centred on selling, so feedback is immediate. No one success or failure will make or break a company. Finding out what the customer wants is essential | One who keeps on trying to make the sale, is customer oriented, and usually individualistic and competitive – you make the sale and someone else does not | Tend to take short-term perspective, going for quantity rather than quality | Immediate feedback of lesson 'sale' by teachers to pupils. More attention paid to parental wishes, and to 'selling' school because of LMS, open enrolment. Increased concentration on 'results', because of testing of attainment targets |
| Bet-your-company culture | High risk, long-term feedback. Billion-dollar decisions take years to assess | Deliberate, careful, thoughtful, willing to bow to the wisdom of experience | Slow to react, can be overcautious, and too hierarchical | Adoption of an educational approach, purchase of materials, hiring and training of staff, implementation and evaluation all take place over long periods of time |
| Process culture | Classic bureaucracy: very low risk, no one decision will break business and little feedback given on actions taken | Deliberate, meticulous, patient, capable of accepting little knowledge of effect of actions, of status by position in hierarchy | Little feedback, may focus on decision process, become preoccupied with petty status wrangles | Effects of policies on pupils may never be apparent, or only have their effect after pupils leave school. Much teaching concerned with relationships, of effects of processes rather than simple outcomes |

**Figure 12.1** Corporate cultures and education.

for these are business writers writing for a business audience, and not for an educational one. For example, the authors state (p. 107) that the creation of cultures in organizations is determined by two factors in the market-place: the degree of risk associated with the company's activities, and the speed at which companies get feedback on whether decisions or strategies are successful. A culture and its values, then, are determined by the nature of the activity, and the kind of market-place in which it finds itself. Educationally, one might agree with this to the extent that an educational culture and its values are (or should be) determined by what it attempts to do. However, after fairly lengthy descriptions of the values of particular companies, they ask themselves the question (Deal and Kennedy, 1988, p. 25) of where the values of a company's culture come from. Their reply is extremely instructive:

> They mostly come from experience, from testing what does and does not work in the economic environment.

In other words, the values of such companies are second-order values, determined by their utility. The message is clear: if particular values work in developing a company which is successful in the search for profit and growth, then these values should be promoted. Such values do not derive, as I suggest they should do in education, from first-order considerations of the development of individual, social and political potentials and the building of a just society. This is further brought out when on p. 159 Deal and Kennedy suggest that there are only five situations where a company should consider reshaping a culture, and hence changing its values. These situations are:

1. when the environment is undergoing fundamental change, and the company has always been highly value-driven;
2. when the industry is highly competitive and the environment changes quickly;
3. when the industry is mediocre or worse;
4. when the company is truly at the threshold of becoming a large corporation;
5. when companies are growing rapidly.

The message to the reader is again quite clear, and underscores yet again the second-order nature of a company's values. If the environment changes, then so must the values. For an educationalist committed to the first-order nature of values, the situation is more problematical. If the essence of education involves issues like the development of individual potentials, and the creation of a just community, then it matters as a matter of tactics and implementation that the environment changes, but it should not affect the values themselves. They should remain inviolate, their attainment made easier or more difficult by situational contingencies, but essentially unchanged.

Deal and Kennedy's treatment of leadership, conceptually tied as it is to its role in their cultures, is therefore not without its problems for education as well. Their concept of an organizational culture, as we have seen, rests upon the notion of its being manufactured and manipulated for particular purposes. In this manufacture and manipulation, the leader – their 'hero' in the organization – has the central role of providing the vision and inspiration to transform the conceptualization of the purpose of the organization for the rank and file. Whilst this function is facilitative in that it stimulates followers to have a higher regard for their own abilities, and to take on more responsibility, it nevertheless very clearly sees leadership in terms of permanent positions of leader and led. It is a persuasive account of leadership which has had its effects upon the educational literature. Take, for instance, writers like Duignan and Macpherson (1987), who suggest (pp. 51, 57) that

> ... educative leadership is part of the process of modifying or maintaining an organizational culture ... Educative leadership helps to articulate, define and strengthen those endearing values, beliefs and cultural characteristics that give an organization its unique identity in the minds of participants ... educative leaders use the tools of culture to build an ethos to create shared assumptions about responsibilities and relationships, and to gain the commitment of groups to the achievement of tangible and intangible goals and objectives.

There is much to agree with in such a description, in that it accepts that those in cultures must come to identify themselves with the values of their culture, and to accept responsibility within it. Such a vision, however, whilst acknowledging the moral and transformative functions of leadership, still locates its central stand within a notion of someone's dream or vision leading others, and continuing to lead others. And yet, as Simon (1987, p. 372) points out,

> ... dreams are never neutral; they are always SOMEONE'S dreams, and to the degree that they are implicated in organizing the future for others, they always have a moral and political dimension.

Such a vision has within it seeds of paternalism and elitism which, whilst possibly unproblematical for a business organization, sit uneasily in an educational organization committed to ultimate goals of personal, social and political development.

Educational organizations, then, have to set out the criteria by which leadership within them is defined and practised. It can be, as functionalist theories would assert, little more than containing the functions of management – the translating and implementing of directives. Concentration in the literature and the training then tends to move towards appreciations of the use of power by leaders, and the mechanism by which they persuade, cajole, or enforce a particular measure. If this is the case, one tends to find extensive reference to the writings of people like French and Raven (1959), or those of Etzioni (1961), with their different categorizations of power. The result, however, is, as Watkins (1989, p. 11) has pointed out, that 'too often what is in reality a power relationship is obscured by the label of leadership'.

Such references provide those heading hierarchies with an appreciation of the tools and resources at their disposal for the realization of their and the organization's objectives, but they should also sensitize critically aware readers to two things. The first is that management as the use of different forms of power conceptualizes relationships within the school in a manipulative, means-to-end manner. People are not seen or valued as ends in themselves, but are being used, through the varieties of power available, to achieve other ends. There is not within this kind of relationship the degree of trust, the meeting of minds in equality, which should be central to an ethical and educational institution. The second thing of which people should be aware is that, necessarily, there is a dialectic proceeding here concerning the nature of power and its place in an educational setting. As Clegg (1977, p. 25) has put it,

> The assumption of 'resource' based explanations of 'power' ought also to entail an exposition of how some people come to have access to these 'resources' while some others do not. The prior possession of resources in anything other than equal amounts is something which a theory of 'power' has to explain.

The distribution and use of power within an organization, then, are inherently ethical and political questions, ethical in terms of the way in which we view and treat people, political in terms of both the relationships between people within the organization, and relationships between parties within society at large. A literature which uncritically spends its time suggesting types of power resources to be used by leaders is not being ideologically neutral, but is taking up an ideological position of accepting the current status quo, one which asserts that leadership is to be viewed in a value-neutral, non-problematic and functional manner, one which is given its purpose from outside of the organization, and which its 'leader' then implements bureaucratically. Educationally, this is derived, at least in part, from the largely hierarchical, class-based and bureaucratic inheritance of most schools. Such ideological baggage is part and parcel of most people's experience within schools, and needs to be recognized, criticized and in many cases jettisoned before a model more clearly educational can be appreciated and adopted. Such functional and power-based perspectives are clearly very different conceptions of leaderships from ones which see it as value-committed, which derive their *raison d'être* from an analysis of the meaning of education. Such an analysis, whilst acknowledging all the functions that *schooling* must perform, places its emphasis upon the criteria that *education* must achieve. These criteria, I suggest, are nine in number.

1. Leadership must be critical.
2. Leadership must be transformative.
3. Leadership must be visionary.
4. Leadership must be educative.
5. Leadership must be empowering.
6. Leadership must be liberating.
7. Leadership must be personally ethical.
8. Leadership must be organizationally ethical.
9. Leadership must be responsible.

The nine criteria are interdependent. If schools are primarily concerned with the personal, social and political development of their inhabitants, then leadership must be centrally concerned with these issues as well. Leadership must then be critical because it must aim to improve the lives and practices of those within the organization, and it can only do this by looking at the status quo and seeing what needs changing. Thus it is necessarily transformative, educative and visionary, for it seeks to change for the better, and does this by presenting both an analysis of the present, and a vision of the future. In so doing, it raises the consciousness of those within the organization, so that they can see their own position, and what needs to be done. It thus attempts to liberate itself and the other members of the organization from the kinds of historical and intellectual constraints described above. Moreover, by treating people as ends in themselves, and not as means to organizational ends, and by keeping the focus on the realization of a just and democratic community, it is ethical at both personal and organizational levels. Through this, it must be responsible, for as Foster (1989, p. 56) says,

> Leadership carries a responsibility not just to be personally moral, but to be a cause of civic moral education, which leads to both self-knowledge and community awareness.

But more than this, it enables others to become leaders and thereby not only to be liberated, but also to accept their share of responsibility in the running and conduct of both institution and society.

This is not to say that such a conception of leadership is without its tensions. If one asks of leadership that it be visionary *and* liberating, it must still be acknowledged that there will be a tension between the vision of the individual acting as leader, and the vision of those others within the school, for they may well have different views of the future and of the organization. Visionaries all too easily become charismatic, then fascist and authoritarian, as they prosecute their personal conceptions. It is comforting to say, as Hartsock (1983, p. 8) does, that 'to lead is to be at the centre of the group rather in front of the others', but whilst this expresses the essentially democratic nature of transformative leadership, it assumes a unity of purpose within a group which may not exist. Similarly, whilst such a model of leadership suggests a facilitative role, it does not spell out how far a leader must go in facilitating an approach which he or she finds difficulty in agreeing with. Allowing someone else to take over the leadership function in this situation would almost certainly be seen as an abnegation of responsibility and a surrendering of personal ideals rather than as the empowerment of others. Finally, the larger demands of society must be acknowledged, which may see school leadership as *neither* visionary nor liberating, in the sense described in this chapter.

However, acceptance of the need for the development of a democratic and participative school community does not necessarily imply a total unity of purpose by its inhabitants, or by those outside. It can exist within an atmosphere of diverse and contrary aspirations and opinions, but it must draw upon the democratic rhetoric used by political parties and society at large to ensure a tolerance of others' opinions, an acceptance of the possibility of personal fallibility, and in so doing make room for disagreements and communication between those within the school community. The concept of leadership must acknowledge the reality of the head or the principal, and appreciate that he or she must perform a delicate balancing act between the prosecution of personal vision, the engendering of empowerment and responsibility, and the demands of those outside of the school community. If an ultimate aim of educational leadership is such that different people come to assume leadership and responsibility for different situations, this must be conditioned by the reality of societal demands, the present nature of the school, and the human beings within both of them. Such ideals are not likely to be fully realized in the short or medium term, but the process, if taken step by step, is still capable of reaching nearer its goal.

An initial step in this direction is to return to and appreciate the subjectivity of values. Leadership conceptualized as the one-sided prosecution of specific values implements an objective set of management values, which transforms few situations and liberates none. Leadership conceptualized as an extreme facilitative role, acknowledging and helping the realization of any and all aspirations, implements a relativistic set of managerial values, which leads not to community but to anarchy, for it builds no concept of which direction to take. But leadership conceptualized as the holding of determinate values, but in an open, self-critical and tolerant manner, suggest a form of leadership which can make the bridge between the structures already in place in an educational establishment, and can generate new perspectives and new leaders within the school community.

From the acceptance of the subjectivity of judgement, and the limited nature of any individual's appreciation of a situation, can come the beginnings of the realization of such a school. One example of this comes from Murgatroyd and Reynolds (1984), who suggest that within the school community, non-executive leadership can be generated in at least four different ways.

Firstly, such leaders may challenge the assumptions of a staff concerning who should do what in an organization, or what it is possible to change. Examples of these might be in terms of those assumed capable of making informed judgements about new curricula, or concerning the intellectual abilities of children.

Secondly, such leaders may go further and not only provide a challenge to present assumptions, but also show how alternative assumptions may be put into practice. In terms of assumptions about children's abilities, this may be in the form of implementing a challenging curricular innovation which demonstrates that children can cope with greater intellectual demands.

Thirdly, by embarking on a new project, an individual can demonstrate that failure can not only be tolerated, but is also an essential part of the personal learning process. This attitude of attempting innovation, of not fearing failure, but instead of viewing it in a positive manner, then encourages others to try the same thing.

Finally, by initiating change at a personal level, such innovators reduce reliance on external authority and change, and in so doing encourage a more accurate match of solutions to local problems, as well as making it more likely that change, because it is created at the local level, will be more owned by participants and therefore more enthusiastically and successfully adopted.

Such innovations, initiated perhaps by informal leaders, but encouraged and sponsored by the formal leader, produce a number of benefits, both practical and ethical. Firstly, by acknowledging the subjectivity of judgement, practical organizational policies are indicated which draw on as much of the total experience within the community as possible. Rather than consultation being limited to a few senior professionals, it suggests that many are able to contribute something to the solution of the problem at hand. Ethically, such an appreciation of subjectivity guards against an overweaning confidence by the individual in his or her judgement, and instead suggests a tentativeness in personal assertion, the need for a readiness to listen to others, and a tolerance of divergent views. Such are the essential preconditions for a school which is truly a community and which strives to be genuinely democratic.

Secondly, the development of an ethos within the school which encourages the participation of all, and accepts their right and need to address issues which affect that community, has a number of practical effects. Because more people participate, more information is generated, and there is created a stronger possibility that a proposed solution is really suitable for the problem at hand. Further, because of such participation, greater ownership of solutions is generated, and there is much more likelihood of a wide consensus about the ultimate resolution adopted. Finally, participation is beneficial ethically because it is precisely the mechanism which is needed to further the personal, social and political development of the school's inhabitants. Indeed, the encouragement of participation involves the school community in a benign circle: the more a participant culture is cultivated, the more that participation is encouraged, and the greater the development of the community as a whole. Participation increases the motivation of those involved to become more involved. This is, then, a strong reply to the kind of arguments developed by Michels (1949) and Schumpeter (1942), that a participant, democratic community cannot develop, either because of the apathy of those within, or because of their limited expertise in the techniques of leadership. In the first case, it can be argued that apathy is more a symptom of the inadequacy of the organization than of any personal constitutional deficiency. As Rizvi (1989, p. 220) suggests,

> Evidence of apathy is clearly an index of the extent to which contemporary institutions have fallen short of the democratic ideal, not a proof of its impracticality.

In the second case, increased participation allows for the encouragement, nurturing and training of precisely those qualities which followers are supposed to lack. When a school community generates the kind of ethos which facilitates the development of leadership qualities in its participants, there is no reason to believe that Michels' argument will hold good. As with the apathy argument, it is more a comment on the socializing influences of present institutions than on the necessity of their effects.

## CONCLUSION

An individual appointed as head or principal in a school at the present time will almost certainly be perceived as leader not only by external authorities, but by interested parties both within and without the school as well. It would be foolish to suggest that this does not give that individual a *de facto* kind of leadership, just as it would be foolish to believe that many so appointed cannot and do not assume the role very adequately. Some of the more extreme literature ignores these facts and consequently seems distanced from the reality of school management. Schools have formally constituted hierarchies, and people accept them and work within them, and give those within them due regard and respect. A head or principal, then, is the obvious candidate from which leadership should begin. The problem, is, as outlined at the beginning of this chapter, that a variety of vices and constraints exist to seduce this individual into pursuing a vision of leadership very different from that described in this book. At best, it will be one which many see as the best role for a head, the kind that Patricia White (1983) calls a 'lynchpin' head. This kind of head is seen as the prime mover in the school, one who inspires and leads from the front. As White (1983, p. 123) says

> The final realisation of this ideal would be a whole education system with an appropriately trained head steering each institution. These heads would form the elite corps of the educational world, leading and inspiring their colleagues and pupils.

This kind of head will have many qualities to admire, many of which one would want for democratic heads. Like them, they would be dedicated, hardworking, enthusiastic, caring, resourceful, determined, aware of government policy and how it will affect the school. But the ends to which the lynchpin head aims are different from those of the democratic head. Whereas lynchpin heads see their role as leading from the front for the duration of their careers, democratic heads are working towards an institution which models a participatory democratic society, where each member has an opportunity to exercise influence and power, ideally on an equal basis with other members. This will mean that democratic heads will want to involve staff and pupils in the school's running, not to produce better results and have a happier staff and pupils, but to educate the school's members in their rights and responsibilities as citizens. They will want to provide opportunities for others to discuss matters of policy and implementation, not to ensure that prior preparation avoids confrontation and opposition, nor even to ensure that all knowledge is pooled to produce better results, but rather to provide school members with the opportunity to develop themselves and their community. Through such continued and increasing participation of all those concerned with the community of the school, leadership is dispersed and devolved. This process does not have to be an all-or-nothing affair, nor need it happen overnight: it suggests, however, that this vision is one which all within the school should understand and strive towards. The principal of the school may have not only to convince and educate him- or herself, but to convince and educate others as well. This, then, is not a utopian vision, but one which accepts that change, if it is to be long-lasting, is best conducted bit by bit, rather than all at an ideological rush.

The challenging thing for a school and its inhabitants is, as with so many other issues, to begin to think the unthinkable, and then to begin to act upon it. Such thoughts and acts begin from a deep-seated optimism in the potential of human beings, a belief that they can rather than that they cannot. It accepts the uncertainty of the truly educational enterprise as one of excitement and challenge, rather than as one to be avoided by too-precise specification of behaviour and curriculum. It sees lack of success not as failure but as a learning experience from which to build more success. It believes that, rather than providing the answers, the school and its management should be more concerned with raising the questions, and then facilitating their resolution.

# Bibliography

Almond, G. A. and Verba, S. (1965) *The Civic Culture.* Boston: Little, Brown & Co.

Alutto, J. A. and Belasco, J. A. (1972) A typology for participation in organisational decision making. *Administrative Science Quarterly* **17.**

Anderson, J. G. (1968) *Bureaucracy in Education.* Baltimore: Johns Hopkins Press.

Apple, M. (1982) *Education and Power.* London: Ark.

Aquila, F. D. (1983) Japanese management in schools: boon or boondoggle? *Clearing House* **57.**

Aries, P. (1962) *Centuries of Childhood.* London: Jonathan Cape.

Armytage, W. H. G. (1970) *Four Hundred Years of English Education,* 2nd edn. Cambridge, UK: Cambridge University Press.

Aronson, E., Blaney, N., Stephen, C., Sikes, J. and Snapp, M. (1978) *The Jigsaw Classroom.* Beverly Hills, CA: Sage Publications.

Asch, S. E. (1951) Effects of group pressures upon modifications and distortions of judgments. In Guetzkow, H. (ed.) *Groups, Leadership and Men.* Pittsburgh: Carnegie.

Auld, R. (1980) William Tyndale Junior and Infants School Public Inquiry: A Report to the ILEA. In Bush, T., Glatter, R., Goodey, J. and Riches, C. (eds) *Approaches to School Management.* London: Harper and Row.

Axelrod, R. (1984) *The Evolution of Cooperation.* New York: Basic Books.

Baker, K. (1986) Speech given to the North of England Educational Conference, at Rotherham, UK.

Barber, B. (1984) *Strong Democracy: Participatory Politics in a New Age.* Berkeley, CA: University of California Press.

Barry, C. H. and Tye, F. (1975) *Running a School.* Hounslow, Middlesex: Temple Smith.

Barton, J., Becher, T., Canning, T., Eraut, E. and Knight, J. (1980). Accountability and education. In Bush, T., Glatter, R., Goodey, J. and Riches, C. (eds) *Approaches to School Management.* London: Harper and Row.

Belbin, R. M. (1981) *Management Teams – Why they Succeed or Fail.* London: Heinemann.

Bernbaum, G. (1976) The role of the Head. In Peters, R. S. (ed.) *The Role of the Head.* London: Routledge and Kegan Paul.

Blake, R. R. and Mouton, J. S. (1985) *The New Managerial Grid.* Houston: Gulf.

Bobbitt, F. (1913) Some general principles of management applied to the problems of city school systems. In Parker, S. C. (ed.) *The Supervision of City Schools.* Twelfth Yearbook of the National Society for the Study of Education. Part 1. Bloomington, IL: Public School Publishing Company.

Bobbitt, F. (1918) *The Curriculum.* Boston: Houghton Mifflin.

Bobbitt, F. (1926) The orientation of the curriculum makers. In Rugg, H. (ed.) *The Foundations and Technique of Curriculum Construction*. Bloomington, IL: Public School Publishing Co.

Borke, H. (1971) Interpersonal perception of young children: egocentrism or empathy? *Developmental Psychology* **15**.

Bottery, M. (1990) *The Morality of the School: the Theory and Practice of Values in Education*. London: Cassell.

Bowles, S. and Gintis, H. (1976) *Schooling in Capitalist America*. London: Routledge and Kegan Paul.

Brennan, T. (1981) *Political Education and Democracy*. Cambridge, UK: Cambridge University Press.

Broadfoot, P. (1979) *Assessment, Schools and Society*. London: Methuen.

Brown, D. and Solomon, D. (1983) A model of prosocial learning. In Bridgeman, D. L. (ed.) *The Nature of Prosocial Development*. New York: Academic Press.

Brown, J. A. C. (1984; first published 1954) *The Social Psychology of Industry*. Harmondsworth, Middlesex: Penguin.

Callahan, R. E. (1962) *Education and the Cult of Efficiency*. Chicago: University of Chicago Press.

Campbell, R. F., Fleming, T., Jackson Newell, L. and Bennion, J. W. (1987) *A History of Thought and Practice in Educational Administration*. New York and London: Teachers College, Columbia University.

Campbell, R. J. (1985) *Developing the Primary School Curriculum*. Eastbourne: Holt.

Chalk, F. and Jonassohn, K. (1990) *The History and Sociology of Genocide*. New Haven: Yale University Press.

Chalmers, R. F. (1982) *What is This Thing Called Science?* 2nd edn. Milton Keynes: Open University Press.

Chitty, C. (1989) *Towards a New Education System: the Victory of the New Right?* Lewes: Falmer.

Clegg, S. (1977) Power, organisation theory, Marx and critique. In Clegg, S. and Dunkerley, D. (eds) *Critical Issues in Organisation*. London: Routledge and Kegan Paul.

Cohen, L. (1981) Political literacy and the primary school: A Dutch experiment. *Teaching Politics* **10**.

Cohen, L. and Manion, L. (1981) *Perspectives on Classrooms and Schools*. Eastbourne: Holt, Rinehart and Winston.

Cole, G. D. H. (1919) *Self-Government in Industry*. London: G. Bell & Sons.

Conway, J. A. (1980) Leadership styles and job-satisfaction in primary schools. In Bush, T., Glatter, R., Goodey, J. and Riches, C. (eds) *Approaches to School Management*. London: Harper and Row.

Crutchfield, R. S. (1955) Conformity and character. *American Psychologist* **10**.

Cunningham, P. (1988) *Curriculum Change in the Primary School since 1945*. Lewes, East Sussex: Falmer.

Curti, M. (1959) *The Social Ideas of American Educators*. Totowa, NJ: Littlefield, Adams.

Davies, B. (1984) Children through their own eyes. *Oxford Review of Education* **10**.

Davis, O. L. (1990) Who is the curriculum customer? *Curriculum* **11** (1).

Deal, T. and Kennedy, A. (1988) *Corporate Cultures.* Harmondsworth: Penguin.

Demause, L. (1974) The evolution of childhood. In Demause, L. (ed.) *The History of Childhood.* London: Souvenir.

DES (Welsh Office) (1977) *Education in Schools: a Consultative Document.* London: HMSO.

DES (1981) *The School Curriculum.* London: HMSO.

DES (1983) *Young People in the 1980s: a Survey.* London: HMSO.

DES (1985) *Education for All* (The Swann Report). London: HMSO.

DES (1988) *Education Act.* London: HMSO.

de Tocqueville, A. (1961) *Democracy in America.* New York: Schocken Books.

Dickson, A. (1975) Foreword. In Goodlad, S. (ed.) *Education and Social Action.* London: Allen and Unwin.

Dill, W. R. (1964) Decision-making. In Griffiths, D. E. (ed.) *Behavioural Science and Educational Administration.* 63rd Yearbook of the National Society for the Study of Education. Chicago: University of Chicago Press.

Docking, J. (1990) *Primary Schools and Parents.* London: Hodder and Stoughton.

Donaldson, M. (1978) *Children's Minds.* London: Fontana.

Dore, R. (1976) *The Diploma Disease: Education, Qualifications and Development.* London: Allen and Unwin.

Downey, M. and Kelly, A. V. (1986) *Theory and Practice of Education,* 3rd edn. London: Harper and Row.

Drucker, P. (1968) *The Practice of Management.* London: Pan.

Duignan, P. and Macpherson, R. (1987) The educative leadership project. *Educational Management and Administration* **15.**

Duke, B. C. (1986) The liberalisation of Japanese education. *Comparative Education* **22** (1).

Dunn, J. (1988) *The Beginnings of Social Understanding.* Oxford: Basil Blackwell.

Eisner, E. (1985) *The Art of Educational Evaluation.* Lewes: Falmer.

Etzioni, A. (1961) *A Comparative Analysis of Complex Organisations.* New York: Free Press.

Fay, B. (1975) *Social Theory and Political Practice.* London: Allen and Unwin.

Fiedler, F. (1987) *New Approaches to Effective Leadership.* New York: John Wiley and Sons.

Fischer, F. and Siriaani, C. (eds) (1984) *Critical Studies in Organization and Bureaucracy.* Philadelphia: Temple University Press.

Foster, W. (1989) Towards a critical practice of leadership. In Smyth, J. (ed.) *Critical Perspectives on Educational Leadership.* Lewes: Falmer.

Franklin, R. (ed.) (1986) *The Rights of Children.* Oxford: Basil Blackwell.

Freire, P. (1972) *Pedagogy of the Oppressed.* Harmondsworth: Penguin.

French, J. R. P. and Raven, B. (1959) The bases of social power. In Cartwright, D. (ed.) *Studies in Social Power.* Ann Arbor, MI: University of Michigan Press.

Friedman, M. (1962) *Capitalism and Freedom.* Chicago: University of Chicago Press.

Friedman, M. and Friedman, R. (1980) *Free to Choose.* New York: Harcourt, Brace, Jovanovich.

Gamble, A. (1988) *The Free Economy and the Strong State.* London: Macmillan.

Gilder, G. F. (1982) *Wealth and Poverty.* London: Buchan and Enright.

Gouldner, A. (1954) *Patterns of Industrial Democracy.* Glencoe, IL: The Free Press.

Graham, D. and Clarke, P. (1986) *The New Enlightenment: the Rebirth of Liberalism.* London: Macmillan.

Graves, N. B. and Graves, T. D. (1983) The cultural context of prosocial development: an ecological model. In Bridgeman, D. L. (ed.) *The Nature of Prosocial Development.* New York: Academic Press.

Green, D. G. (1987) *The New Right.* Brighton: Wheatsheaf.

Greenfield, T. B. (1980) Theory about organisation: a new perspective and its implications for schools. In Bush, T., Glatter, R., Goodey, J. and Riches, C. (eds) *Approaches to School Management.* London: Harper and Row.

Gunn, J., Holdaway, E. and Johnson, N. (1988) The power of principals. *The Canadian Administrator* **27** (4).

Halsey, A. H. (1983) Schools for democracy? In Ahier, J. and Flude, M. (eds) *Contemporary Education Policy.* London: Croom Helm.

Handy, C. (1984) *Taken for Granted? Looking at Schools as Organizations.* London: Longman.

Handy, C. (1985) *Gods of Management* (revised edition) London: Pan.

Handy, C. and Aitken, R. (1986) *Understanding Schools as Organisations.* Harmondsworth: Penguin.

Harling, P. (1984) School decision-making and the primary headteacher. In Harling, P. (ed.) *New Directions in Educational Leadership.* Lewes: Falmer.

Harris, K. (1979) *Education and Knowledge.* London: Routledge and Kegan Paul.

Harris, P. L. (1989) *Children and Emotion.* Oxford: Basil Blackwell.

Harris, R. (1980) *The End of Government . . .?* London: Institute of Economic Affairs. Occasional Paper 58.

Hartsock, N. (1983) *Money, Sex and Power.* New York: Longman.

Haviland, J. (1988) *Take Care, Mr Baker!* London: Fourth Estate.

Hayek, F. A. (1944) *The Road to Serfdom.* London: Routledge and Kegan Paul.

Hayek, F. A. (1960) *The Constitution of Liberty.* London: Routledge and Kegan Paul.

Hayek, F. A. (1973) *Law, Legislation and Liberty,* vol. 1. London: Routledge and Kegan Paul.

Hayek, F. A. (1976) *Law, Legislation and Liberty,* vol. 2. London: Routledge and Kegan Paul.

Hayek, F. A. (1979) *Law, Legislation and Liberty,* vol. 3. London: Routledge and Kegan Paul.

Heater, D. (1990) *Citizenship: The Civic Ideal in World History, Politics and Education.* London: Longman.

Hillgate Group (1986) *Whose Schools? A Radical Manifesto.* London: Hillgate Group.

Hobson, P. (1984) Some reflections on parents' rights in the upbringing of their children. *Journal of Philosophy of Education* **18.**

Holt, M. (1987) *Judgment, Planning and Educational Change.* London: Harper and Row.

Hoover, K. and Plant, R. (1989) *Conservative Capitalism in Britain and the United States.* London: Routledge.

Horio, T. (1988) *Educational Thought and Ideology in Modern Japan.* Tokyo: University of Tokyo Press.

Hoyle, E. (1986) *The Politics of School Management.* Sevenoaks, Kent: Hodder and Stoughton.

Hoyles, M. (1979) Childhood in historical perspective. In Hoyles, M. (ed.) *Changing Childhood*. London: Writers and Readers Publishing Cooperative.

Hughes, M. (1975) *Egocentrism in Pre-School Children*. Unpublished doctoral dissertation. Edinburgh University.

Illich, I. (1973) *Deschooling Society*. Harmondsworth: Penguin.

Jackson, P. W. (1968) *Life in Classrooms*. London: Holt, Rinehart and Winston.

Jahoda, G. (1972) *Children and Alcohol: a Developmental Study*. London: HMSO.

Janis, I. (1972) *Victims of Groupthink: a Psychological Study of Foreign-Policy Decisions and Fiascoes*. Boston: Houghton Mifflin.

Jay, A. (1967) *Management and Machiavelli: an Inquiry into the Politics of Corporate Life*. London: Holt, Rinehart and Winston.

Jeffs, T. (1988) Preparing young people for participatory democracy. In Carrington, B. and Troyna, B. (eds) *Children and Controversial Issues*. Lewes: Falmer.

Johnson, D. B. (1982) Altruistic behaviour and development of self in infants. *Merrill-Palmer Quarterly* **28.**

Jordan, B. (1989) *The Common Good*. Oxford: Basil Blackwell.

Joseph, Sir K. (1974) *The Times* (21 October).

Joseph, Sir K. (1976) *Stranded on the Middle Ground*. London: Centre for Policy Studies.

Kanter, R. M. (1983) *The Change Masters*. London: Counterpoint/Unwin.

Katz, M. B. (1975) *Class, Bureaucracy, and Schools*. New York: Praeger.

Katz, M. B. (1977) From voluntarism to bureaucracy in American education. In Karabel, J. and Halsey, A. H. (eds) *Power and Ideology in Education*. Oxford: Oxford University Press.

Kelman, H. C. (1958) Compliance, identification and internalisation: three processes of attitude change. *Journal of Conflict Resolution* **2.**

Kelman, H. C. and Hamilton, V. L. (1989) *Crimes of Obedience*. New Haven: Yale University Press.

King, E. J. (1986) Japan's education in comparative perspective. *Comparative Education* **22** (1).

Kohlberg, L. (1981) *The Philosophy of Moral Education*. New York: Harper and Row.

Kohn, M. (1977) *Class and Conformity*. Chicago: University of Chicago Press.

Kuhn, T. (1970) *The Structure of Scientific Revolutions*. Chicago: University of Chicago Press.

LaNoue, G. R. (1972) *Educational Vouchers: Concepts and Controversies*. New York: Teachers College Press.

Lawton, D. (1980) *The Politics of the School Curriculum*. London: Routledge and Kegan Paul.

Lawton, D. (1983) *Curriculum Studies and Educational Planning*. Sevenoaks, Kent: Hodder and Stoughton.

Levinson, E. (1976) *The Alum Rock Voucher Demonstration*. Santa Monica, CA: Rand Corporation.

Lipsky, M. (1980) *Street-Level Bureaucracy*. New York: Russell Sage Foundation.

Loney, M. (1986) *The Politics of Greed*. London: Pluto Press.

Lupton, T. (1983) *Management and the Social Sciences*. Harmondsworth: Penguin.

McGregor, D. (1960) *The Human Side of Enterprise*. New York: McGraw-Hill.

Mackintosh, J. (1977) *Inside British Politics*. Manchester: Granada Television.

Maclure, S. (1988) *Education Re-formed.* Sevenoaks, Kent: Hodder and Stoughton.

Macquarrie, J. (1972) *Existentialism.* London: Hutchinson.

Marx, K. (1965) *The German Ideology.* Moscow: Foreign Languages Publishing House.

Masatsugu, M. (1982) *The Modern Samurai Society.* New York: American Management Associations.

Mayo, E. (1946) *The Human Problems of an Industrial Civilization.* Cambridge, MA: Graduate School of Business Administration, Harvard University.

Merton, R. K. (1952) Bureaucratic structure and personality. In Merton, R. K., Gray, A. P., Hockey, B. and Selvin, H. C. (eds) *Reader in Bureaucracy.* Glencoe, IL: The Free Press.

Michels, R. (1949) *Political Parties.* Glencoe, IL: The Free Press.

Milgram, S. (1974) *Obedience to Authority.* London: Tavistock.

Mill, J. S. (1963) *On Liberty* (1859). Published in a selection by Fontana. Glasgow: William Collins and Sons.

Minford, P. (1984) State expenditure: a study in waste. *Economic Affairs* (April–June).

Montgomery, D. (1976) Workers' control of machine production in the nineteenth century. *Labor History* **17,** 485–509.

Moore, M. and Lawton, D. (1978) Authority and participation. In Lawton, D., Gordon, P., Ing, M., Gibby, B., Pring, R. and Moore, T. (eds.) *Theory and Practice of Curriculum Studies.* London: Routledge and Kegan Paul.

Morgan, G. (1985) *Images of Organisations.* London: Sage.

Mouzelis, N. P. (1975) *Organization and Bureaucracy: An Analysis of Modern Theories.* revised edn. London: Routledge and Kegan Paul.

Mueller, E. (1972) The maintenance of verbal exchanges between young children. *Child Development* **43.**

Murgatroyd, S. and Reynolds, D. (1984) Leadership and the teacher. In Harling, P. (ed.) *New Directions in Educational Leadership.* Lewes: Falmer.

Newsom Report (1963) *Half our Future.* London: HMSO.

Nias, J. (1980) Leadership styles and job satisfaction in primary schools. In Bush, T., Glatter, R., Goodey, J. and Riches, C. (eds) *Approaches to School Management.* London: Harper and Row.

Noddings, N. (1984) *Caring: A Feminine Approach to Ethics and Moral Education.* Berkeley, CA: California University Press.

Nozick, R. (1974) *Anarchy, State and Utopia.* Oxford: Basil Blackwell.

Ohta, T. (1986) Problems and perspectives in Japanese education. *Comparative Education* **22** (1).

Ouchi, W. (1981) *Theory Z.* Reading, MA: Addison Wesley.

Paisey, A. (1983) *Organisation and Management in Schools.* London: Longman.

Paisey, A. (1984) Trends in educational leadership thought. In Harling, P. (ed.) *New Directions in Educational Leadership.* Lewes: Falmer.

Pajak, E. (1991) Supervision: a central office perspective. *Curriculum* **12** (1).

Pascale, R. T. and Athos, A. G. (1982) *The Art of Japanese Management.* London: Allen Lane.

Pateman, C. (1970) *Participation and Democratic Theory.* Cambridge, UK: Cambridge University Press.

Peters, T. and Waterman, R. (1982) *In Search of Excellence.* London: Harper and Row.

Piaget, J. (1977) *The Moral Judgment of the Child.* Harmondsworth: Penguin.

Piaget, J. and Inhelder, B. (1956) *The Child's Conception of Space.* London: Routledge and Kegan Paul.

Picken, D. B. (1986) Two tasks of the Ad Hoc Council for Educational Reform in Socio-Cultural Perspective. *Comparative Education* **22** (1).

Plowden Report (1967) *Children and their Primary Schools.* Central Advisory Council for Education. London: HMSO.

Pollard, A. (1988) Controversial issues and reflective teaching. In Carrington, B. and Troyna, B. (eds) *Children and Controversial Issues.* Lewes: Falmer.

Pollock, L. A. (1983) *Forgotten Children.* Cambridge, UK: Cambridge University Press.

Pool, D. L., Shweder, R. A. and Much, N. C. (1985) Culture as a cognitive system: differentiated rule understandings in children and other savages. In Higgins, E. T., Ruble, D. N. and Hartup, W. W. (eds) *Social Cognition and Social Development.* Cambridge, UK: Cambridge University Press.

Popper, K. (1966) *The Open Society and its Enemies* (2 vols). London: Routledge and Kegan Paul.

Power, F. C., Higgins, A. and Kohlberg, L. (1989) *Lawrence Kohlberg's Approach to Moral Education.* New York: Columbia University Press.

Protherough, R. (1984) Shaping the image of the great headmaster. *British Journal of Educational Studies* **32** (3).

Pusey, M. (1976) *Dynamics of Bureaucracy.* Brisbane: John Wiley.

Rawls, J. (1971) *A Theory of Justice.* Cambridge, MA: Harvard University Press.

Reimer, E. (1971) *School is Dead.* Harmondsworth: Penguin.

Rizvi, F. (1989) In defence of organisational democracy. In Smyth, J. (ed.) *Critical Perspectives on Educational Leadership.* Lewes: Falmer.

Rogers, C. (1983) *Freedom to Learn for the 80s.* Columbus, OH: Charles E. Merrill.

Rose, M. (1985) *Industrial Behaviour.* London: Pelican.

Rothbard, M. (1978) *For a New Liberty: The Libertarian Manifesto,* 2nd edn. London: Collier-Macmillan.

Rutter, M., Maughan, B., Mortimore, P. and Ouston, J. (1979) *Fifteen Thousand Hours.* London: Open Books.

Sadler, M. (1979) How far can we learn anything of practical value from the study of foreign systems of education? In Higginson, J. H. (ed.) *Selections from Michael Sadler: Studies in World Citizenship.* Liverpool: Dejall and Meyorre International Publishers Ltd.

Schein, E. H. (1988) *Organizational Psychology,* 3rd edn. Englewood Cliffs, NJ: Prentice-Hall.

Schmidt, W. H. O. (1973) *Child Development.* New York: Harper and Row.

Schubert, W. H. (1990) Curriculum centralisation and decentralisation: historical perspectives. *Curriculum* **11** (2).

Schumpeter, J. (1942) *Capitalism, Socialism and Democracy.* London: Allen and Unwin.

Schutz, W. C. (1958) The interpersonal underworld. *Harvard Business Review* No. 36.

Scott, W. R. (1978) Theoretical perspectives. In Meyer, M. W. *et al.* (eds) *Environments and Organizations.* San Francisco: Jossey-Bass.

Scruton, R. (1984) *The Meaning of Conservatism,* 2nd edn. London: Macmillan.

Sedgwick, F. (1990) The management of poetry in education. *Curriculum* **11** (1).

Seldon, A. (1977) *Charge.* London: Temple Smith.

Seldon, A. (1986) *The Riddle of the Voucher.* London: Institute for Economic Affairs.

Selznick, P. (1949) *TVA and the Grassroots.* Berkeley, CA: University of California Press.

Shatz, M. and Gelman, R. (1973) The development of communication skills: modifications in the speech of young children as a function of listeners: *Monographs of the Society for Research in Child Development* **38** (5), serial no. 152.

Sherif, M. (1935) A study of some social factors in perception. *Archives of Psychology* **27** (187).

Shimahara, N. K. (1986) The cultural basis of student achievement in Japan. *Comparative Education* **22.**

Shorter, E. (1976) *The Making of the Modern Family.* London: Collins.

Simon, B. (1988) *Bending the Rules.* London: Lawrence and Wishart.

Simon, R. (1987) Empowerment as a pedagogy of possibility. *Language Arts* **64** (4).

Slavin, R., Sharan, S., Kagan, S., Lazarowitz, R. H., Webb, C. and Schmuck, R. (1985) *Learning to Cooperate, Cooperating to Learn.* New York: Plenum Press.

Smith, A. (1976) *An Inquiry into the Nature and Causes of the Wealth of Nations.* Campbell, R. H. and Skinner, A. S. (eds). Oxford: Clarendon Press.

Stevens, O. (1979) Politics and juniors: the political thinking of younger children. *Teaching Politics* **8.**

Stogdill, R. M. (1970) Personal factors associated with leadership: a survey of literature. In Gibb, C. A. (ed.) *Leadership.* Harmondsworth: Penguin.

Stradling, R. (1977) *The Political Awareness of the School Leaver.* London: Hansard Society.

Swidler, A. (1979) *Organizations without Authority.* Cambridge, MA: Harvard University Press.

Taylor, F. W. (1911) *Principles of Scientific Management.* London: Harper and Row.

Thatcher, M. (1987) *Woman's Own* (31 October).

Titmuss, R. M. (1987) Social welfare and the art of giving. In Abel-Smith, B. and Titmuss, K. (eds) *The Philosophy of Welfare: Selected Writings of Richard M. Titmuss.* London: Allen and Unwin.

Tonnies, F. (1957) *Community and Society.* East Lansing, MI: Michigan State University Press.

Tout, T. F. (1960) The emergence of a bureaucracy. In Merton, R. K., Gray, A. P., Hockey, B. and Selvin, H. C. (eds) *Reader in Bureaucracy.* Glencoe, IL: The Free Press.

Tucker, R. C. (1981) *Politics as Leadership.* Columbia, MO: University of Missouri Press.

Tyler, R. (1950) *Basic Principles of Curriculum and Instruction Syllabus for Education 360.* Chicago: University of Chicago Press.

Vroom, V. H. (1984) A normative model of managerial decision making. In Pugh, D. S. (ed.) *Organization Theory.* Harmondsworth: Penguin.

Vroom, V. H. and Deci, E. L. (1985) *Management and Motivation*. Harmondsworth: Penguin.

Wardle, D. (1976) *English Popular Education 1780–1975*. Cambridge, UK: Cambridge University Press.

Watkins, P. (1989) Leadership, power and symbols in educational administration. In Smyth, J. (ed.) *Critical Perspectives on Educational Leadership*. Lewes: Falmer Press.

Watson, H. (1985) *The Democratisation of Schooling*. Geelong: Deakin University Press.

Weber, M. (1947) *The Theory of Social and Economic Organisation*. T. Parsons (ed.) Oxford: Oxford University Press

Weber, M. (1970) *From Max Weber*. Gerth, H. H. and Wright Mills, C. (eds). London: Routledge and Kegan Paul.

Webster, D. H. (1982) Awe in the curriculum. In Priestley, J. G. (ed.) *Religion, Spirituality and Schools*. Exeter: School of Education, University of Exeter.

Webster, D. H. (1985) Commitment, spirituality and the classroom. *British Journal of Religious Education* **8** (1).

White, J. P. (1972) Indoctrination and intention. In Snook, I. A. (ed.) *Concepts of Indoctrination*. London: Routledge and Kegan Paul.

White, M. (1987) *The Japanese Educational Challenge*. New York: Free Press.

White, P. (1983) *Beyond Domination*. London: Routledge and Kegan Paul.

Whiting, B. B. (1983) The genesis of prosocial behaviour. In Bridgeman, D. L. (ed.) *The Nature of Prosocial Development*. New York: Academic Press.

Whyte, W. H. (1960) *The Organisation Man*. Harmondsworth: Penguin.

Wolf, M. (1983) *The Japanese Conspiracy*. Sevenoaks, Kent: New English Library.

Wolfendale, S. (ed.) (1989) *Parental Involvement*. London: Cassell.

Wood, D. (1988) *How Children Think and Learn*. Oxford: Basil Blackwell.

Wragg, E. C. (1987) *Teacher Appraisal: a Practical Guide*. London: Macmillan.

Wringe, C. A. (1981) *Children's Rights*. London: Routledge and Kegan Paul.

# Index